Culture and
Customs of
El Salvador

Recent Titles in
Culture and Customs of Latin America and the Caribbean

Culture and Customs of El Salvador

Roy C. Boland

Culture and Customs of Latin America
and the Caribbean
Peter Standish, Series Editor

GREENWOOD PRESS
Westport, Connecticut • London

Library of Congress Cataloging-in-Publication Data

Boland, Roy.
    Culture and customs of El Salvador / Roy C. Boland.
        p.   cm.—(Culture and customs of Latin America and the Caribbean, ISSN 1521–8856)
    Includes bibliographical references and index.
    ISBN 0–313–30620–6 (alk. paper)
        1. Ethnology—El Salvador.   2. El Salvador—Social life and customs.   I. Title.   II. Series.
GN564.S2 B65   2001
    306'.097284—dc21   00–033124

British Library Cataloguing in Publication Data is available.

Library of Congress Catalog Card Number: 00–033124

ISBN: 978-0-313-36097-8

First published in 2001

Greenwood Press, 88 Post Road West, Westport, CT 06881
An imprint of Greenwood Publishing Group, Inc.
www.greenwood.com

Printed in the United States of America

The paper used in this book complies with the
Permanent Paper Standard issued by the National
Information Standards Organization (Z39.48–1984).

10 9 8 7 6

Copyright Acknowledgments

The author and publisher gratefully acknowledge permission for the use of the following material:

From "Penitential Sonnet I," by David Escobar Galindo and from "Turris Babel," by Francisco Gavida, translated by David Escobar Galindo. Reprinted by permission of David Escobar Galindo.

Unless otherwise noted, photographs are used by courtesy of Roy C. Boland.

To Manlio Argueta and David Escobar Galindo,
poets and patriots,
and to Titi Escalante and Margarita Wilson,
dos flores.

Contents

A photo essay follows p. 79.

Series Foreword

"CULTURE" is a problematic word. In everyday language we tend to use it in at least two senses. On the one hand we speak of cultured people and places full of culture, uses that imply a knowledge or presence of certain forms of behavior or of artistic expression that are socially prestigious. In this sense large cities and prosperous people tend to be seen as the most cultured. On the other hand, there is an interpretation of "culture" that is broader and more anthropological; culture in this broader sense refers to whatever traditions, beliefs, customs, and creative activities characterize a given community—in short, it refers to what makes that community different from others. In this second sense, everyone has culture; indeed, it is impossible to be without culture.

The problems associated with the idea of culture have been exacerbated in recent years by two trends: less respectful use of language and a greater blurring of cultural differences. Nowadays, "culture" often means little more than behavior, attitude, or atmosphere. We hear about the culture of the boardroom, of the football team, of the marketplace; there are books with titles like *The Culture of War* by Richard Gabriel (Greenwood, 1990) or *The Culture of Narcissism* by Christopher Lasch (1979). In fact, as Christopher Clausen points out in an article published in the *American Scholar* (Summer 1996), we have gotten ourselves into trouble by using the term so sloppily.

People who study culture generally assume that culture (in the anthropological sense) is learned, not genetically determined. Another general assumption made in these days of multiculturalism has been that cultural differences should be respected rather than put under pressure to change.

But these assumptions, too, have sometimes proved to be problematic. For instance, multiculturalism is a fine ideal, but in practice it is not always easy to reconcile with the beliefs of the very people who advocate it: for example, is female circumcision an issue of human rights or just a different cultural practice?

The blurring of cultural differences is a process that began with the steamship, increased with radio, and is now racing ahead with the Internet. We are becoming globally homogenized. Since the English-speaking world (and the United States in particular) is the dominant force behind this process of homogenization, it behooves us to make efforts to understand the sensibilities of members of other cultures.

This series of books, a contribution toward that greater understanding, deals with the neighbors of the United States, with people who have just as much right to call themselves Americans. What are the historical, institutional, religious, and artistic features that make up the modern culture of such peoples as the Haitians, the Chileans, the Jamaicans, and the Guatemalans? How are their habits and assumptions different from our own? What can we learn from them? As we familiarize ourselves with the ways of other countries, we come to see our own from a new perspective.

Each volume in the series focuses on a single country. With slight variations to accommodate national differences, each begins by outlining the historical, political, ethnic, geographical, and linguistic context, as well as the religious and social customs, and then proceeds to a discussion of a variety of artistic activities, including the press, the media, the cinema, music, literature, and the visual and performing arts. The authors are all intimately acquainted with the countries concerned: some were born or brought up in them, and each has a professional commitment to enhancing the understanding of the culture in question.

We are inclined to suppose that our ways of thinking and behaving are normal. And so they are . . . for us. We all need to realize that ours is only one culture among many, and that it is hard to establish by any rational criteria that ours as a whole is any better (or worse) than any other. As individual members of our immediate community, we know that we must learn to respect our differences from one another. Respect for differences between cultures is no less vital. This is particularly true of the United States, a nation of immigrants, but one that sometimes seems to be bent on destroying variety at home, and, worse still, on having others follow suit. By learning about other people's cultures, we come to understand and respect them; we earn their respect for us; and, not least, we see ourselves in a new light.

Peter Standish
East Carolina University

Acknowledgments

THIS BOOK has been written with the support, guidance and information provided by family, friends and colleagues. Particular debts are recorded in some of the endnotes. I wish to express special gratitude to Rina Osegueda and Yolanda Gussman, whose personal recollections and testimonies have been invaluable. I thank Salvador Dubón, Guillermo Cucalón, Luis Andreu, Juan José Fernández and their families in El Salvador for their hospitality. I am grateful to the following scholars for their generous assistance: Ricardo Roque Baldovinos, John Boland, Germán Cáceres, Carlos Cañas, Laurie Clancy, Rafael Rodríguez Díaz, Robert Gaston, Ana Francis Góngora, Alastair Hurst, Alun Kenwood, Oscar Melhado, Katherine Miller and Margarita Shepherd. My warm thanks go to Clásicos Roxil in Santa Tecla; Grant and Cutler in London; and the USA Information Office and the Fundación María Escalón de Núñez in San Salvador for their excellent services. I am indebted to Mario and Patricia Vargas Llosa for their kindness, to Peter Standish for his confidence in me and to Wendi Schnaufer for her superb professionalism.

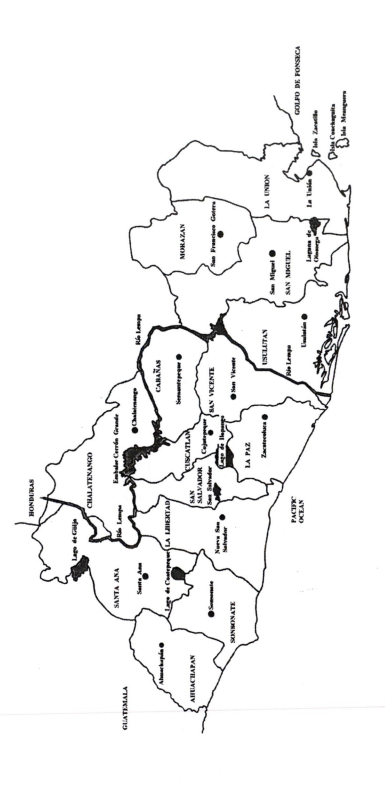

EL SALVADOR

Introduction

VERY FEW countries in Latin America have been as marginalized as El Salvador has throughout its 150 years as an independent, sovereign republic. Until the mid-1970s the country made international news only when a volcano erupted, an earthquake struck or another military coup overthrew its president. To North Americans, Europeans and even other Latin Americans, El Salvador was the classic banana republic: small, poor, underdeveloped, corrupt, violent and governed by an alliance of military strongmen, millionaire ranchers and well-fed priests and bishops. Few tourists ventured there—wedged between Guatemala, Honduras and Nicaragua, the country had few stretches of golden sand and there were no five-star resorts with mariachis or samba dancers to lure the first-world tourist.

When El Salvador eventually made the front pages of the world's newspapers and became a lead story in prime time television, its reputation as a banana republic was dramatically confirmed. The escalation of violence in the late 1970s led to the outbreak in 1980 of a civil war that ushered in twelve years of carnage and devastation. Up to 1,000 murders per month were recorded at the height of the conflict. El Salvador's notoriety was heightened when it became a pawn in the Cold War between the superpowers. Both the United States and the Soviet bloc poured in massive military assistance. The international media captured the chilling images: the severed head or bloodied torso of a soldier lying on the curbside, the rotting corpse of a guerrilla in the bush, the massacre of dozens of innocent men and women who had come to mourn their murdered archbishop. Two major movies conveyed to the world the tragedy unfolding in the sad, little republic: *Sal-*

vador (1986, directed by Oliver Stone, starring James Woods) and *Romero* (1989, directed by John Duigan, starring Raul Julia).

Peace came at last to El Salvador in 1992, and since then the country has been engaged in an arduous process of reconciliation and reconstruction. As one of Latin America's most perceptive commentators, the Peruvian writer Mario Vargas Llosa, has observed, "Falling down is inevitable when one is learning to walk along the path to democracy."[1] Although there are numerous social, economic and political pitfalls obstructing the path to democracy in El Salvador, what bodes well for the future is that the culture of terror that haunted the country for decades has now been replaced by a culture of peace. Twice since 1992 the people have gone to the polls to elect a president, and both times the election has been as free as in any other recently established democracy. Poverty, crime, inequality and unemployment are still grave problems, but a fundamental respect for civil and human rights seems to have become part of political life.

In spite of the remarkable transformation taking place, the memory of the atrocities committed in the past remains fresh in the minds of most Salvadoreans. This book endeavors to address the country's embattled past—from the Spanish conquest to the most recent civil war—frankly and objectively. However, the principal objective is to bring to light another side of El Salvador, what may be called its hidden face: a cultural richness and diversity that its bloodstained history has obscured. Salvadoreans themselves tend to dismiss their cultural achievements. Indeed, in the course of researching this book the author was struck by the way in which many leading intellectuals were ready to apologize for the limited quantity and modest quality of their cultural endeavors. If this book has any contribution to make to a fuller understanding of Salvadorean society, it is that its inferiority complex about its culture is misplaced and unnecessary. The fact is that El Salvador has produced an impressive array of artists—particularly in the fields of literature, painting and music—whose achievements are all the more remarkable given the conditions under which they have had to labor.

Salvadoreans also tend to be rather coy about their traditional customs, explaining that they are not very picturesque or attractive by comparison with those in such countries as Mexico, Peru, Argentina or Guatemala. Any discussion of traditional customs must consider the problematic question of the country's Indian heritage, which is problematic in the sense that many Salvadoreans are not sure whether to be proud or embarrassed about its apparent invisibility. For historical reasons to be explained in due course, Indian customs have been suppressed in El Salvador from the day that the Spaniards entered the country in 1524. The principal pre-Hispanic language,

Nahuat, has virtually disappeared, and traditional Indian dress is hardly ever seen. Yet one does not need to scratch very far below the surface of Salvadorean society to strike a rich vein of ancestral customs and manners dating back to pre-Hispanic times. Many traditions—oral storytelling, myths, legends, superstitions, music, dance, gastronomy and crafts—bear the imprint of the pre-Hispanic past.

To be sure, it is also difficult to find any cultural expression of El Salvador's Indian heritage that has not been "diluted" or "enriched"—depending on one's point of view—by subsequent Spanish customs and beliefs. In this regard El Salvador constitutes one of Latin America's most *mestizo* (mixed Spanish and Indian) societies. As the author's grandfather, Colonel Félix de J. Osegueda (1896–1972), used to remind him, "En El Salvador todos somos un poco indios" (In El Salvador we are all a little bit Indian). The chapters that make up this book illustrate this truth.

NOTE

1. *Time*, March 26, 1984, 30.

Chronology

1859	The nation's official title becomes The Republic of El Salvador
1863	El Salvador goes to war with Guatemala
1865	Execution of General Gerardo Barrios, former liberal president
1870	Beginning of the Coffee Republic
1873	An earthquake devastates San Salvador
1881–82	Abolition of communal and municipal ownership of land
1885	Military coup
1890	Military coup
1894	Military coup
1898	Military coup
1906	El Salvador goes to war with Guatemala
1907	El Salvador goes to war with Honduras and Nicaragua
1913	Assassination of President Manuel Enrique Araujo
1917	Worst earthquake on record destroys San Salvador
1927	End of the Coffee Republic
1930	Foundation of the Communist Party of El Salvador
1931–44	Dictorship of General Maximiliano Hernández Martínez
1932	Communist uprising; the Great Slaughter and execution of Farabundo Martí
1948	The Revolution of 1948
1949	Colonel Oscar Osorio becomes president
1956	Colonel José María Lemus wins rigged presidential elections
1960	The army invades the National University; military coup against President Lemus; foundation of the Christian Democratic Party
1961	Colonel Julio Adalberto Rivera becomes president of El Salvador
1964	José Napoleón Duarte becomes mayor of San Salvador

1967   General Fidel Sánchez Hernández becomes president of El Salvador

1969   Soccer War between El Salvador and Honduras

1972   Colonel Arturo Armando Molina wins rigged presidential elections; José Napoleón Duarte is tortured and exiled

1975   Murder of poet-revolutionary Roque Dalton

1976   General Carlos Humberto Romero becomes president of El Salvador; Monseñor Oscar Arnulfo Romero becomes archbishop of San Salvador

1979   Military coup

1980   Murder of Monseñor Oscar Arnulfo Romero; formation of FMLN; outbreak of civil war

1981   FMLN launches "Final Offensive"; Major Roberto D'Aubuisson founds ARENA

1982   Alvaro Magaña becomes provisional president of El Salvador

1984   José Napoleón Duarte becomes president of El Salvador

1986   Earthquake devastates San Salvador

1989   Alfredo Cristiani (ARENA) elected president of El Salvador; FMLN launches another "Final Offensive"; assassination of six Jesuits, a cook and her daughter on the campus of the Jesuit University

1990   Government of Alfredo Cristiani and the FMLN leadership agree to pursue peace negotiations

1992   Signing of Chapultepec Peace Accords; end of the civil war; democracy established in El Salvador

1994   Armando Calderón Sol (ARENA) elected president of El Salvador

1997   Héctor Silva (FMLN) elected mayor of San Salvador

1998   Hurricane Mitch causes devastation in Central America

1999   Francisco Flores (ARENA) elected president of El Salvador

Culture and
Customs of
El Salvador

1

Context

FROM THE KINGDOM OF CUSCATLÁN TO THE REPUBLIC OF EL SALVADOR

THE REPUBLIC OF EL SALVADOR underwent a series of transformations before assuming its current political status and administrative structure.[1] Before the Spanish Conquest most of the country formed part of the Indian kingdom of Cuscatlán. Cuscatlán means "land of precious things," perhaps in reference to the fertile soil, to the chocolate made from the cocoa used as currency by the Indians, or to the general splendor of the countryside. After entering Cuscatlán in 1524, the *conquistadores* (Spanish conquerors) founded the village of San Salvador in 1525 in honor of "Christ, the Holy Saviour of the World," who became the patron saint and national symbol of El Salvador. After moving a number of times in the first two decades after the Spanish invasion, San Salvador eventually arrived at its present location. Emperor Charles V gave it the title of city in 1546. By 1552 the Spaniards had divided the former kingdom of Cuscatlán into two provinces: San Salvador, situated in the western valley of Zalcuatitán, and Sonsonate, 40.3 miles southwest with an outlet to the sea in Acajutla. Although the two provinces developed separately, both were dependent politically upon the captanía-general (captaincy-general) of Guatemala, the largest and most significant administrative region of the Spanish empire in Central America. San Salvador was more strategically situated toward the center of the country, and it evolved much more rapidly than Sonsonate did. By 1785 it had earned the privileged status of *intendencia*, a region administered by a governor, and it incorporated the district of Santa Ana in the northwest, San Vicente in the center and San Miguel in the east.

Following independence from Spain in 1821 and a very brief, turbulent period under Mexican rule, San Salvador was proclaimed a state of the Federal Republic of Central America in 1824. That same year its boundaries were enlarged with the amalgamation of Sonsonate. The republic collapsed in 1840. On February 18, 1841, San Salvador adopted its own constitution, under which it became a free, single, independent nation. It was not until January 24, 1859, however, that the nation adopted the official title of Republic of El Salvador, and it has remained a sovereign republic since then.

El Salvador is divided into fourteen administrative divisions known as *departamentos* (departments), with each one possessing a *cabecera* (regional capital). Under the constitution (there have been fifteen since 1824, the last one approved in 1983) the nation has a republican, democratic, representative government that is divided into three branches: the executive, the legislature and the judiciary. The head of state is a president elected by universal suffrage for a five-year term. Each of the fourteen departments is administered by a governor appointed by the president. The fourteen departments are divided into *municipios* (municipalities or counties) administered by mayors, who are directly elected. The municipalities are subdivided into numerous, sometimes ill-defined *cantones* (hamlets) and *caseríos* (clusters of houses).

THE LANDSCAPE

The Chilean poet Gabriela Mistral, the Nobel Prize winner for literature in 1945, baptized El Salvador *El Pulgarcito de las Américas* (Tom Thumb of the Americas) because of its shape and size. Nestled like a child in a mother's bosom between parallels 13° and 14°10' north latitude and meridians 87° and 90° west longitude, El Salvador is the smallest Hispanic country in the Western Hemisphere. Identifying regionally with the other four Central American republics (Guatemala, Honduras, Nicaragua and Costa Rica), El Salvador is the only one without an Atlantic coast, a fact that has proved both a blessing and a drawback. On the one hand, the country has been spared the ravages of malaria that have periodically afflicted the Atlantic lowlands of the other republics. On the other hand, it was not able to benefit from the lucrative trading routes that once plied the Atlantic Ocean, and in more recent times it has missed out on the tourist dollars of vacationers who seek the white sands, sun and rum of the Caribbean.

Approximately the size of Massachusetts or Wales, and able to fit twenty-one times into Peru, El Salvador covers an area of 8,124 square miles.

It measures about 162 miles from east to west and 62 miles from north to south. The country is so tiny that it possesses only one major national and international airport. With the aid of a sturdy four-wheel-drive car it is possible to travel all of El Salvador in one day. It has political boundaries to the west with Guatemala, from which it is separated by the Paz River and Lake Güija; to the north with Honduras, where three rivers—the Lempa, the Sumpul and the Torola—demarcate a sometimes disputed border; and to the east with Nicaragua, where the Goascorán River and the Gulf of Fonseca act as natural divisions. The Gulf of Fonseca, teeming with sea life and covering an area of 1,131 miles, also separates El Salvador from the southeast of Honduras. Not surprisingly, disputes over fishing rights erupt from time to time between Nicaragua, Honduras and El Salvador. The Gulf of Fonseca has always been regarded of strategic importance in Central America, and both Great Britain and the United States at one stage considered it as an alternative site to the Panama Canal.

Geographically, El Salvador is divided into three parallel regions that run from east to west. A thin coastal plain of approximately 20 miles at its widest point skirts the Pacific Ocean, extending from Bocana del Río Paz on the Guatemalan border to Punta Amapala in the Gulf of Fonseca. This narrow coast, originally extremely fertile and the site of the almost defunct cotton industry, now bears the ecological scars of overexploitation and erosion. A few important port cities remain, such as Acajutla and La Libertad, as do a smattering of fishing villages and some long-established *haciendas* (ranches). This coastline's most prominent feature is the stark, black sand of its beaches, where palm trees shade the low-thatched huts of the country clubs that well-heeled *salvadoreños* (Salvadoreans) frequent during weekends and holidays.[2]

The second region is the Meseta Central (Central Highlands), a kaleidoscopic chain of mountains, volcanoes, valleys, rivers, geysers, lava flows and lakes that encompasses about 75 percent of the country. This area contains twenty volcanoes, a few of them still active. The highest, Volcán Santa Ana, soars majestically to 7,759 feet, while Volcán San Salvador, which reaches 6,398 feet, seems to stand like a perpetual sentinel over the capital city. When the Spaniards founded the original village of San Salvador, they dubbed this area *el valle de las hamacas* (the valley of the hammocks) because the constant seismic instability made them feel as if they were swinging in a hammock. The country's youngest volcano, Volcán Izalco, measures 6,184 feet. It was spat out of the ground in 1770 amid roars and thunderclaps that seemed to presage the end of the world. Sailors named this volcano *el faro del Pacífico* (the lighthouse of the Pacific) because its glowing sparks and embers seemed designed to light up the sea.

Most of El Salvador's cities, towns and villages are situated in the Meseta Central because the volcanic ash fertilizes the rich soil. Some of the valleys between the craters and cones seem like a patchwork quilt of coffee plantations, fields of sugarcane and clusters of banana trees. In some parts the combination of volcanic soils and recently developed irrigation schemes allow for up to three yearly harvests of beans, *maize* (corn) and vegetables.

Majestic they may be, but the towering volcanoes are a constant reminder that nature has not always been kind to El Salvador. Since time immemorial volcanoes have meant eruptions, lava flows, tremors, fires and earthquakes. The first recorded earthquake was in A.D. 260, when Volcán Ilopango erupted, wreaking havoc over an area of 3,861 square miles. San Salvador itself has been devastated by earthquakes five times since 1756. The last occasion was in 1986, when an earthquake measuring 7.5 on the Richter scale caused $US1 billion in damage and left 2,000 dead, 10,000 wounded and 200,000 homeless or destitute. The most destructive earthquake in the country's history happened in 1917 when the capital was utterly devastated, an event movingly and graphically recorded by a visitor to the country, the Colombian poet Porfirio Barba Jacob, in his book *El terremoto de San Salvador* (Earthquake in San Salvador).[3] A volcanic eruption almost totally destroyed the eastern city of San Miguel in 1655, legend claiming that only the image of Lucifer in the parish church was spared by the inferno. In 1936 an earthquake destroyed the major city of San Vicente. In 1951 a spate of violent tremors seriously damaged the town of Santiago de María, an important commercial center in the department of Usulután. It is one of the great ironies of its embattled history that until the outbreak of the most recent civil war in the 1980s, its tourism authorities promoted El Salvador as *el país de la sonrisa* (the smiling country). According to the poet David Escobar Galindo, given the twin blights of war and earthquakes that have regularly rocked El Salvador, a more fitting epithet would have been *el país de la mueca* (the grimacing country).[4]

The third and northernmost region of El Salvador is the Sierra Madre (Northern Highlands), a wild and extensive mountain range along the border with Honduras that comprises about 15 percent of the national territory. The highest peak is El Pital (8,957 feet), a nonvolcanic mountain. This region was once abundant in forest and game, but now it is barren and rugged. It contains some of the most primitive, deprived pockets of population in El Salvador. In some particularly remote areas, as in the case of a *bolsón* (cluster of huts) known as Santa Anita, *campesinos* (peasants) have been caught in a judicial no-man's-land following the 1992 settlement by the International Court of Justice in The Hague of a border dispute between El Salvador and

Honduras. In Santa Anita about sixteen marginalized families, formerly Honduran but now officially Salvadorean, scratch out a wretched existence, subsisting on a daily diet of adulterated coffee, salt and corn tortillas.[5]

Apart from its volcanoes and mountains, El Salvador's outstanding physical characteristic consists of its rivers and lakes. Around 590 rivers, streams and creeks crisscross the country. However, only one—the Lempa River—is navigable. El Salvador's largest and most important river, the Lempa bisects the country into two clearly defined regions, Poniente (West) and Oriente (East), a division that has had significant historical and political repercussions. Entering El Salvador at the north western border with Guatemala, the Lempa winds its way through 202 miles of Salvadorean territory, traversing the Northern Highlands, flowing through the Central Highlands and running south toward the Pacific Ocean, into which it empties at Bocana Río Lempa between the departments of Usulután and San Vicente. The basin of the Lempa and its tributaries occupies approximately 49 percent of the national territory, while the basins of River Grande de San Miguel (45 miles), the River Paz (35 miles) and the small River Goascarán occupy among them almost 22 percent. Numerous other small rivers and streams are scattered throughout the rest of the country. El Salvador's plentiful water supplies have provided the basis for natural-energy production. Major hydroelectric schemes such as Presa 5 de Noviembre and Presa del Cerrón Grande operate in the northwest on the Lempa. Geothermal plants have also been built at strategic locations in the same area, where thermal springs, geysers and fumaroles abound. Considerable damage, in some cases irreparable, was done to the country's hydroelectric infrastructure during the recent civil war.

Within its cramped boundaries El Salvador abounds in lagoons and lakes of volcanic origins. Many of them, in fact, formed as a result of craters filling with rain. In the country's extreme northwest lies Lake Güija, two-thirds of which belongs to El Salvador, the other third to Guatemala. To the west, on the foothills of the Santa Ana volcano, is Lake Coatepeque, a spectacular sight indeed. Its crater measures 394 feet in depth at an altitude of 2,428 feet. The largest lake is Ilopango, which means "golden maize" in the Indian language that was spoken in the ancient kingdom of Cuscatlán. Ilopango measures 25 square miles and lies at an altitude of 1,450 feet. Although it is only 10 miles from San Salvador, it lies about 1,191 feet below the capital. Now a scenic area popular with vacationers, Ilopango has been subject to seismic disturbances in the past. In 1880 a volcano rose out of the lake. In the course of time the cone has grown taller and the lake has changed shape and size.

CLIMATE, FLORA AND FAUNA

Although a variety of microclimates exists in El Salvador, in general the country enjoys a tropical climate with a relatively narrow range of temperatures that is dependent upon altitude. Annual average temperatures range between 89.6°F and 64.4°F, with the temperature dropping about 1.6°C with each increase of 984 feet in altitude. The average for San Salvador is 82.4°F but in the highest mountain areas the minimum temperature can drop to the freezing point. Salvadoreans divide the territory into three zones: *tierra caliente* (hot land) along the coast, *tierra templada* (temperate land), which encompasses most of the country, and *tierra fría* (cold land) in the Northern Highlands along the Guatemalan and Honduran borders. The coast can be suffocatingly hot and humid during the so-called *verano* (summer or dry season) between mid-November and mid-April. The *invierno* (winter or wet season), which lasts between mid-May and mid-October, is characterized by periods of heavy and prolonged rainfall, including spectacular electrical storms. Annual rainfall ranges from 68 inches on the coast to as much as 96 inches in the Northern Highlands. The country has one of the highest rainfall rates in Latin America.

Two thousand years ago luxuriant vegetation covered El Salvador. Giant hardwoods with such exotic names as *guarumos, amates* and *ceibas* cloaked the area between the coast and the Central Highlands. Between the center and the eastern parts of the country another mantle of huge trees, including the towering *conacaste*, formed a dense tropical jungle. Unfortunately, because of inappropriate farming techniques, overexploitation and the ravages of the civil war, only about 5 percent of the country currently contains original forest, and a real danger of desertification threatens certain zones. The abundant wildlife inhabiting the country at the time of the Spanish Conquest has also dwindled. Many species of monkeys, anteaters, peccaries (feline mammals that resemble pigs), ocelots, ducks and otters are extinct or near extinction. In the case of Laguna de Jocotal Reserve in the department of San Miguel, for instance, more than 99 percent of the total wildlife has disappeared.

Nevertheless, since the end of the civil war El Salvador has begun to acquire an ecological consciousness. This is evidenced by the creation of the Ministry of the Environment and the passing of tough environmental legislation which is aimed at curbing the excesses of large businesses and developers that exploit the country's natural resources, especially its rivers, lakes and few remaining national parks and reserves. The most famous tropical forest is El Imposible, which is in the southwest department of Ahuachapán.

Here, many endangered species of birds and animals live and reproduce, including black buzzards, wild turkeys, crested eagles, three-toed anteaters, red-billed pigeons, small tigers, horn-rimmed owls, white-nosed coatis (a type of large raccoon), rattlesnakes and various species of toads and frogs. Montecristo National Park, on the border between Guatemala, Honduras and El Salvador in the northwest corner of the department of Santa Ana, consists of 2,000 acres of rainforest. Known also as Bosque Nebuloso (Misty Forest), this reserve is famous for its aerial plant life, including dozens of species of orchids that are now being exported to the United States and to other Central American countries. Montecristo is also the habitat of blue butterflies, pumas, wild boars and deer. It is also one of the few breeding grounds for the *quetzal*, the sacred bird of the ancient Mayas who inhabited Central America. Cerro Verde National Park in the department of Santa Ana contains more than 120 species of birds, including over a dozen kinds of hummingbirds.

The María Escalón Núñez Cultural Foundation identifies three other principal parks or reserves: Nancuchiname in the department of Usulután, Walter Thilo Denninger in the department of La Libertad and Barra de Santiago in the department of Ahuachapán.[6] In spite of all the damage caused in the past to the environment, numerous species of flora and fauna are still found in these protected areas and in other parts of the country. The principal tree species are cedar, mahogany, laurel, medlar and *madre cacao* (mother of cacao), some of which local craftsmen utilize to make furniture. The legendary balsam tree is still found on the coast. Its sap is extracted to manufacture perfume, soap and medicine. To this day it is still mistakenly called "balsam of Peru" because during colonial times it was transported to Peru en route to Spain. The *maquilishuat,* a tropical tree whose branches flower in delicate pink shades, and the fiery-colored *flor de fuego* (flower of fire) are sprinkled throughout the country. Coconut and banana trees are fairly numerous, while other types of fruit-bearing trees include the mango, guava, tamarind and the plumlike *jocote.*

One of the most precious mammals to survive is the spider monkey, while the *urraca* (a kind of magpie with a blue breast and a gray head) is one of the rarest birds found in the country. Opossums and iguanas are found in many places, although they are sometimes trapped and cruelly barbecued while still alive. In the lakes and lagoons there is an abundance of wild ducks, white herons and royal herons, while the cries of parrots, cockatoos, parakeets, toucans and macaws can still fill the forests.

Aquatic animals and fish exist in varying numbers in El Salvador. Although sadly dwindled, crocodiles, alligators and turtles survive in lakes and rivers. There are many varieties of both freshwater and seawater fish, as a visit to a local market, a pier or a fishing village readily proves. Crabs, crayfish, oysters, eels, anchovies and shrimp are found. The range of fish extends from sharks, swordfish, lampreys and catfish to perch, bass, mackerel, snapper and mullet. Only shrimp, however, is caught in sufficient numbers for export. Today shrimp is the country's third largest agricultural export after coffee and sugar, earning almost $US28 million in 1995.

AGRICULTURE

El Salvador's traditional image as a "garden country" is changing considerably, although agriculture continues to be one of the country's economic mainstays. During the colonial period (1524–1821), three crops were cultivated, marketed and exported successfully: cocoa, balsam and indigo.[7] In 1585 the province of Sonsonate was called *la tierra del cacao* (the land of cocoa). To this day the coastal region southwest of Izalco is still known as *la costa del bálsamo* (the balsam coast). For a number of reasons—international competition, the decimation of Indian labor by disease, and a conflict between the Spanish and Indian perception of the significance and use of the land—both cocoa and balsam virtually disappeared by the end of the eighteenth century. Since the last civil war there has been a small resurgence of the balsam industry. Approximately $US1.25 million was earned in exports in 1995.[8]

Indigo was by far the most important crop throughout the colonial period. At one stage the province of San Salvador provided over 95 percent of all indigo produced in Central America. Indeed, so dependent was San Salvador on indigo that a major catastrophe could have occurred when the bottom fell out of the international market with the development of cheap, synthetic chemical dyes in Europe in the 1870s. The economic savior for the now-independent Republic of El Salvador was coffee, which was called "king coffee" or *el grano de oro* (the golden grain) because of the regal beauty of its beans and its overwhelming economic significance.

Coffee was probably introduced into El Salvador in the early years of the nineteenth century. It was first grown commercially by a Brazilian schoolteacher, Antonio Coelho, who bought a small farm, La Esperanza (Hope), in 1840 and began to develop new, efficient methods of cultivation. Coffee, which grows best at altitudes between 1,476 and 4,265 feet, took readily and generously to the country's climate and topography. By 1881 it was already being exported to the United States. Indeed, for the period between 1871 and 1927 the country was known as the Coffee Republic. El Salvador became a monocultural nation whose economic and political fortunes were bound inextricably to the price of coffee on the international market. The principal coffee-growing regions are west of the Lempa River in the departments of Santa Ana, Sonsonate, San Vicente, La Libertad, La Paz, Cuscatlán and Ahuachapán, while east of the Lempa there are coffee-growing areas in Usulután and San Miguel.

Although nonrural industries have now overtaken coffee in terms of the national GNP (Gross National Product), El Salvador is still Central America's major coffee producer, ranking fourth overall in Latin America. Its export quality is considered one of the finest in the world (although a coffee connoisseur may find the product for internal consumption disappointing). An indication of the significance of coffee is that its price is quoted every day on page two of the most important national newspapers, *La Prensa Gráfica* and *El Diario de Hoy*. A downturn in the international price of coffee can have serious consequences for the Salvadorean economy, as in fact occurred during the crisis of 1986, when coffee exports declined abruptly from $US61.5 million to $US39.6 million. By 1995 the coffee industry had recovered sufficiently from the international crisis and the disruptive effects of the civil war to post export earnings of just over $US363 million, almost four times as much as the combined total for the country's principal commercial products of sugar, shrimp, sesame, fruits, honey and balsam. In 1997 export earnings soared to $US518 million, although El Niño's shadow hangs over future crops.[9] As they have since the 1870s the large coffee growers continue to wield considerable influence politically through memberships in the current governing party, the Nationalist Republican Alliance (ARENA), the Salvadorean Coffee Growers Association (ACES) and the Association of Coffee Processors and Exporters (ABECAFE). The coffee growers also possess influential connections to the country's conservative mass media, which take every opportunity to identify the industry's commercial and political fortunes with the national interest.

Although coffee has dwarfed all other commercial crops, in recent times cotton and sugar have contributed significantly to the national coffers. Cotton, which provided the pre-Columbian population with the raw material for their cloth, has been grown commercially on the country's coastal plains during various periods. After a boom period during the American Civil War, when cotton was exported to the United States, it almost disappeared until the 1920s. It experienced a revival during World War II. Following a land-rush operation the industry blossomed through the 1950s. The high point was reached in 1964–65, when 302,100 acres were under cultivation. In financial terms cotton accounted for 24 percent of El Salvador's exports in 1964. The cotton industry continued to prosper until 1979, when exports reached $US87 million.[10] The subsequent civil war had a cataclysmic effect upon cotton, causing it to virtually disappear as a viable industry. This is perhaps poetic justice for the incalculable ecological damage that greedy cotton planters have done to the coastal plains. To facilitate cotton growing, large tracts of forest were erased, thousands of acres of soil were exhausted and subsistence farmers were driven off their traditional lands.

Sugar, which has been grown in El Salvador since the sixteenth century, is El Salvador's second most important commercial crop after coffee. The American embargo on Cuba has proved a boon to the sugar industry, which in 1998 earned over $US65 million in exports.[11] The Asociación de Cañeros (Association of Sugarcane Growers) is very active in defending the interests of the country's 3,500 producers, whose farms are in small pockets throughout the Central Highlands in the departments of San Miguel, La Libertad, San Vicente and Sonsonate. Only a few small farms still utilize traditional mills known as *trapiches*, which are sometimes ox-driven devices, to produce *dulce de panela*, a brown sugar cake popular among the *campesinos*.

Apart from coffee and sugar, which earn substantial revenue from exports (principally to the United States, Germany and Japan), most other crops are grown for internal consumption. Only a few so-called nontraditional fruits, such as melons and pineapples, have been cultivated successfully for the international market. An overcrowded country of almost 6.2 million people, with the highest population density in Latin America (about 720 per square mile), El Salvador has quite a voracious appetite for the dazzling array of fruits and vegetables that are found in the swarming street markets of its towns and villages. About 50 percent of the produce is homegrown; the other 50 percent comes from other Central American countries, especially from Guatemala. Almost every street corner has vendors who offer their wares from baskets that are balanced on their heads or placed neatly on the ground.

Maize, beans and rice continue to be the staple diet of the *campesinos*, but the taste for these ancestral foods crosses class boundaries. Even the most luxurious households in El Salvador include them in their daily menus. The *campesinos* grow these crops on their subsistence plots that are scattered throughout the hills, mountains and volcanoes of the Salvadorean countryside. Cattle (over 1 million head) and pigs (over 400,000) are the principal sources of meat. There are also small but thriving chicken and turkey industries. Meats, cheese and eggs, however, are beyond the means of the majority of Salvadoreans.

INDUSTRY

The recent civil war accelerated a process in El Salvador that had been in evidence since the 1960s: the advance of manufacturing and of the so-called service industries. The economist Oscar Melhado goes so far as to suggest that El Salvador's image as a coffee republic belongs to the past.[12] Due to the strategy of import substitution that was adopted by the governments of the 1960s and 1970s, and subsequent to the ravages inflicted upon the countryside during the last civil war, El Salvador underwent a belated industrial revolution. Light industries, such as textiles, footwear, tobacco, aluminium, chemical products, detergents, medicines and processed foods, made a dynamic entry into the national scene. The civil war did not affect the industrial sector as severely as it did agriculture. In fact, the industrial sector increased more than 20 percent with respect to its contribution to the GNP. Since the end of the war in 1992 the upward trend of manufacturing has continued, particularly in the sector known as *maquilas* (foreign-owned textile or electronic-processing plants that transport software, textile and clothing for assembly in El Salvador and then reexport it back to the United States, Taiwan, China or Japan). Between 1991 and 1996 the total foreign revenue generated by *maquila* exports boomed from $US120.9 million to $US656 million. This spectacular leap in the *maquila* industry was due largely to the establishment of free-trade zones and industrial complexes that pay no tariff duties on the condition that all the goods assembled leave the country. El Salvador's *maquila* exports currently face increasing competition from Mexico, which receives favored treatment from the United States through NAFTA (North American Free Trade Agreement).

The traditional agricultural profile of El Salvador has been undergoing such a face-lift that some commentators now argue that in macroeconomic terms it is becoming a country dominated by the service industries, a phenomenon normally associated with first-world countries. Public administration, property rentals, entertainment, restaurants and other personal services account for 60 percent of the GNP, by contrast with agriculture, which makes up about 15 percent. This trend is likely to continue because of the domination of the national economy by the capital city, which has a large industrial base and a growing middle class that demands first-world services. If the political stability that has now settled upon the country since 1992 continues, and if the neoliberal, private-enterprise policies of the conservative government currently in office pay dividends, in a few years El Salvador will have undergone a complete economic transformation. Facts, figures and projections, however, cannot disguise the fact that El Salvador is a small, poor, overpopulated, developing country where the struggle for food, land, work and liberty is a daily reality for the vast majority of its population.

HISTORY

Pre-Columbian History

The American continent, the last to be colonized by Paleolithic humans, was probably settled around 12,000 B.C. In the ensuing millennia gradual waves of migration spread into Mesoamerica, the region between Mexico and Panama. Between 4000 and 1600 B.C., American Indians (Amerindians) in Mexico and Guatemala gradually evolved from hunter-gatherers to agricultural farmers who cultivated *maize*, beans, gourds, chilies and a limited amount of fruits. If a modern observer could go back in time, what would be most striking is that the ancient Amerindians experienced a lifestyle similar to that of the remote communities of *campesinos* in the mountains and hills of El Salvador, who live in huts of wattle and daub, shell corn, weave baskets and textiles, and seldom wander far from their villages. As in many parts of El Salvador today, ancient villages were surrounded by *milpas* (small cornfields) whose produce was stored in underground silos.

Because of its geographic and historical marginalization from the traditional seats of power and influence in the Americas, archaeological and ethnographic research on El Salvador is still fairly limited.[13] However, it has been established that El Salvador was settled predominantly during three periods: the Preclassic (1200 B.C.–A.D. 250), the Classic (A.D. 250–900) and the Postclassic (A.D. 900–1524). In the course of approximately 3,000 years before the arrival of the Spaniards, El Salvador underwent various waves of migrations and conquests from the Mayan and Mexican empires to the north. Although there is some uncertainty regarding the precise chronology, the racial composition and the languages of pre-Columbian El Salvador, it is most likely that the country was settled by successive and sometimes simultaneous waves of Amerindians from two dominant groups: the Maya-Quichés from the region that encompasses modern Guatemala, Honduras and southeast Mexico, and the Nahuas from southern and central Mexico. The Maya-Quichés arrived between A.D. 500 and 800, the golden age of Mayan civilization. The Nahuas entered the country in increasingly large numbers after A.D. 900 and went on to become the most powerful racial, cultural and linguistic group by the time of the Spanish Conquest.

When the *conquistadores* arrived, they found a territory divided into three *señoríos* (kingdoms). The largest was Cuscatlán, which was bordered by the

Paz River on the west and by the Lempa River on the east. It covered an area of approximately 2,896 square miles. It is estimated that Cuscatlán—a name still applied affectionately to El Salvador in Central America—contained about 1,200 households in fifty-nine different towns and villages. Cuscatlán was governed by a powerful ethnic group called the Pipiles, a branch of the Nahuas who had entered El Salvador from Mexico during the preceding six centuries. The term *Pipil*, meaning "child" or "little old man," was coined by the Nahuas who accompanied the *conquistadores* in 1524. These Nahuas believed that their Salvadorean cousins spoke a dialect that they associated with the sound of children or of old people. To distinguish between the language of Mexicans and Cuscatlecos (citizens of Cuscatlán), the term Nahuatl is employed for the former and Nahuat for the latter.

Another Pipil kingdom at the time of the Spanish Conquest was that of Los Izalcos, which covered a region of about 965 square miles and incorporated fifteen principal towns in the southwest. Although nominally independent when the Spaniards arrived, Los Izalcos had fallen under the sphere of influence of the more powerful *señorío* of Cuscatlán. Between them the two Pipil kingdoms covered about 75 percent of modern El Salvador. To the east of the Lempa, in the area embraced by the departments of San Miguel, La Unión and Morazán, was the kingdom of Chaparrastique (Place of Beautiful Orchids), which was under the control of the Lencas, an early branch of the Maya-Quichés who may have been the original settlers of El Salvador.

Many other smaller ethnic groups, all related to the Maya-Quichés, were subsumed within the three kingdoms that the Spaniards encountered. The Chorti and the Pokomam were in the west. The Ulúa were in the southeast. The Mangue were in the far eastern region. It is calculated that as many as a million people may have lived in El Salvador at the time of the Spanish Conquest, although around 130,000 is a more realistic estimate. There was regular warfare among the three kingdoms, and some of the smaller tribes occasionally rebelled against their more powerful neighbors, but it appears that there was sufficient harmony in ancient El Salvador for the development of flourishing commercial relations among the various groups. The main commodity was cocoa, but *maize*, balsam and cotton were also traded across the Lempa, which was navigable by canoe. As in Mexico, cocoa beans were utilized as a rudimentary form of money. A rabbit was worth ten beans, a slave was worth 100 beans, and eight sapodilla plums were worth four beans.

The *conquistadores* were initially drawn to El Salvador from their bases in Mexico and Panama by its reputation as a rich, fertile land. Led by Pedro de Alvarado, one of Hernán Cortés's most dashing but ruthless lieutenants, the conquest of El Salvador was a particularly savage affair. After entering the kingdom of Cuscatlán from Guatemala on June 6, 1524, with 250 Spaniards and 6,000 *indios amigos* (Indian allies), Alvarado used his superior firepower to rout the Pipiles at the celebrated Battle of Acajutla on June 8. Furious at not finding the expected quantities of gold, Alvarado adopted a scorched-earth policy. He subjected the Indians to cruel punishment and death. However, stout resistance by the legendary chieftain Atlacatl prevented him from capturing the Pipil capital. After being badly injured in battle, Alvarado left the enterprise of conquest in the hands of his brothers Gonzalo and Diego, who founded the original village of San Salvador in April 1525. The members of the Alvarado clan and their followers spent the next few years quelling Indian rebellions. By 1528, after the famous capture of Cinacantlán, an Indian stronghold on the coast where the port of La Libertad now stands, the kingdom of Cuscatlán west of the Lempa was "pacified."

The conquest of El Salvador was complicated by the fact that another expeditionary force entered the Lenca kingdom of Chaparrastique from the east in 1530. Led by Martín de Estete, who was acting on behalf of the ambitious governor of Nicaragua, Pedrarias Dávila, this other band of *conquistadores* crossed the Lempa into Cuscatlán and founded an alternative capital, Ciudad de los Caballeros, a few miles from the village of San Salvador. Apparently intent on establishing a new province based on the slave trade under the jurisdiction of Nicaragua, Estete sparred and parried with the Alvarado-led forces for a few weeks until he realized the futility of his enterprise and returned to Nicaragua. Aware of the need for a bastion east of the Lempa, the Alvarados established the village of San Miguel de la Frontera, the forerunner of the modern city. The *conquistadores* were now in a position to wage a war of pacification on Chaparrastique. In spite of fierce guerrilla warfare by the legendary Lenca chieftain Lempira, within ten years Chaparrastique had succumbed to the Spaniards. By 1540 the Spanish Conquest was basically complete, but not before a pattern of civil conflict, military repression and antagonism with Central American neighbors had been set for the next 450 years of Salvadorean history.

The colonial history of El Salvador lasted until 1821. As in the rest of the Americas one overriding fact stands out: the violent, implacable incorporation of the indigenous groups into a new racial, religious, cultural, political and economic order.[14] Due to the waves of dispossession, disease, violence and hardship that followed the bloodshed of the Spanish Conquest, the native population of El Salvador collapsed dramatically. By the middle of the sixteenth century it had dropped to no more than 60,000. Particularly hard hit was the Lenca population east of the Lempa, whose social structure was much less cohesive than that of the Pipiles in the west. Indeed, it has even been suggested that in El Salvador the ravages of measles, chicken pox, malaria and yellow fever were so devastating, and the policy of pacification and assimilation by the Spaniards so ruthless, that many of the Indians who did not die lost the will to live. The historian David Browning, for example, states that in 1550 there were seventy Indian villages with a population of 30,000 in a particular area east of the Lempa. By 1590, eighteen of these villages had disappeared and the population had fallen to 8,300. Historians also record a steep decline in the indigenous birthrate throughout El Salvador in the years following the Spanish Conquest.

In 1542 Spain promulgated the Laws of the Indies in response to a campaign by Bartolomé de las Casas, who defended the Indians' right to be treated as human beings subject to the laws of God and the king. Nevertheless, de facto slavery continued to exist in El Salvador until the end of the sixteenth century. Formerly proud Indian warriors were branded with irons and reduced to *tamemes* (beasts of burden), while the women were taken as concubines by the Spaniards. Small numbers of Indians were also transported to Peru, where they were sold as slaves. Black slaves were also brought from Africa to act as foremen over the Indians in Salvadorean cocoa and balsam plantations. It is also recorded that some Spanish planters ordered their black slaves to breed with Indian women so that their children could be brought up as slaves. Such attitudes toward the Indians laid the foundations for the subsequent ethnic composition of El Salvador, with full-blooded Pipiles, Lencas and other tribes gradually disappearing and giving way to a new *mestizo* (mixed-blood) race of Spanish and Indian parentage. The genes of the few thousand African slaves were spread and diluted among the *mestizo* population. Consequently, El Salvador today is one of the most *mestizo* nations in Latin America.

Colonial Life and Government

From the moment of its incorporation as a colony of the Spanish empire, El Salvador was burdened by what was to become its defining characteristic: its marginalization. To govern its widespread empire Spain established a series of *audiencias* (tribunals), which combined the functions of a court of law and a legislative assembly. Cut off until 1549 from the power centers in Panama, Peru and Mexico, El Salvador was administered until 1549 from the Audiencia de Los Confines, a remote jurisdiction within the confines of Honduras. From 1549 to the outbreak of the War of Independence against Spain (1811), the most important decisions affecting El Salvador were taken from the Audiencia de Guatemala, which was subsequently raised to the level of a *capitanía-general*. One of the first decisions that the Spanish authorities made concerning El Salvador was to establish a colonial institution known as the *encomienda* (a plantation or estate), whereby a landowner known as an *encomendero* was assigned a number of Indians to work for him and provide him with a *tributo* (a tax based on their labor). As in the other parts of the Spanish empire, however, the system of *encomienda* and *tributo* quickly degenerated into slavery.[15]

Almost devoid of silver and gold, El Salvador was very soon in danger of losing its most ambitious and adventurous settlers to the Peruvian gold rush. Consequently, the Spanish authorities encouraged the settlers to remain by granting them large *encomiendas* where they could utilize Indians to farm two commercial crops: balsam and cocoa. The Indians who grew balsam and cocoa in their traditional lands were also forced to pay their *tributo* in kind. These two crops were the colony's economic mainstay for the first seventy-five years. They were exported in large quantities to other parts of the Spanish empire. The virtual disappearance by 1750 of balsam and cocoa in colonial El Salvador, however, is symptomatic of the country's history. Too many Indians died from disease and exploitation to make the industries viable, and Spain soon discouraged the cultivation of cocoa in El Salvador in favor of Guayaquil and Venezuela, which were closer to its main trading routes in the Pacific and the Atlantic.

Unfortunately, during the sixteenth century the foundations were laid for a political and economic system that would retard development and progress in El Salvador. The system was one of dependence between Spain's representatives in Guatemala and a hierarchy of clients and hangers-on headed by the *alcaldes mayores* (lord mayors) in the provinces of San Salvador and Sonsonate. Both lord mayors were responsible to the captaincy-general of Guatemala, which had ultimate political and economic control over El Salvador. Some of the richest cocoa and balsam plantations in El Salvador were owned by *encomenderos* in Guatemala. While Guatemala grew rich on El Salvador, the lord mayors of San Salvador and Sonsonate developed a network of patronage that allowed them, their relatives, their friends and other leading colonial functionaries to accumulate wealth and privileges. As in other parts of the Spanish empire the *encomienda*, which was in reality a disguised form of slavery, was eventually replaced by the *repartimento*, in theory a fairer system under which the Indians had to provide periodic labor on farms for a small wage. Through bribes and nepotism, however, landowners could often avoid payment to the Indians.

In keeping with the pattern of colonial government in Peru and Mexico, *cabildos* (town councils) were established in El Salvador. The *cabildos* had the authority to sell land to wealthy Spaniards. The landowners used this opportunity to establish *haciendas*, which were often enlarged by the cheap purchase or usurpation of traditional Indian land. By the end of the sixteenth century the colonial authorities also created the so-called *pueblos de indios*, which were villages established ostensibly for the purpose of evangelizing and civilizing the natives. To administer the *pueblos de indios* the lord mayors set up a system of indirect rule, forming *cabildos de indios* (Indian councils) that were headed by *caciques*, native chiefs who often became accomplices in a well-oiled machinery of exploitation and extortion. In 1710 an edict was passed that made the Spanish language a prerequisite for membership in the *cabildos*, thus imposing even tighter controls upon the daily lives of the Indians and striking a further blow against indigenous pride and identity. Each Indian village was given the name of a patron saint (for example, Santo Domingo, Santa Catarina) and a *cofradía* (brotherhood) was organized to pay the salaries of the parish priests (mainly Dominicans and Franciscans) who had begun to arrive in increasing numbers.

Following the collapse of the cocoa and balsam industries, Salvadorean landowners were fortunate to discover a new major commercial crop: *añil* (indigo dye), which became the colony's principal source of revenue until the late nineteenth century. The Pipiles had cultivated *jiquilite* (indigo plant) in small quantities for sale to the northern tribes of Mexico. The extremely high quality of Salvadorean indigo created a strong demand for it in Holland and England, which were prepared to pay a high price for it. Throughout most of the seventeenth and the eighteenth centuries it was the profits from indigo that provided the means to purchase the gold, silver, wine, china and fine cloths that helped make life comfortable for the Salvadorean elite. During the years of the indigo boom, El Salvador became the second richest region in Central America after Guatemala. Although the Spanish monarchy prohibited the utilization of Indian labor in the harsh, insalubrious indigo plantations and mills, the lord mayors turned a blind eye to the exploitation of the natives and the usurpation of their land. By 1738, when the use of Indian laborers in the indigo plantations was legalized, entire Indian villages had been destroyed and thousands of natives had died from fever and other infectious diseases.

On the other hand, the wealth that the indigo industry generated for the Salvadorean landowners was restricted by two factors: the continued marginalization of Central America within the Spanish empire, and the monopolistic control of Central American trade by the merchants of Guatemala. Because of Spain's policy of mercantilism, all international trade to and from the colonies had to pass through a few selected ports and follow prescribed trading routes, all of which bypassed the Central American coastline. To make matters worse, Central America was serviced only by a secondary route between Seville and the Gulf of Honduras. The situation was aggravated further by the growth of English piracy in the Caribbean throughout the sixteenth and seventeenth centuries, which made maritime trade in the region a hazardous affair. Consequently, the number of trading vessels leaving Central America with Salvadorean indigo were few and irregular. There was a sharp drop from 118 ships between 1550 and 1559 to a mere 17 ships between 1700 and 1749. At one stage there was a gap of eight years between arrivals of ships. Not surprisingly, Salvadorean indigo growers began to question and criticize Spanish trading policy in Central America. The protests became louder and fiercer when the so-called Bourbon Reforms were enacted during the reign of Charles III (1759–88). The reforms were supposed to free trade and increase economic activity in Spanish America, but they actually led to tighter controls over the increased number of ships laden with indigo that were leaving for Spain. Following the French Revolution, Spain became involved in European affairs, including a war against England, and this meant the imposition of higher taxes upon Salvadorean landowners and an interruption of the indigo trade for four years.

Salvadorean indigo planters were preeminently native-born *criollos* (born of Spanish parents in El Salvador). They bitterly resented what they regarded as profiteering by the Guatemalan merchants who, in league with royal functionaries, controlled the indigo trade. The Guatemalans owned the lending houses upon which the Salvadoreans depended for financing the cultivation and production of indigo. The Guatemalans also determined the price at which the precious dye could be purchased. The collective monopoly of Guatemalan merchants extended to other Salvadorean industries such as iron, which by the end of the eighteenth century had become a major source of revenue in the northwest region of Metapán. The monopolistic practices of the Guatemalan merchants played a major role in fostering an independence movement in El Salvador, and there is no doubt that a historical memory of the power that Guatemala once wielded over El Salvador still influences the relationship between the two countries.

Independence

There are two valuable documents that permit the reconstruction of Salvadorean society in the crucial period leading up to independence from Spain. The first, *Descripción geográfico-moral de la diócesis de Guatemala*

(Geographic and moral description of the diocese of Guatemala), was written by Archbishop Don Pedro Cortés y Larraz after he visited thirty-four towns around the Lempa between November 1761 and July 1762. The second, *Estado general de la provincia de San Salvador* (General conditions in the province of El Salvador) was composed between 1806 and 1807 by Antonio Gutiérrez y Ulloa, an *intendente* (governor) who took a special interest in the lives of the people under his jurisdiction. From these two sources it can be established that the population of El Salvador (combining San Salvador and Sonsonate) on the eve of the wars of independence in Latin America (1811–21) was approximately 250,000. About 50 percent of the people were *mestizos*, 40 percent were Indians and less than 3 percent were Spaniards. The latter category was divided into *peninsulares* (born in Spain) and *criollos*. Both *peninsulares* and *criollos* were equal before the king, and although there were some tensions between them, these were not as deep as in other parts of the Spanish empire since both groups were united in their resentment of Guatemalan hegemony over El Salvador. Spanish was by now the primary language, but Indian languages were commonly heard.

At the turn of the nineteenth century there was still no school in the city of San Salvador, and only about 250 school pupils were in the whole of El Salvador. Since there was no institution of higher learning, young people had to go to Guatemala to pursue further studies at the University of San Carlos. Indian *curanderos* (faith healers or witch doctors) plied their trade. Belief in *nahuales* (animal totems) was widespread among the Indians, who usually attached an animal reference to their Christian name (for example, Juan Venado means John Deer).

The economic exploitation of the indigenous population was an everyday reality. Numerous Indians had abandoned their *pueblos* and fled to the countryside *para vivir con libertad* (to seek a life of freedom). Both the *mestizos* and the Spaniards looked down upon the Indians, while the Spaniards felt racially and culturally superior to the *mestizos*. There were about 440 cattle and indigo *haciendas* that were owned by no more than 300 wealthy, mainly *criollo* families. About 80 percent of the population, a combination of Indians and *mestizo* peasants, eked out an existence on the *haciendas* as illegal squatters, small tenant farmers or peons. Apart from the five main cities (San Salvador, Sonsonate, San Vicente, Santa Ana and San Miguel), a network of smaller settlements had spread throughout the territory. These settlements included Metapán, Zacatecoluca, Chalatenango, Cojutepeque and Usulután. There were 122 *pueblos de indios*, many of which were by this stage semi-abandoned or taken over by *mestizos*.

El Salvador, therefore, was an isolated, agrarian, hierarchical, racially divided pocket of the Spanish Empire, but it had steadily developed a sense of separate identity by the time the Napoleonic invasion of Spain in 1808 opened the door to Latin American independence. The ideals of the French Revolution, the heroic example of the American Revolution and the stirring deeds of the great liberator Simón Bolívar in South America reached as far as El Salvador, where patriotic *criollos*, disillusioned with Spain and resentful of Guatemala, supported a revolutionary movement in 1811 that was led by a visionary priest named José Matías Delgado and his nephew Manuel José Arce. After ten turbulent years, during which El Salvador became a bulwark of Central American independence, the captaincy-general of Guatemala finally rejected Spanish rule in 1821. A confused, traumatic period ensued when all of Central America, with the exception of San Salvador and the district of San Vicente, were incorporated into a short-lived Mexican empire that was founded by a would-be Napoleon of the New World, General Augustín Iturbide. Following a failed bid by Salvadorean leaders to seek admission into the United States in 1822, El Salvador joined Honduras, Nicaragua, Costa Rica and Guatemala on July 1, 1823, in the formation of the Independent United Province of Central America, which was soon renamed the Federal Republic of Central America. Manuel José Arce was its first president.

The political system that was established lent itself to a bitter merry-go-round of conflict between a centralizing government at the federal level and five inward-looking governments at the regional level. This situation was exacerbated by the lingering suspicions that the other states retained of Guatemala. In addition, each state had internal problems of their own. In El Salvador a charismatic Indian chieftain, Anastasio Aquino, rebelled against the government in 1833 and declared himself king of the Nonualcos in the department of Zacatecoluca. Thousands of Indians rallied to Aquino's call for land and justice. Although he was soon defeated and executed, his rebellion was a warning to El Salvador's leaders that serious measures were required to alleviate the lot of the Indians and poor *mestizos* in the countryside. In spite of further Indian revolts in 1842 in Ahuachapán and in 1854 in Tejutla, there was no meaningful or lasting endeavor to respond to the Indians' claims for a just distribution of land and properly remunerated work. If enlightened leadership had been displayed during these early years by its *caudillos* (the military strongmen in charge of the country's political fortunes), perhaps El Salvador's future might not have been so traumatic.

Unfortunately, at both state and federal levels Central America's energies at this crucial stage of its history were drained by a debilitating conflict between liberals, who favored free trade and advocated limits upon the influence of the Catholic Church, and conservatives, who supported protectionist economic policies and defended church involvement in affairs of state. Following a chaotic series of coups, countercoups, assassinations, executions and invasions of each other's territories by various states, the Central American Federation collapsed in 1840. Of all the *caudillos*, Francisco Morazán, a liberal who at different times was president of the federation, Honduras or El Salvador, had been the greatest champion of a united Central America. Although there would be sporadic attempts to revive it in subsequent years, the dream of union basically ended with Morazán's execution in 1842.

Following its formation as an independent nation in 1841, El Salvador fell into an orgy of political infighting between Morazán's liberal heirs and the conservatives, who were supported by a Guatemalan strongman, Rafael Carrera. During his long years in power Carrera wielded considerable influence in El Salvador, installing a series of puppet presidents. The confrontation between conservatives and liberals in El Salvador and in the rest of Central America was shelved temporarily in 1856, when a joint military expedition was launched to expel the infamous filibuster John Walker from Nicaragua. However, this respite was short-lived. In 1863 the most celebrated Salvadorean liberal president, Gerardo Barrios, declared war against Carrera. Barrios hoped to put an end to Guatemalan interference in Salvadorean affairs and to revive Morazan's vision of a united Central America. However, Barrios was defeated, and he was executed in 1865 by a Carrera puppet, the conservative Francisco Dueñas. The confrontation between liberals and conservatives in El Salvador continued until the mid-1880s, and fear of Guatemalan hegemony in Central America led to another war in 1885 in which the Guatemalan president, Justo Rufino Barrios, was killed.

In the midst of all this turmoil the government of El Salvador held a census in 1858, the results of which provided some illuminating facts. Outbreaks of smallpox and cholera were common, malaria was widespread, and primitive medical facilities impaired the general health of the population. Life expectancy was short, with less than 5 percent living beyond the age of fifty. Child labor was rife, male peasants over fifteen years of age were compelled to work as road builders for two days a week, and the *caudillos* recruited soldiers for their armies by forced levies of able-bodied Indians and poor *mestizos*. Women peasants worked alongside the men in the fields, and they also specialized in certain arts and crafts, such as pottery, weaving and hatmaking.

By the 1870s San Salvador was gradually developing the trappings of a capital city. A population of about 30,000 was serviced by a cathedral and up to ten churches, a university, a seminary, various hospitals, and an aqueduct that measured five miles. There was gas lighting in the main streets and some handsome colonial mansions for the city's elite. The seat of government was an attractive, neoclassical building. Weekly mail service connected El Salvador to the rest of Central America, and mail could be dispatched to other parts of the world by steamship. The first telegraph was installed in 1879. An earthquake in 1854 had arrested the city's development, but life was back to normal by 1859, at least for the elite, who could be seen promenading along Plaza Santo Domingo and sampling fine French food at Doña Luisa's restaurant.

The Coffee Republic

The coffee boom between the 1870s and the 1920s gave a name to a well-defined period in El Salvador's history: the Coffee Republic.[16] By 1875 coffee had overtaken indigo as the country's principal commercial product, and by 1890 the "golden grain" accounted for as much as 80 percent of Salvadorean exports. With the potential bonanza from coffee becoming immediately apparent, successive governments sought to promote its cultivation by generous incentives to growers and exporters, who were virtually exempt from taxes. While there is no doubt that coffee brought huge profits and benefits to El Salvador on a macroeconomic scale, it also had a negative impact upon its economic development. The almost total reliance upon a single crop exposed the country both to the vagaries of nature and to the inconstancy of the financial markets of North America and Europe. This monoculture had particularly grave consequences for El Salvador during times of international crisis, such as during the Great Depression, and during periods of internal political turmoil, such as during the civil war of the 1980s.

On paper the benefits during the years of the Coffee Republic were impressive. Realizing that economic development required political stability, the political, military and clerical establishments formed an alliance with the new coffee-growing oligarchy to usher in a period of *orden y progreso* (order and progress). Although one president was assassinated during this period (Manuel Enrique Araujo in 1913), and coups were still common, sufficient presidential terms were long enough to provide the country with a sense of steady, confident administration. The presidency of Rafael Zaldívar, for instance, lasted nine years (1876–85), and between 1913 and 1927 the Meléndez-Quiñónez dynast held the reins of power. Moreover, after armed conflicts with Guatemala in 1906 and with Honduras and Nicaragua in 1907, El Salvador's relations with its Central American neighbors improved considerably. The Central American Peace Conference in 1907 led to the establishment of the Central American Court of Justice.

All the presidents between 1911 and 1931 were civilians, and although there were differences of style among them, they were all liberals espousing *laissez faire* ("hands off") principles for the coffee industry. The government actively supported the planters and exporters by building railways and developing the port facilities in Acajutla, La Libertad and La Unión. It also passed antivagrancy laws to encourage peasants to work in the plantations, and it established the Guardia Nacional (National Guard) to keep law and order in the countryside. Perhaps the most notable achievement of the Coffee Republic was to instill a sense of nationhood among the citizenry by a series of important measures. In 1879, Giovanni Aberle set to music the national anthem, "Saludemos la patria orgullosos" (Let us proudly salute our country), with lyrics by the poet Juan José Cañas. The so-called Liberal Constitution of 1886 was promulgated, enshrining the values of the Coffee Republic for the next fifty years. Other initiatives included the replacement of foreign currency with official Salvadorean money, the centralization of government in the capital, the professionalization of the army, the establishment of an operational judicial system and the foundation of a network of consulates to represent El Salvador's interests abroad.

On the negative side of the ledger, one of the most infamous pieces of legislation in El Salvador's history was passed during the Coffee Republic. In 1881, President Zaldívar abolished the *tierras comunales* (communal lands owned by Indians or *mestizos*) to maximize the potential of the coffee industry. The next year the *ejidos* (land owned by the municipalities) were abolished. The result of this legislation was that almost overnight about a quarter of El Salvador passed into the hands of the coffee planters, who were able to buy or usurp parcels of land that thousands of Indians and *mestizos* farmed. In a country where land tenancy, however precarious, was necessary for the survival of peasants who grew subsistence crops (*maize*, beans, rice and sweet potatoes), this meant a revolutionary change in the social and cultural profile of El Salvador. The seeds were sown for the creation of the notorious Fourteen Families, who through strategic marriages and alliances controlled the country's economic and political destiny for the next hundred years. Whereas until the abolition of the *tierras comunales* and the *ejidos* there were few farms exceeding fifty to seventy-five acres, by 1900 the *hacienda* had become part and parcel of the Salvadorean landscape. For instance, in 1910 Angel Guirola owned a *hacienda* of 765 acres, Rafael Guirola Duke had one of 667 acres and the heirs of Félix Dárdano had one of 444 acres. It was also common for big landowners to possess their own coffee mills and export houses, which promptly led to a monopoly of the coffee industry. The elite of the Coffee Republic resided in luxurious villas in the capital.

They traveled by steamer to New York and Paris. Their sons went to the best American universities, and their daughters went to the most prestigious finishing schools in Europe.

The concentration of the coffee industry in the hands of a few impresarios created economic inequities that were aggravated by the government's policy on taxation. The government removed direct taxes on the coffee industry, choosing instead to raise revenue through import duties on goods brought into the country from Europe and the United States. While the elite could afford to pay the tax on luxury goods, the long-suffering peasantry had to bear an increasingly severe taxation burden on such essential items as cotton shirts and machetes, on which a levy of 120 percent was imposed. By 1885, 75 percent of state revenue was raised from import duties. Yet the life of Indians and poor *mestizos* continued to deteriorate. The health system continued to languish, and education reached a minimal proportion of the population. Indeed, it was government policy to limit educational reforms on the basis that literacy and learning could stimulate the underprivileged either to ask too many questions or to begin wondering whether there may be alternatives to the daily grind of work on a coffee plantation or a workshop.

It is a sad reflection upon the Coffee Republic that any significant social and educational reforms were left to *asociaciones mutuales*, which were guilds of shoemakers, tailors, printers and blacksmiths that launched literacy campaigns and founded a network of night schools for their members and their families. One of the most important reforms was the institution of La Universidad Popular (The University of the People), which offered weekly lectures on such issues as health, education, politics and workers' rights. The guilds can be credited with raising the political consciousness of peasants and workers.

As the gap between poor and rich continued to widen, violence against the coffee planters and their overseers became a common feature of Salvadorean life. Racial tensions between Indians and *mestizos* resurfaced, and the Indians formed brotherhoods to protect their interests. By the 1920s El Salvador was rapidly turning into a cauldron of social, economic, ethnic and political conflicts. The reigning Meléndez-Quiñónez dynasty sought to control the situation by violent repression, either through the often brutal intervention of the National Guard or through a progovernment association known as Liga Roja (Red League), which harassed opponents. Concerned about the ethnic tensions, the government also entered into a series of strategic alliances with disaffected Indian communities, such as with the powerful Nahuizalcos who lived west of the Lempa.

Influenced by the Mexican and Russian Revolutions, artesan guilds in El

Salvador turned into trade unions in the 1920s. Their manifestos included references to armed struggle. The Federación Regional de Trabajadores (Regional Federation of Labor) was formed in 1923, and its membership soon mushroomed to tens of thousands of workers under leaders who were sympathetic to the ideals of communism and anarchosyndicalism. The political temperature in the country heated up when the United States invaded Nicaragua in 1926. Salvadorean students joined workers in opposition to what was denounced as American imperialism in Central America. Such an explosive set of circumstances—oligarchical privilege, government repression, rural misery, trade-union activism, student militancy and anti-imperialism—brought the Coffee Republic to the brink of collapse by the time presidential elections were held in 1927.

There were high hopes for the new president, Pío Romero Bosque, one of the most principled and reform-minded politicians in El Salvador's history. Don Pío, as he became known, embarked upon a program to raise the moral standards of society and politics in the country, even if this meant provoking the ire of the Meléndez-Quiñónez dynasty and the coffee oligarchy. His ideas were inspired by one of El Salvador's most revered and influential intellectuals, Alberto Masferrer (1868–1932). In his celebrated tomes, *El dinero maldito* (The curse of money) and *El mínimum vital* (The essential minimum), Masferrer argued for the establishment of a new public culture that would be founded on the principles of mutual respect and shared responsibilities among all the sectors of Salvadorean society: rich and poor, Indian and *mestizo*, town and country. He envisioned a well-ordered nation with an efficient health system and a basic wage that would permit all Salvadorans to enjoy a healthy diet. He advocated women's rights, and he warned against domestic violence and the dangers of alcohol, which since independence had been used by the government to raise revenue through a "rum tax." Unfortunately, the entrenched opposition of the oligarchy and the cataclysmic effects of the Great Depression thwarted both don Pío and Masferrer.

Almost totally dependent upon coffee, El Salvador's national economy collapsed when the bottom fell out of the international market for its precious commodity. The massive retrenchment of peasants in the countryside, the wholesale destruction of small businesses in towns and cities, and the confiscation of small farms by debtors led to waves of strikes and antigovernment demonstrations. The violent retaliation by the national security forces aggravated the situation. The ranks of the Communist Party of El Salvador, which was founded in 1930, were swelled by an angry influx of unemployed peasants and workers who were supported by students, teachers and civil servants. Moreover, entire Indian communities, particularly those from the western coffee-growing districts where the Great Depression had struck hardest, joined the Communist Party. Since communal ties dating back to pre-Columbian times were still strong among the Indians, the ideals of communism seemed to offer a practical solution to the crisis that was engulfing them. Led by Farabundo Martí, a charismatic guerrilla who had fought with the legendary Augusto César Sandino against the Somoza regime in Nicaragua, the Communist Party of El Salvador was supported by the forces of international communism, which believed that the conditions in this tiny republic were ideal for a successful revolution.

Notwithstanding the explosive situation facing the country, don Pío Romero Bosque held presidential elections on schedule in 1930. It is to his credit that they are regarded as one of the cleanest on record in Salvadorean history. However, his successor, Arturo Araujo, a would-be reformer influenced by the British Labour Party, could not stem the twin tides of revolution and repression. A military coup in December 1931 overthrew Araujo, after a mere nine months in power. The country was then plunged into one of its bloodiest periods under one of its most infamous dictators.

The Great Slaughter and *El Martinato*

The new president was General Maximiliano Hernández Martínez, a ruthless eccentric nicknamed *El Brujo* (The Witch Doctor) because he was a practicing theosophist (a devotee of a secret doctrine) who believed in telepathy and reincarnation. His detractors claimed that he had a higher regard for animals than for humans. Through a combination of repression, rigged elections, constitution tampering, a patriarchal attitude, and plain good luck, Martínez governed El Salvador for thirteen years. In a historical perspective *El Martinato* (The Martínez Clampdown), as his dictatorship became known, is significant in that it ushered in almost half a century of direct military rule.

Barely a year after coming to power, Martínez gave the order for *La Matanza* (The Great Slaughter) when a widespread peasant uprising began on the night of January 22–23 in the western districts. This led to the brutal massacre of up to 30,000 men, women and children.[17] Although the historical evidence leaves no doubt that the Communist Party of El Salvador organized the uprising under the auspices of international communism, the mainspring for the revolt was the hardship and oppression under which the peasants had to labor on the coffee plantations, a situation made totally unbearable following the Great Depression. Encouraged by their *caciques*, Feliciano Ama of Izalco and Felipe Neri of Nahuizalco, the vast majority of the Indian communities west of the Lempa joined the insurrection. From the outset, however, what was supposed to become an unstoppable national revolution became mired in logistical incompetence and a lack of coordination. The *jefe máximo* (supreme leader), Farabundo Martí, was captured even before the planned date of the uprising, leaving the waves of machete-wielding peasants directionless and at the mercy of Martínez's security forces. Described by none other than Martínez as a a generous and disinterested man, Martí was executed on February 1 after swearing allegiance to Sandino in Nicaragua and to communism.[18] Most of the other communist leaders in El Salvador were also summarily executed, as were the two Indian *caciques* who had supported the revolt.

The Great Slaughter had dramatic consequences for El Salvador. Not only did it eliminate most of the country's existing indigenous population, but it also created a reluctance on the part of the few remaining Indians to draw attention to themselves by speaking Indian tongues, wearing traditional dress or practicing native customs. To a large extent, therefore, the Great Slaughter of 1932 helps to explain why there are so few outward signs of indigenous culture in El Salvador today. In addition the massacre of communists, other left-wing militants and sympathizers explains why, in spite of the continuation of profound socioeconomic inequalities, it took another generation for a new left-wing vanguard to emerge in El Salvador.

An admirer of the dictators Benito Mussolini and Adolf Hitler, General Martínez ran El Salvador like a police state, using his own party, Legion Pro-Patria (Legion of the Motherland), as the political basis for his dictatorship. The fear of communism in Latin America and the desire to win Martínez over to the Allied cause encouraged the United States to recognize his regime and to provide him with economic assistance. When the wily Martínez declared war on the Axis in 1941, he was promptly rewarded with two loans for more than $US4.5 million. For all his brutality, like most dictators Martínez did record some positive achievements. The creation of the Banco Central de Reserva (Central Reserve Bank) in 1934 meant that whereas in the past the Salvadorean government had to rely on private banks for printing money, it could now issue its own national currency. The *colón* was set at the rate of $US 2.50, at which it was to remain for the next fifty years. To earn the support of the coffee oligarchy, upon whose continued prosperity the stability of his regime depended, Martínez also set up the Banco Hipotecario (Loans and Mortgage Bank).

Martínez displayed a populist touch with a series of measures that were designed to widen the political base of his regime. He established the Cajas de Crédito Rurales (Rural Credit Societies) to assist the interests of the small farmers, most of whom had been badly hit by the Great Depression. A program known as *mejoramiento social* (social improvement) provided cheap housing for a limited number of families, and he also implemented a restricted package of land redistribution. Salvadorean artisans were very grateful to the dictator when he passed legislation that protected local crafts against foreign-manufactured products. Although most of Martínez's reforms were little more than paternalistic window dressing, they softened the monstrous image that he acquired following the Great Slaughter.

Nevertheless, by the early 1940s the repressive, personalized nature of Martínez's regime had not only alienated even his closest supporters among the oligarchy and the military, but it had also galvanized disparate opposition groups in the capital, including students, teachers, intellectuals, mutual societies, civil servants, market vendors, shop owners and dissident army officers. The execution of the leaders of a failed coup on April 2, 1944, and jackboot tactics against his expanding number of enemies provoked a strike that paralyzed San Salvador at the end of April and the first week of May. When a student with American nationality was killed during the anti-Martínez demonstrations, the American Embassy put pressure upon the dictator, who was forced to resign on May 8. Martínez departed for exile in Honduras. He lived there until 1966, when one of his own servants hacked him to pieces with a machete.

1948–61: The Era of Lost Opportunity

Following a confused period of four years that was marked by corruption and repression, the so-called Revolution of 1948 was launched by an ardent group of youthful officers who regarded themselves as the bridge between traditional military values and civilian ideals of modernity and reform. A short-lived Governing Revolutionary Council (December 1948–March 1950) that was composed of military figures and civilians is remembered especially for its heady mixture of rhetoric and idealism that culminated in a new constitution in 1950. Focusing on the state's democratic obligation to reconcile economic modernization with social justice, including the right to work of all citizens, the constitution inspired some important if limited reforms by the next two presidents, Major Oscar Osorio (1949–56) and Colonel José María Lemus (1956–60).

Wary of the radical reformism that happened in Guatemala in 1944, which eventually led to the overthrow of President Jacobo Arbenz in 1954 by U.S.-backed right-wing exiles, Osorio sought to curb the idealism of his younger officers. Not wishing to alienate the oligarchy, he ensured that the temporary bonanza accruing from high coffee and cotton prices was used only for strictly limited programs such as social security, hospital and medical care, urban housing and rural land settlement. His government also laid the foundations for the selective industrialization of El Salvador, with shoes, textiles, cement and chemical products produced for the Central American and U.S. markets. Such reforms, while welcome, largely benefited a small urban sector that in due course came to comprise a privileged middle class, which was based predominantly in San Salvador. The country continued to bear the characteristics of a dependent third-world society. The army controlled its political fortunes, and a mere 8 percent of the population hoarded over 50 percent of the national revenue. The flight of capital to banks in the United States and Europe was a significant factor in retarding economic and social progress. More money left El Salvador between 1945 and 1955 than from all the other Central American republics combined.

By the end of the 1950s El Salvador was showing ominous signs of reverting to the odious model of General Martínez. The country had become a virtual one-party state under PRUD (Revolutionary Party of Democratic Unification). Opponents of the regime were persecuted or exiled, and loyal military officers were rewarded with important posts within the government or the party.[19] By 1960 El Salvador was in crisis because of a collapse of the coffee and cotton markets, and President Lemus cast nervous glances at recent events in Cuba, where Fidel Castro had come to power. As the situation became increasingly intolerable, a united opposition of students, trade unionists, political dissidents and a revived Communist Party formed against the Lemus regime. Believing that the National University in San Salvador was the intellectual source of opposition against him, Lemus made the mistake of sending his security forces to the campus. On September 2, 1960, the Lemus forces savagely beat students, professors and the university president himself. This move cost Lemus the already wavering support of leading members of the oligarchy, whose own sons and daughters were among the victims. On October 26 a group of reform-minded officers launched a coup against the beleaguered president, and a retaliatory coup by military hardliners followed on January 25, 1961.

Yet again, another period of Salvadorean history came to a sad, ignominious conclusion. The opportunity for genuine, lasting reform that was promised by the Revolution of 1948 had been foiled by unenlightened military leadership, the self-interest of the oligarchy and El Salvador's monocultural dependency.

Stalled Reforms and War with Honduras

The decade after Lemus's demise was dominated by two more military presidents, Colonel Julio Adalberto Rivera (1961–67) and General Fidel Sánchez Hernández (1967–72). In view of U.S. president John F. Kennedy's Alliance for Progress, which aimed to promote good will, democracy and development in Latin America, both presidents were under pressure to apply the familiar formula of limited reforms. The aftershocks of Fidel Castro's revolution were spreading throughout the Caribbean and Central America. The more pragmatic members of the military and oligarchical establishments realized that social and economic changes were needed in El Salvador if the Cuban experience was not to be repeated there. In 1963 President Rivera introduced a compulsory income tax so that, at least in theory, some of the profits reaped by the oligarchy could be used to improve the lot of the poor, particularly in the neglected countryside. In 1965 a minimum rural wage was established in spite of an outcry among some rich coffee-growers that such a measure would encourage "demagogery."

Both Rivera and Sánchez Hernández were elected under the banner of a new party, the PCN (Party of National Conciliation), that the military and their oligarchical allies created to oversee a cautious democratization of the Salvadorean political system. Laws promulgating the basic democratic freedoms of thought, expression and assembly were enacted. The autonomy of the National University was reestablished. Trade-union activity was permitted. Rivera became the last president to be elected under the winner-take-all electoral formula because of the introduction in 1963 of proportional representation. This reform meant that for the first time in Salvadorean history each party's representatives in municipal and legislative assemblies would be determined by the number of votes cast in its favor. Although elections could still be manipulated by the military and the oligarchy, the door was now open for some semblance of political pluralism. Consequently, in 1964 José Napoleón Duarte, the leader of the opposition PCD (Christian Democratic Party), was elected mayor of San Salvador. Amid grumblings from die-hard conservatives, the government respected Duarte's victory. It was because of his commitment and effectiveness as mayor that Duarte gained the national profile necessary to launch his bid for the presidency in 1972.

A gradual movement toward regional economic integration had started in 1950. The inauguration of the Central American Common Market in 1964 signaled a crucial development that would have dramatic consequences for El Salvador before the end of the decade. By 1960 the minuscule republic was bursting at the seams. It had a population density of 463 per square mile, whereas the figure for the rest of Central America was a mere 94 per square mile. On the other hand, El Salvador's population of 3 million was not large enough to provide a sustainable market for its domestic industries. By establishing a free-trade zone, a customs union and the rationalization of industrial development in the region, the Central American Common Market soon proved of immense benefit to El Salvador. By 1965, 30 percent of all Central American trade was controlled by El Salvador, and the export of textiles increased from $US2.1 million in 1960 to $US16.5 million in 1970. In the course of the decade the manufacture of electrical appliances became an important industry, earning $US4.2 million in 1970.

The program of Central American economic integration suffered from a major drawback. Whereas El Salvador and Guatemala, the two most industrialized countries, earned considerable rewards, Honduras and Nicaragua, the two least-developed ones, saw their relative economic situation go backward. Honduras, in particular, felt aggrieved with the uneven pace of development. It soon began to nurture a deep resentment of El Salvador, which controlled 50 percent of all Honduran trade in Central America. In one of the great ironies of Central American history a poor country like El Salvador "was beginning to take on, vis-à-vis Honduras, the relationship typical of an advanced country with an underdeveloped satellite."[20] To make matters worse, by 1969 El Salvador's population had grown to more than 3.5 million, with 40 percent under the age of fifteen. San Salvador's population alone had mushroomed from 280,000 in 1961 to 350,000 in 1969. Such demographic pressures, in addition to the fact that a privileged 2 percent of the people owned over 60 percent of the land in El Salvador, meant that by 1969 about 300,000 Salvadorean peasants had crossed the border into Honduras.[21]

Throughout 1968 and 1969 Honduras was in the midst of an economic crisis. There were crippling strikes and long-standing demands for land reform by peasant leaders, who regarded the Salvadoreans as poachers. Rich Honduran landowners, interested in expanding their own plantations, fanned the anti-Salvadorean sentiments among the peasantry. Tensions between the two countries escalated in April and May 1969, when the Honduran government implemented an agrarian-reform plan that included a provision for expelling thousands of Salvadorean "illegals." It was unfortunate that immediately afterward, on June 8 and June 15, two World Cup soccer elimination matches were scheduled between the two countries. In spite of the saber rattling on both sides of the border, the matches were played. Honduras won the first match in Tegucigalpa by one goal to none. El Salvador won the second match in San Salvador by three goals to none. With Honduras eliminated from the World Cup by "big brother" El Salvador in a deciding match staged in Mexico on June 29, anti-Salvadorean feelings reached fever pitch. Meanwhile, the arrival of angry, confused columns of Salvadorean refugees confirmed the worst possible suspicions against Hondurans. The so-called Soccer War erupted on July 14. Before the OAS (Organization of

American States) could broker a cease-fire on July 18, up to 80,000 Salvadorean refugees had returned home, and some 4,000 people from both sides had been killed. A major consequence of the war was that the Central American Common Market was suspended for almost twenty-five years.

El Salvador Plunges into Civil War

The initial period of elation following the Soccer War was characterized by heady talk of national unity that was based on a widespread plan of agrarian reform. The mass media raised hopes of a *patria renovada* (reborn country) for the tens of thousands of refugees who were seeking land, work and education. Once again such idealism was short-lived. In the presidential elections of 1972 José Napoleón Duarte, the popular mayor of San Salvador and the candidate of a united bloc of centrist and left-wing parties, was deprived of victory by blatant vote rigging. Aware of the dangers of repeating the mistakes of the past, yet another patriotic group of young military officers launched a coup against the president elect, Colonel Arturo Armando Molina, the candidate of the PCN, the party of the military and the oligarchy. The coup failed. Duarte, who had been savagely beaten, was forced into exile, and El Salvador reverted to its traditional pattern of repression and persecution by military dictators.

Colonel Molina (1972–77) tried to salvage some credibility by initiating a feeble attempt at land reform in San Miguel and Usulután, but large landowners quickly stopped it. In the forty years since the Great Slaughter a new and reinvigorated left-wing leadership, inspired and in many cases trained by Castro and Che Guevara, had evolved in El Salvador. Molina was now confronted with the opposition of such groups as the FPL-FM (Popular Liberation Forces of Farabundo Martí) and the ERP (People's Revolutionary Army). These succesors of Farabundo Martí, who had by now acquired legendary status, advocated armed struggle and guerrilla warfare as the only solutions to political corruption, social injustice and economic exploitation. They had also learned the lesson of history: ragtag bands of peasants and Indians were no match for ruthless security forces. So they actively began to obtain military, financial and other political assistance (education, propaganda, refuge) from the Soviet Union and its satellites.

As it became apparent that a revolution was indeed possible in El Salvador, Molina and his successor, General Carlos Humberto Romero (1976–79), supported and encouraged the activities of paramilitary groups whose activities earned them the designation of *escuadrones de la muerte* (death squads). Their names were indicative of their function: Orden (Order), Falange (the title of the Spanish Fascist Party), and Union de Guerreros Blancos (Union of the White Warriors). As the decade progressed a wide spectrum of radical left-wing groups, ranging from social democrats to Marxist-Leninists, became increasingly active in El Salvador. Their membership came from student organizations, intellectual groups, trade unions, peasant collectives and women's groups. Militant Christians and priests who were influenced by liberation theology (see Chapter 3) joined the left-wing tide of opposition, which found an intellectual and spiritual home in the Jesuit University of El Salvador. With the country ideologically and politically split into two hostile groups, it is not surprising that El Salvador became an orgy of kidnappings, assassinations, bombings and massacres. The country vied for international headlines with Nicaragua, where the infamous Somoza regime was overthrown by the leftist Sandinistas in 1979. U.S. president Jimmy Carter, a champion of human rights, led the chorus of outrage against the spiraling violence in El Salvador. Both sides were guilty of atrocities. The most shocking event in the first years of confrontation occurred in May 1979, when the armed forces perpetuated the Massacre in the Cathedral, and in December 1980, when soldiers brutally murdered four American churchwomen.

Following another coup by concerned young military officers in October 1979, El Salvador was governed by four successive military-civilian juntas for the next two and a half years. The last junta included Duarte, the man who would dominate Salvadorean politics until 1988, as provisional president. The checkered period of junta rule was noteworthy for a bold attempt to launch a comprehensive land-reform package. The plan redistributed 16 percent of the country's farmland, including 14 percent of all coffee plantations, 31 percent of all cotton plantations and 24 percent of all sugar plantations. Further reform was sabotaged by the fierce opposition of the oligarchy and the country's collapse into full-scale civil war. A member of a death squad assassinated Archbishop Oscar Arnulfo Romero, the legendary "voice of the voiceless," while he was celebrating mass in a hospital chapel on March 24, 1980. The following day dozens of innocent mourners at his funeral were massacred. The events triggered twelve years of fratricidal conflict. During this tragic period more than 70,000 people died, and hundreds of thousands of exiles and refugees left, mainly for the United States but also for Canada, Europe and countries as far away as Australia and New Zealand.[22]

The government's hopes of a quick victory against the left-wing insurgents were quickly dashed by the military coordination displayed by the FMLN (Farabundo Martí National Liberation Front), an umbrella of the five principal guerrilla groups, that in the preceding years had built up popular support in the deprived rural areas. By January 1981 the FMLN felt confident enough to launch a "Final Offensive" throughout El Salvador. Although it failed, it demonstrated to the government and the armed forces that the war would be a long, savage affair. The internationalization of the conflict was inevitable, given that its outbreak coincided with the Cold War between the United States and the Soviet Union. Convinced that the United States national security was as much at stake in El Salvador as in Nicaragua, where he was backing the right-wing contras against the Marxist Sandinistas, President Ronald Reagan negotiated with Congress to send massive economic and military aid to three successive Salvadorean governments. The governments were the juntas (1979–82), the provisional regime of President Alvaro Magaña (1982–84), and President Duarte (1984–88).

With American support the Salvadorean armed forces grew from 17,000 troops in 1980 to 56,000 in 1987. Elite officers and battalions also received anti-insurgency training in the United States. Beginning with $US25 million in 1981, by 1984 American assistance to the Salvadorean government had grown to $US197 million. A substantial percentage of this money was utilized to purchase sophisticated equipment, including helicopters and planes that were vital to the war effort against the guerrillas, who launched hit-and-run raids against bridges, factories, dams and electricity pylons in the countryside, particularly in the central, northwest and northeastern regions. By 1984 the FMLN had grown to about 12,000 experienced, well-trained guerrillas. It also received financial, logistic and military aid from the Soviet Union and its Eastern European allies via Cuba and Nicaragua. By 1984 the war had become a vicious stalemate, and the world was constantly shocked by reports of atrocities by both sides.

Although ARENA (Nationalist Republican Alliance), a new right-wing party founded by the hawkish Major Roberto D'Aubuisson, continued to urge a scorched-earth policy against the guerrilla forces that were entrenched in inaccessible mountains, President Duarte was sufficiently moved by the bloodletting to make overtures to the FDR (Democratic Revolutionary Front), the political wing of the FMLN. Subsequently, between 1983 and 1989 there was a series of international initiatives known as Contadora (involving Mexico, Venezuela, Colombia and Panama) and Esquipulas I and II (restricted to the five Central American republics) that sought to bring a negotiated end to the civil war in El Salvador. Unfortunately, both sides proved intractable. When Duarte, who was ill with terminal cancer, reached the end of his presidency, the bloodletting in El Salvador continued. The country was able to survive thanks to the economic assistance of the United States, the humanitarian aid from European countries and the remittances of Salvadorean exiles and refugees, which reached as much as US$1.4 billion a year.

Toward the end of 1989 the FLMN-FDR leadership made a last attempt to attain a military victory and embarked on another "Final Offensive." For eight days in November, San Salvador and the major eastern city of San Miguel faced the brunt of a massive guerrilla attack that left over 2,000 dead. With the failure of the "Final Offensive," it became obvious to even the most obdurate hard-liners on either side that a negotiated solution had to be found. The new U.S. president, George Bush, favored this position. The inauguration of Alfredo Cristiani, the new Salvadorean president, offered a propitious moment to make a concerted effort for peace, as this was the first time since 1931 that one civilian president had passed the baton to another one. An intelligent, pragmatic businessman with a realistic vision of El Salvador's place in the world and, in particular, in Central America, Cristiani was able to moderate the policies of his party, ARENA, and offered the olive branch to the FMLN-FDR leaders, who readily embraced it. Although the war continued unabated, both sides agreed to the presence of international human-rights observers. The peace process was a prolonged one. The United Nations sponsored a quite hectic, often heated round of international diplomacy between 1990 and 1992. The long-awaited peace accord was finally signed in Chapultepec, Mexico, in January 1992.

In the peace accord both sides pledged to honor the basic democratic principle of the separation of the judiciary, legislative and executive powers. They agreed to respect human rights and to accept the subordination of the military establishment to a democratically elected civilian government. The FMLN accepted the terms that called for the dismantling of its military structure, the destruction of its weaponry and its incorporation into a democratic, parliamentary process. The government agreed to introduce extensive political and military reforms, including the replacement of the infamous National Guard and the police force with a new National Civil Police that incorporated former members of both the guerrillas and the armed forces who had undergone education in democracy and human rights. An important aspect of the accord specified that the government would implement a program to redistribute land among former guerrillas and former soldiers on a just and equitable basis. Finally, both sides welcomed the presence of a United Nations peace mission (ONUSAL) to supervise the peace process. The constitution of 1983 remained, but amendments were introduced to reflect the fundamental principles of the peace accord.

In the years since Chapultepec the fundamental principles of the accord have been largely respected. Notwithstanding some prophets of doom, El Salvador does seem to have entered a new era of reconciliation and democratization. There are promising signs that the oligarchy is finally aware that the old order of privilege and exploitation must change. The two presidential elections since 1992 have been won by civilian candidates from ARENA: Armando Calderón Sol in 1994 and Francisco Flores in 1999. On both occasions in the FMLN fought the elections vigorously, but it accepted defeat just as graciously in the best democratic tradition. ARENA acknowledged the victory of the FMLN candidate, Héctor Silva, as mayor of San Salvador in 1997 and in 2000. Debate in the current legislative assembly, where ARENA holds twenty-nine seats and the FMLN thirty-one seats, is no less heated and no more impolite than in Congress in the United States or the House of Commons in England. El Salvador still is, of course, a developing country with chronic third-world problems. Not surprisingly, crime (including up to twenty murders a day) is of grave concern in a society where such a high percentage of the population lived by the law of the gun for so long, and where war provided the only education to so many young men and women. Nevertheless, the manner in which a culture of democracy and peace is becoming established in El Salvador offers considerable hope for the future.

NOTES

1. Among the best introductions to the history, geography and society of El Salvador are Alastair White, *El Salvador* (London: Ernest Benn Limited, 1973); Richard A. Haggerty, ed., *El Salvador: A Country Study* (Washington, DC: Library of Congress, 1990); Kevin Murray and Tom Barry, *Inside El Salvador* (Albuquerque: Resource Center Press, 1995). For a comprehensive account of Salvadorean history in Spanish see *Historia de El Salvador, I & II* (San Salvador: Ministerio de Educación, 1994). Jeff Brauer, Veronica Wiles, Julian Smith and Steve Wiles, *Conozca El Salvador* (Charlottesville: On Your Own Publications, 1997), includes a useful introduction to the country.

2. The Spanish term *salvadoreño* may be translated as "Salvadorean" or "Salvadoran." The former is used in this book.

3. Originally published in 1917, this valuable book was reissued by CONCULTURA in 1997.

4. This epithet was coined by David Escobar Galindo in an interview with the author in San Salvador on January 10, 1998.

5. For a description of life in Santa Anita see Carmen Tamacas, "Pobreza compartida," *La Prensa Gráfica*, February 9, 1998, 10–11.

6. *Guía informativa y metodológica. Mapa de flora y fauna de El Salvador* (San Salvador: Fundación María Escalón de Núñez/Ministerio de Educación, 1998).

7. An indispensable study for the history of land, agriculture and society is David Browning's *El Salvador: Landscape and Society* (Oxford: Clarendon Press, 1971).

8. Oscar Melhado, *El Salvador. Retos económicos de fin de siglo* (San Salvador: UCA Editores, 1997), 32. Melhado provides a perceptive, comprehensive economic analysis of El Salvador.

9. For coffee production and export statistics see *Country Profile. Guatemala, El Salvador, 1999–2000* (London: The Economist Intelligence Unit, 1999), 67.

10. Haggerty, *El Salvador: A Country Study*, 123.

11. *Country Profile. Guatemala, El Salvador, 1999–2000*, 67.

12. Melhado, *El Salvador. Retos económicos de fin de siglo*, 20.

13. For an excellent illustrated account of the country's prehistoric past see William R. Fowler, Jr., *El Salvador: antiguas civilizaciones* (San Salvador: Banco Agrícola Comercial de El Salvador, 1995).

14. David Browning, in chapters 2 and 3 of *El Salvador: Landscape and Society*, provides a moving and well-documented account of the ravages of the Spanish Conquest in El Salvador.

15. For a clear, eloquent history of colonial government in Latin America, which is applicable to El Salvador, see Carlos Fuentes, *The Buried Mirror* (London: André Deutsch, 1992), Part II, 93–147.

16. For a concise history of the Coffee Republic, see White, *El Salvador*, 86–97; and Haggerty, *El Salvador: A Country Study*, 9–16.

17. One of the most dramatic accounts of the Great Slaughter is contained in Roque Dalton, *Miguel Mármol*, Kathleen Ross and Richard Schaaf, trans. (Willimantic, CT: Curbstone Press, 1987).

18. Given his historical significance there have been relatively few studies of Farabundo Martí. One of the most illuminating is Jorge Arias Gómez, *Farabundo Martí* (San José, Costa Rica: EDUCA, 1972).

19. Perhaps the best insight into this period of Salvadorean history is provided in a novel by Manlio Argueta, *El valle de las hamacas* (The valley of the hammocks) (San Salvador: UCA, 1992).

20. White, *El Salvador*, 183.

21. For an overview of the war with Honduras, see Thomas P. Anderson, *The War of the Dispossessed: Honduras and El Salvador, 1969* (Lincoln: University of Nebraska Press, 1981).

22. The civil war is the most studied period in Salvadorean history. Hundreds of articles, books, documentaries and films have been produced throughout the world, especially in the United States and Europe. For a select bibliography see Haggerty, *El Salvador: A Country Study*, 270, 276–81.

2

Society and the Economy

IN THE YEARS during which El Salvador's postwar administrations have been tackling the daunting agenda of political and economic reconstruction, society has been undergoing dramatic changes, many of them seemingly beyond the control of the country's policymakers. The landed oligarchy no longer has undisputed control of the economy. The arrogant military establishment must now abide by the rule of law. Hundreds of thousands of emigrants and exiles have chosen not to return to their homeland. Newly empowered women clamour for equal rights at home and in the workforce. Gangs of delinquents roam the city streets. A former revolutionary has become the overcrowded capital's democratically elected mayor. The social contours of El Salvador are being redrawn. While only a lunatic fringe questions the value of democracy, divisions and conflicts abound in this developing nation. Some of its older citizens wonder aloud whether a better, safer, freer nation can ultimately emerge from the current melting pot. However, Salvadoreans with a sense of history point out that it is essential not to lose heart in the face of the inevitable problems that confront a society intent on building a brave, new future from a blood-soaked past.

THE POPULATION: A PROFILE

Since the second half of the eighteenth century El Salvador's population has doubled every twenty or twenty-five years. It reached an estimated figure in excess of 6 million in 1999. There are also more than 2.25 million other Salvadoreans who have migrated or sought exile in the United States, Mexico and elsewhere. In spite of the massive exodus, El Salvador is still the most densely populated country in Latin America, with approximately 630 inhabitants per square mile. The capital, San Salvador, has a population close to 2 million. The city crowds within its boundaries a staggering 17,180 people per square mile. Statistics reveal that the country's future is in the hands of its youth, for 50.2 percent of Salvadoreans are under nineteen, and only 5.1 percent are over sixty-five. The emergence in the last twenty years of a visible, active woman's movement is explained in part by the fact that women now make up 51.4 percent of the population. On the other hand, women fare much worse than men do when it comes to the labor market. Of the approximately 2.25 million Salvadoreans classified as officially "economically active" in 1998, only 38 percent are women.[1]

After a hundred years of consistent increase in the rate of population growth, the percentage dropped during the 1980s from 3.46 percent to just over 1 percent. The rate jumped again to 2.1 percent in 1997. Not surprisingly, the lowest figure (under 1 percent in the war years) is for the departments most heavily affected by the fighting: Cabañas, San Vicente, Cuscatlán, Chalatenango, Usulután, and Morazán. San Vicente provides an indication of the traumatic effects of the war. After experiencing a growth rate of over 2 percent between 1950 and 1960, between the outbreak of the war in 1979 and its conclusion in 1992 the department actually had a rate of −0.33 percent. However, the ordinary men and women of El Salvador continued to reproduce prolifically. The crude birthrate (the annual number of births per 1,000 inhabitants) during the war years was just over 39, double the figure in the major industrial countries. Since the war the crude birth rate has dropped to approximately 33.5.[2]

A major demographic shift was a direct result of the war. Tens of thousands of peasants from the most devastated departments migrated to the major towns, particularly San Salvador, whose population doubled. Accordingly, whereas in 1971 El Salvador was a rural country, with just over 60 percent of the population living in the countryside, by 1997 this proportion had fallen to around 25 percent. Of the total urban population in El Salvador, 67 percent is now concentrated in the capital. Another 10 percent are in the two other major cities, Santa Ana and San Miguel, and 5.7 percent are in Sonsonate and Usulután.[3]

THE NEW ELITE

In spite of the civil war, the land reforms of the 1980s and the economic-liberalization policies of the postwar governments, Salvadorean society remains highly divided between the haves and the have-nots. However, in the last two decades the structure of society and the relationships between and within its various components have changed from top to bottom. Indeed, not even the formerly all-powerful Fourteen Families, which since the foundation of the Coffee Republic in the 1870s controlled the economic wealth of the country, have been immune to the forces that the war and its aftermath unleashed. In the early 1980s a tiny elite of plantation owners (less than 2 percent of the total population) owned about 60 percent of the productive land, and it had a vicelike grip on all sources of revenue, including the industrial and financial sectors. By 1998 a small elite still held economic power, but the elite's character had altered significantly, with the influence of the landed oligarchy dwindling considerably.

Indeed, many of the historic Fourteen Families have now withdrawn from the coffee and sugar industries altogether. Some of them have diversified into commerce, banking, construction, electronics and the booming offshore assembly factories known as *maquilas*. The neoliberal, free-market policies of the postwar ARENA administrations have, in fact, led to the replacement of the traditional coffee and sugar oligarchy with a new industrial and banking elite that has taken advantage of the privatization of major financial and telecommunication sectors. Local investors have been eager to enter into partnerships with the foreign companies that have purchased majority shares of Salvadorean banks, telecommunication operations and electricity-distribution companies. For instance, when Telefónica of Spain bought out the National Telephone Company (CTE) in 1998, a consortium of Salvadorean investors bought 25 percent of the shares. Not long afterward, local bankers and entrepreneurs entered into a partnership with two Taiwanese firms that invested in a new free-trade zone in Olocuilta, between San Salvador and the airport. Members of the new elite point with pride to the tall, postmodern towers with reflective glass that the banks are building in the upper-class districts of San Salvador.

What benefits, if any, will the emergence of a new, urban, industrial elite bring to El Salvador? Firstly, it is apparent that most of the bankers, financiers and industrialists who control the nation's wealth are university educated, many of them in the United States and Europe, and so bring with them the knowledge and experience of the successful application of capitalism. In the words of Guillermo Cucalón, a middle manager in a large automobile corporation in San Salvador, "At long last the capitalists in this country are beginning to understand that they will make more money still if they develop a social conscience."[4] Secondly, while many do enjoy (and flaunt) the privileges attached to being rich in a developing country, it is apparent that only a Neanderthal would want to return to the era of the Coffee Republic and military dictatorships. Thirdly, many of the elite have played an active role in trying to make the new Salvadorean system of democracy work. Many members of the new elite are known to support the incumbent FMLN mayor of San Salvador, the popular Héctor Silva, because "él hace que las cosas funcionen" (he makes things go well).[5] Finally, the wealthy, powerful members of the new elite know that the rules of the game have changed in El Salvador. There is now a congress, constantly growing in experience and confidence, that passes laws to punish corruption and criminality in high places, as more than one wealthy impresario or politician has found out.

THE COUNTRYSIDE AND THE IMPACT OF INTERNATIONAL REMITTANCES

Macroeconomic indicators (the rate of inflation, GNP, fiscal deficit, consumer price index) suggest that the radical, free-market reforms of successive ARENA administrations have lifted El Salvador above most of its Central American neighbors. The rate of infant mortality improved considerably from 123 per 1,000 live births between 1960 and 1965 to 40 during the mid-1990s. Life expectancy at birth rose from fifty-two years to sixty-seven years during the same period. El Salvador is still a third-world country, with the majority of the population classified as poor. Nevertheless, between 1970 and 1998 the poverty index fell from 81.15 percent of the population to less than 60 percent. For an individual the benchmark for relative poverty is the basic wage (approximately 1,260 colónes / $US144 per month in 1998), while for a family it is the so-called canasta básica, a basket containing the ingredients to satisfy the basic needs of a family of 4.5 members.[6] If the American dream is to become a millionaire, the Salvadorean dream is to rise above this poverty threshold.

For the majority of El Salvador's 1.2 million campesinos, life continues to be a constant struggle. Quite apart from the continuing land shortage (around 330,000 people are landless or what is known as "land-poor") most peasants who work in large plantations or cooperatives receive less than the minimum wage and are unable to fill the canasta básica. In addition, medical facilities are scarce, schooling inadequate, credit facilities negligible, and access to safe drinking water limited. The forces of nature contribute to their burden. Floods, mudslides and deforestation are regular blights, while Hurricane Mitch in 1998 wrought havoc in the northern and central rural regions just at the start of the harvest season.[7]

Since the beginning of the war El Salvador has undergone a process of *descampesinización* (rural depopulation and attrition of rural culture) as waves of peasants have sought a safer, more prosperous life elsewhere. All the rural areas have lost significant proportions of their population to San Salvador and to the United States. On the one hand, this phenomenon has led to the paradoxical situation of a labor shortage in the coffee and sugar plantations. However, work is often not available, and when it is, wages do not improve. On the other hand, there has been a dramatic sociocultural impact upon the life of people in the countryside. The massive exodus has led to the break up of nuclear families, and many husbands have abandoned their wives and children. Indeed, many cases have been reported of bigamous husbands (and wives) who have established an alternative home in their new city or country. The extended-family system, a typical feature of village life, has been seriously undermined by the departure of so many young people. Traditional culture and customs, always more robust in the rural areas, have been weakened by the adoption of urban mores in matters of food, drink, dress, entertainment and morality. This is particularly true of the young who, if they have to stay in their village, console themselves by imitating the style and fashion of their "sophisticated" friends and relatives in San Salvador or Los Angeles.

However, there has been a positive dimension to the emigration of such a high proportion of rural folk to the United States (and on a smaller scale to Canada, Australia, Spain and other European countries), for they have kept on loyally sending *remesas* (international remittances) to their relatives back home. In 1998 alone the 2.3 million Salvadoreans residing abroad (about 85 percent in the United States), remitted a total of $US1.4 billion, which was about 50 percent more than in 1994 and more than four times the revenue derived from the export of coffee![8] In fact, remittances are the country's largest source of foreign-currency income, and their impact has revolutionized life in the countryside. Thousands of peasants survive their inhospitable environment thanks to them, while thousands of others have left their villages to set up a business. The traditional adobe houses continue to be a feature of rural El Salvador, but numerous families are now using the *remesas* for upgrading to a house of brick and cement. There have been cases of whole villages using *remesas* to build parks, schools and sporting facilities, as in the case of Intipucá in La Unión. When the Salvadorean emigrés who can afford it come back to visit from Los Angeles, New York, Sydney or Montreal, they invariably bring with them clothes, watches, televisions, radios, stereos, video recorders, computers and of course, hard cash in U.S. dollars. Consequently, not only do the material circumstances of rural Salvadoreans improve, but their lifestyle also changes. It is now very uncommon to find what used to be a symbol of Salvadorean backwardness: a barefoot peasant with a dirty sombrero and a rusty machete. Indeed, the visitor is struck by well-dressed rural Salvadoreans. A minor sign, perhaps, but one that indicates the progress taking place in Salvadorean society.

The dilemma facing politicians, economists and sociologists is the following: what will be the effect upon El Salvador if—or when—the *remesas* stop flowing so regularly? It is doubtful that the children and grandchildren of emigrés will have the same level of commitment to El Salvador. In the space of another generation a cultural shock may strike those *campesinos* who have not invested their *remesas* with an eye to the future.

SAN SALVADOR: SOCIAL CONTRASTS AND THE EXPANDING MIDDLE CLASS

El Salvador has fourteen *cabeceras*, one for each department, but by international standards only one can be classified as a city: San Salvador, the capital. Indeed, in the Salvadorean context the capital city is a megalopolis that has grown into Gran San Salvador (Greater San Salvador). It has eight *municipios*, which are twice as many as when it was founded in 1825. It is a city that has been called a phoenix because it rises again, undaunted, bigger and more crowded, from the ashes of every one of the thirty earthquakes that have struck it since 1574. Santa Ana, the second largest city, may be more charmingly aristocratic with its beautifully preserved colonial buildings, but since the beginning of the twentieth century San Salvador has been the national hub of political, economic, industrial and social activity. Since 1929, when the Great Depression struck the country, people have been drawn to San Salvador in search of work and to fulfill their dream of a better life in the same way that Americans have been drawn to New York and Los Angeles.

Two outstanding sociological features have characterized San Salvador in the modern era: it is a city of migrants—principally the poor and the unemployed—from every corner of the country, and it is the residence of the rich and powerful. Nothing illustrates more starkly the socioeconomic contrast in the nation than the houses of the rich and of the poor in San Salvador. In the most prestigious *colonias* (suburbs), such as San Benito, San Francisco, Santa Elena and Colonia Escalón, the elite live in mansions, most of them with rifle-toting guards, that would not be out of place in Beverly Hills. These wealthy suburbs, with their fashionably dressed residents who travel regularly to the United States for holidays or spending sprees, are a world apart from the *barrios populares* (working-class suburbs), where hundreds of thousands of people are crowded in *tugurios* (shantytowns on the periphery of the city) or in *mesones* (large communal houses situated mainly in the central part of the city). Even people living above the official poverty line are forced by economic circumstance to live in these unpleasant conditions. As late as the 1980s most of these dwellings were lacking in such basic amenities as electricity and sewage, but such deficiencies have now been remedied in many of them.

Indeed, it is a measure of the modest but admirable social progress of postwar El Salvador that even the *champas* (hovels of wood, tin and card-board), which appear overnight in the capital's gullies and creeks, very soon sport improvised electricity lines and water pumps, many now provided by the municipal authorities. Inventive San Salvadoreans call these overnight migrants *paracaídistas* (parachutists) because they seem to fall out of the sky. Another mark of the social changes that are occurring in El Salvador is the attitude of the rich and powerful towards the *paracaídistas*, who often choose to erect their hovels within walking distance of a mansion or a modern mall. Rather than send their personal guards or ask a friendly colonel to eject the *paracaídistas*, as was customary in the past, they will exert pressure upon the municipal authorities to find alternative, more suitable accommodations for them. This change in attitude toward the poor and underprivileged reflects the new social consciousness that has taken root in El Salvador since the civil war.

Perhaps the most graphic metaphor for the situation of the lower classes in El Salvador is the garbage dump in Nejapa, which is situated on the outskirts of the capital. In the midst of this fetid squalor, about fifty families have erected a shantytown of typical *champas*, scavenging a living from the scrap that they resell to local merchants. To the first-world outsider, this may appear to be another depressing example of third-world poverty. Yet to its proud residents, Nejapa means an average income of about $US100 per month or more per family, a dwelling comparable in standard to that of most poor people in San Salvador, a tranquil environment that is free of crime and, above all, an opportunity to get on in life. Moreover, whereas ten or twenty years ago the municipality would have ignored or even persecuted the people in Nejapa, it now actually sends a tanker to the junkyard so that they can have safe water for drinking and bathing. Residents can also make extra money by selling foods and drinks to the garbage-truck drivers and to the people who come from outside to work on the site. Nejapa is evidence that a spirit of solidarity, optimism and entrepreneurship can be found at every level of society in the new El Salvador.[9]

Another important development in Salvadorean society in the last twenty years, and particularly in the postwar period, has been the expansion and consolidation of a middle class, whose members earn from three to eight (or more) times the minimum wage. Although this middle class is also evident in the departmental capitals and among a small group of independent farmers, its representatives reside and work principally in San Salvador. Its ranks include professionals, such as doctors, lawyers, dentists, engineers and architects. The most successful of these professionals constitute a tiny upper-middle class, and they regard themselves as being closer to the elite than to the rest of the middle class. The rest includes government employees, clerks in banks and offices, managers and the better-paid personnel in the fast-food chains (McDonalds, Pizza Hut, Burger King) that have proliferated since the end of hostilities, attendants in the large department stores, teachers and university professors, low- to mid-level managers and proprietors of small businesses.

The Salvadorean middle class has grown remarkably from about 8 percent of the population in the early 1980s to approximately 27 percent in 1998. Most members of the middle class lead no more than a life of basic comfort, with a car, the essential conveniences, and a brick-and-cement house located in an area adjoining the wealthy suburbs. Like most middle-class people in the United States and Europe, they aspire to home ownership. They will visit the handful of well-appointed, American-style malls in San Salvador to buy electronic goods, stylish clothes, medicines and toiletries. They will go to a supermarket for food, especially of the tinned or packaged variety. However, since most middle-class families can afford at least one domestic assistant (usually a young, female peasant who has migrated to the city), they will send her to a public market to buy fresh food and other everyday items. If they have no choice, the wife will go herself.

To the first-world visitor the public markets, such as the famous Mercado Central in dilapidated downtown San Salvador, are colorful, exciting places. In some markets peasant vendors wear traditional indigenous dress and display exotic species of local flora and fauna in handwoven baskets. To the middle-class Salvadorean, on the other hand, markets may be cheap, but they are also dirty, crowded, fly-infested, dangerous places. Rather than viewing it as an expression of typical Salvadorean culture, the middle-class regards a public market as a symbol of backwardness. In fact, a sure sign of upward mobility for middle-class Salvadoreans is when they can afford to swap the sweltering market for the air-conditioned supermarket! Another indication of social ascent among the middle-class is when, instead of requiring *remesas* from a relative in the United States, the role is reversed and the relative receives financial assistance from the family in El Salvador. This is a rare occurrence, but it is not unknown.

The significance of the middle class in El Salvador cannot be underestimated. It not only acts as a political buffer between the elite and the lower classes, but it also provides a realistic goal for those Salvadoreans who are fighting to work up the socioeconomic ladder. It is the increasing accessibility of a middle-class status that distinguishes El Salvador from its even poorer Central American and Caribbean neighbors. And most importantly, middle-class comfort—however modest by comparison with the lifestyle of first-class countries—will encourage its citizens to stay in the country, to work for a better El Salvador, rather than taking their dreams, energy and talent elsewhere.

THE INFORMAL ECONOMY

How can a civilian society remain cohesive and continue to function—indeed, how can profound social unrest, if not revolution, be avoided—in the face of such grave problems? The catalog of shortcomings appears to be an explosive one, particularly in the overcrowded capital. There is poverty, unemployment, underemployment, a low minimum wage, inadequate housing, inefficient social security and limited health and welfare services. And yet any visitor can see what sociologists and economists confirm: that the concept of "poverty" in San Salvador and other major urban centers needs redefinition. The fact is that San Salvador, Santa Ana, San Miguel and other cities appear to be places that are inhabited by poor people who nevertheless appear to be working, plying a trade in a workshop, hawking wares in a teeming marketplace, selling food from a basket, driving rackety minibuses, making cheap clothes, knocking on doors to offer arts and crafts or standing in the middle of the road to offer bananas or mangoes to drivers. Moreover, the vast majority are adequately clothed, and the street cafes always seem to be full of customers.

The explanation for the above is that a considerable percentage of the officially unemployed in El Salvador—around 62 percent—belong to an urban phenomenon known as *la economía informal*, an informal economy that operates alongside the official, formal, taxed, regulated, capitalist economy. Because of the nature of *los informales* (informal workers) the exact statistics are difficult to tabulate, but it is estimated that nationally at least a million people may belong to this alternative economy. Over 40 percent of *los informales* live and work in San Salvador, mainly in small commercial activities such as selling fruit in the street, making shoes in a small shop, fashioning made-to-measure shirts, building furniture or driving microbuses. Most operate individually, but others form *microempresas* (minibusinesses) of up to five people. Their remuneration ranges from the minimum wage to three times that wage per individual. In fact, there are a few instances of successful *informales* who, in earning capacity and lifestyle, belong to the middle class![10]

The informal workers have the benefit of not paying taxes, although market vendors are required to pay a fee to the municipality for the right to set up their stalls, and if they are working from home they have such overheads as electricity and water bills. Another advantage is that they can work unrestricted hours and have no bosses or trade unions to answer to. On the negative side, *los informales* possess no legal status and so lie outside the Salvadorean social-security system, though in this regard they join the majority of the official workforce. So successful have *los informales* become, and so important are they to the national economy, that the government has allowed them to form various legal associations to protect their rights and interests. For instance, approximately 20,000 permanent and itinerant vendors in the central market of San Salvador have established CONAMI (National Committee of Salvadorean Microbusinesses). After enduring what they considered harassment by the municipal authorities, itinerant street vendors of downtown San Salvador founded ANPECOVAL (National Association of Merchants and Sellers of Fastfoods and Snacks).

At this stage of their existence *los informales* live up to their name. They constitute a large, informal collection of independent men and women (and in some cases children) who have used initiative and imagination to survive in a difficult environment. However, the formation of associations and committees to represent their interests is a significant step toward turning their informal economy into a united, popular movement with legally binding rights and obligations. Irrespective of what the future holds for them, *los informales* are evidence of the energy, creativity and entrepreneurship that is present in postwar El Salvador at every level of society.

TOURISM

On paper, El Salvador should be a postcard country. It has tropical color and diversity—volcanoes, lakes, lagoons, beaches and rainforests—packed into its 8,124 square miles. It features a stable currency that is tied to the U.S. dollar, friendly people, a national cuisine that is exotic but surprisingly clean and safe, and a calendar bursting with traditional festivities (see Chapter 5). However, the years of civil war, its current reputation for high crime and its historic marginalization have turned El Salvador into a tourist backwater. A comparison with a Central American neighbor puts the situation in context. One of the safest, most politically stable countries in the developing world, Costa Rica, receives about a million international visitors per year from all around the globe, including high-profile celebrities. On the other hand, only about 350,000 international visitors per year visit El Salvador, the majority of them from the United States and Central America. The Salvadorean Institute of Tourism (ISTU), in collaboration with private tourist operators, is making an effort to improve the country's image as a tourist destination, particularly in Spain and the United States. It is expected that within five to ten years the number of international visitors will reach 500,000.

In the absence of a large international market, authorities have promoted internal tourism by establishing a network of sixteen Turicentros Nacionales (National Centers of Tourism), which are located in some of the most scenic spots in the country. Moreover, every weekend fleets of buses ferry locals at a reduced tariff to these centers. The objective of this policy is to encourage *turismo popular* (popular tourism), particularly from the lower socioeconomic classes who are given the opportunity to get away from the urban centers and enjoy the natural beauty of the country in a relaxed, affordable environment. In 1998 over 2 million Salvadoreans took day trips to these tourist sites.

Since the war, authorities have launched a campaign to protect and promote El Salvador's archaeological sites. The goal is to attract *turismo cultural* (cultural tourism). Although not nearly as splendid as the ceremonial sites in Mexico, Peru and Guatemala, pre-Columbian ruins such as those in San Andrés (twenty miles from San Salvador) and Joya de Cerén (sixteen miles from San Salvador) offer valuable insights into the society and customs of the ancient Pipil kingdom of Cuscatlán. Joya de Cerén, the most recent discovery, is in a superb state of preservation after being buried under yards of ash for 1,400 years. It has been compared to a time capsule that has frozen scenes and objects of everyday, domestic life: fields of *maize*, family dwellings, kitchens, eating utensils, food and flowers. El Tazumal (nine miles from Santa Ana) offers evidence of the lifestyle of the Pokoman Indians, who in the fifteenth century were driven out of the western region into Guatemala after living there for more than three millennia. Until the last few years, only specialists or locals visited El Salvador's archaeological sites. However, the country has now joined the famous Ruta Maya (Mayan Route), an international program that links the major sites of Mayan civilization in Mexico and Central America. It is hoped that such initiatives will open El Salvador to international tourism.

THE ARMED FORCES

For over six decades of the twentieth century the armed forces were the undisputed political masters in El Salvador, tolerating minimal public dissent and using undemocratic means to impose eight presidents upon the nation between 1931 and 1979. Rather than a class, high-ranking military officers were a caste apart, enjoying a unique status in Salvadorean society. By virtue of their office the generals and colonels of the military establishment lived in a style comparable to the elite. They owned lucrative coffee plantations and joined the executive boards of banks and other government institutions. While rank-and-file soldiers were poor recruits, often peasants forced into service, the cadets who went to the legendary Captain General Gerardo Barrios Military Academy usually came from the lower-middle class. The military offered them an exceptional opportunity for social advancement. Upon graduation they could expect a swift, profitable rise up the hierarchy. In fact, regular ascent in rank, pay and perks was virtually guaranteed to each graduating *tanda* (class), since the custom was for each group of graduates to receive promotion collectively over the ensuing thirty years. Members of a *tanda* who remained loyal to an outstanding leader could expect to be rewarded by him, as occurred in the case of Major Roberto D'Aubuisson's class of 1963. Until his death in 1993 D'Aubuisson, the founder of ARENA, the party that has held the presidency since 1989, regarded his *tanda* as a mutual-benefit society. They supported his ambitions, and he looked after their interests.

One of the most taxing problems confronting El Salvador since the signing of the peace accords in 1992 has been how to ensure the permanent incorporation of the traditionally autocratic, pampered armed forces into the democratic, civilian structure of society. In the years since, there have been some strains and tensions, climaxing in a series of confrontations in 1994 and 1995 when disgruntled veterans occupied the National Congress, took deputies as hostages and blocked the country's main highways. Overall, however, a pragmatic attitude by the principal parties—the armed forces, the conservative ARENA government and the FMLN opposition—has paved the way for a workable accommodation between the civilian and military authorities. The main political parties have respected the institutional autonomy of the armed forces, which continue to function as a caste apart, with their historic privileges virtually intact. The *tanda* system remains in operation, although in more discreet fashion. The military budget has been maintained at a high $US100 million per year, and in spite of occasional questions by the opposition in Congress, the government has granted financial independence to the high command. However, the armed forces have accepted that the rules of the game have changed. In the absence of provocative measures by the civilian authorities, they have been prepared to respect the executive power of the presidency and the legislative function of Congress. Moreover, since 1992 the United States, whose political, economic and moral influence in El Salvador is immense, has made it clear that it expects the military to play—and to be allowed to play—an appropriate role in a democratic society. Nevertheless, the acid test for the armed forces may come if a left-wing FMLN government comes into power. Will the former antagonists who fought so bitterly for control of the country for over a decade be able to accept each other's legitimacy in the new El Salvador?

The signs are positive that irrespective of which political party gains power in the future the armed forces will consolidate their place in the democratic system. Every practical effort is being made to fulfill the fundamental principles of the peace accords, including the removal of public security from the sphere of military control and the fair distribution of land and other financial benefits of postwar reconstruction to both the demobilized members of the armed forces and the former FMLN combatants. In April 1994 the government passed a law that restricted the constitutional obligations of the armed forces to the defense of national sovereignty and territorial integrity. In principle an absolute separation was thus established between the military establishment and the civilian police, who are charged with public security and the protection of civilian rights. However, the role of the armed forces has had to be reviewed in light of the soaring crime rate, which has become one of the most serious social problems in El Salvador. Deportees from the United States, many of them with a criminal record, have joined the ranks of *maras* (street gangs), which have caused considerable consternation in urban areas, particularly in San Salvador. In addition, murders, kidnappings, highway robberies, automobile thefts, drug trafficking and money laundering have been filling the headlines with embarrassing frequency. To make matters worse, organized crime has been linked to the civilian police. At one stage the authorities had to replace the entire police force in the north-central town of Aguilares. Under the circumstances public opinion has led to special presidential decrees that authorized the military to collaborate with the police to maintain internal law and order, particularly in high-crime areas. Although there are concerns that this move could encourage the armed forces to abuse their power, it appears that the democratic system in El Salvador is evolving sufficient flexibility and trust to permit military involvement in civilian society.

To the outside observer the daily scenario of crime, violence, police corruption and arguments about the role of the armed forces in El Salvador may suggest a society in a state of decomposition. Yet the opposite is true: these problems are symptoms of a developing nation that is striving, however painfully, to establish itself as a civilian, democratic society after decades of military rule. Formerly, in times of social stress the government would call the army into the streets, and victims would be jailed, tortured, even murdered with impunity. The present system is developing legal strategies and a network of constitutional checks and balances to establish lasting foundations for an orderly society.

THE CHANGING ROLE OF WOMEN

There is a general perception among Latin Americans that El Salvador is one of the most patriarchal, chauvinistic countries in the Spanish-speaking world. Salvadorean men have a legendary reputation for being *machista* (aggressively masculine), and women have been traditionally stereotyped as their *alfombras* (doormats). It is quite common to hear an angry woman shout at her partner, "¡No soy tu alfombra!" (I am not your doormat!). To what extent these characterizations are valid is a matter for sociological interpretation, but one stark statistic certainly provides insights into the female condition in El Salvador. According to an official report in 1994, 80 percent of households are the scene of violence against women, be it physical, psychological or sexual. Indeed, so prevalent is the battered-wife syndrome that the typical Salvadorean home has been described as *un nido de violencia* (a nest of violence).[11]

Other statistics reveal that in most areas of life, such as literacy, education and employment, Salvadorean women are worse off than men. Social workers and counselors report high rates of rape, incest, underage pregnancies and bungled abortions, especially among women in the lower socioeconomic sectors. Moreover, the social dislocation that the war caused through male deaths, injuries and emigration aggravated another major problem in the country: the high proportion of men who abandoned their wife and children, never to be seen again. Consequently, El Salvador now has a higher number than ever of women who act as *jefas de familia* (heads of household), particularly among the working classes. For instance, 80 percent of the women in the huge informal economy are the heads of households, and 80 percent of a workforce of more than 50,000 people in the *maquila* industry are women.[12] Consequently, today in El Salvador almost 60 percent of the heads of household are women. However, government and free enterprise have moved slowly in recognizing the social needs of the important female work-force in El Salvador.

On the other hand, although progress has been slow, there is evidence that the situation for women has improved since the 1980s. First and foremost, there appears to be an attitudinal shift occurring. The civil war caused a perceptible change in the traditional Salvadorean male chauvinism, particularly among the ranks of the former guerrillas, who witnessed thousands of women fighting, struggling and dying on equal terms with the men. In a country in which it is difficult to name even one outstanding female leader since independence, it is noteworthy that a number of female guerrillas rose to positions of prominence, such as Marianela García Vilas (known simply as "Marianela") and Virginia Peña Mendoza (called "Susana"), both of whom fell in combat. On the other side of the political fence, hundreds of middle- and upper-class women demonstrated exemplary courage when confronted with the murder, torture and kidnapping of family members by the guerrillas. Moreover, women from every class, background and ideology had to bear the burden of caring for children and parents in the absence of partners—soldiers, guerrillas, politicians, businessmen, students and teachers—with some level of involvement in the conflict. The tone of respect, and in some cases awe, with which Salvadorean men tend to refer to the fortitude and resilience that women show in times of stress is certainly striking. The writer Manlio Argueta, for instance, refers to them as "the centre of the household, the sun round which revolve the twin planets of poverty and hope."[13] Whether this admiration will translate into more positive gender relations at home and in the workplace is another matter.

The atrocity of war also had the effect of politicizing women, most of whom had previously accepted the traditional view that political and social responsibilities were men's business. One of the first organized movements to appear on the scene was CO-MADRES (a pun meaning mothers and solidarity among women), which in 1984 won the Robert F. Kennedy Human Rights Award for its campaign to obtain justice for the *desaparecidos*, the thousands of men and women who were "disappeared" by the military and the death squads during the war. Numerous members of CO-MADRES suffered persecution, torture and death during the war. Rape and other forms of sexual abuse were routine forms of "softening up" the women for interrogation. In the course of their investigation CO-MADRES, whose membership crossed social, educational and economic boundaries, soon became aware that Salvadorean women faced an appalling series of disadvantages related to family life, sexual relations, the workplace, health and education.

Consequently, by the end of the war what had begun as a human-rights movement had been redefined into a feminist movement that focused on the rights of Salvadorean women.[14]

Since CO-MADRES, other women's groups have formed in El Salvador, among them DIGNAS (Women for Dignity and Life), MAM (Mélida Anaya Montes Women's Movement), and IMU (Institute for Women's Research, Training and Development). Although the various groups are independent, they have endeavored to project a common manifesto, which is neatly summarized in MAM's goal to transform the disadvantage, discrimination and subordination that women endure in the sexist, patriarchal society of El Salvador.[15] Although the vast majority of Salvadorean women have never heard of the feminist Germaine Greer, "first-wave feminism" or "second-wave feminism" in the United States and Europe, their philosophy and agenda echo most of what liberated women in the first world now take for granted, but their goals are in the context of Salvadorean social and economic reality. Accordingly, the Salvadorean women's claims include an end to incest, rape and sexual harassment, the establishment of sex education, sexual equality and lesbian rights, the benefits of land, credit and technical assistance, a recognition of women's rights to ownership of land and equality of salary with men and the right of female representation in the national police force. Although many Salvadorean men—and conservative women—express discomfort, mockery, resentment or open hostility toward the women's movement, it has had some significant successes. For instance, since 1989 a number of women have been elected to Congress, including the former high-profile education minister, María Cecilia Gallardo de Cano. The government has established the Institute for the Development of Women (ISDEMU), the principal objective of which is the legal protection and counseling of women who suffer violence in the home. Of particular significance in a country where men who are divorced or separated—or have simply absconded—are reluctant to accept any financial responsibility for their children, legal measures have now been enacted to enforce the principle of responsible fatherhood.

NOTES

1. These statistics have been provided by Dr. Roque Baldovinos, director of the team that is compiling the *Encyclopaedia of El Salvador* (San Salvador: Universidad Centroamerica José Simeón Cañas). I thank Dr. Baldovinos and his team of researchers, particularly Luis Armando González and Luis Romano, for their collaboration.

2. Ibid.

3. Ibid.

4. Guillermo Cucalón, in an interview with the author in San Salvador, January 10, 1998.

5. Ibid.

6. Statistics provided by Dr. Roque Baldovinos.

7. For a report on the damage caused by Hurricane Mitch, see Tim Padgett, "The Catastrophe of Hurricane Mitch," *Time*, November 16, 1998, 44–48.

8. *Country Profile. Guatemala, El Salvador, 1999–2000* (London: Economic Intelligence Unit, 1999), 61. For an analysis and projection of the effects of the *remesas* on Salvadorean society, see Segundo Montes, *El Salvador 1989. Las remesas que envían los salvadoreños de Estados Unidos. Consecuencias sociales y económicas* (San Salvador: UCA, 1990). Segundo Montes was one of the six Jesuits assassinated on the UCA campus on November 16, 1989.

9. For a report on Nejapa, see F. Kovaleski, "Slim Pickings in San Salvador," *The Guardian Weekly*, August 2, 1998, 17.

10. For an in-depth analysis of the informal economy in El Salvador see Aquiles Montoya, *Informalidad urbana y nueva economía popular* (San Salvador: UCA, 1995).

11. See María Eugenia Ochoa, coordinator, *Identificación de las necesidades prácticas y estratégicas de las mujeres de las regiones de trabajo del M.A.M.* (San Salvador: M.A.M., 1996).

12. Statistics provided by Dr. Roque Baldovinos.

13. Manlio Argueta, *Cuzcatlán donde bate la mar del sur* (Tegucigalpa: Editorial Guaymuras, 1986), 146.

14. A valuable study of the women's movement in El Salvador is Lynn Stephen's, *Women and Social Movements in Latin America: Power from Below* (Austin: University of Texas Press, 1997), 27–107.

15. See Ochoa, *Identificación de las necesidades*, 4–6.

3

Religion

BACKGROUND: THE CROSS AND THE SWORD

AS OCCURRED in the rest of the New World the conquest of Central America was conducted under the twin banners of the Cross (the Catholic Church) and the Sword (the military might and political power of the Spanish Empire).[1] The first priest arrived in El Salvador in 1528, adding his evangelizing zeal to the military bravado of the *conquistadores*. To the vast majority of soldiers and priests alike the Indians were savages in dire need of conversion to the Catholic faith, in whose name well-documented atrocities were committed throughout the Americas. Indeed, King Philip II himself estimated that by 1581 more than a third of the Indian population had been killed in his domains.

Some men of God, such as the legendary Bartolomé de las Casas (1474–1566), strove to defend the Indians against the odious policies of civilization and Christianization. It was Father de las Casas's denunciation of the barbarous treatment of the Indians in Central America and the Caribbean that led to Spain's promulgation of the Laws of the Indies in 1594. Their intention was to curb the abuses of greedy conquerors and fanatical priests, but the New World was too far away for the laws to be rigorously implemented. Not surprisingly, it was in El Salvador, one of the most remote corners of the Spanish Empire, that some of the harshest treatment was meted out to the Indians. Apart from the thousands of Pipiles, Lencas, Ulúas and Chortis killed, many more thousands perished from lethal European diseases or from the damage that slavelike labor inflicted on their bodies and minds. The best

survival tactic for the remaining Indians was to adopt the ways of their conquerors, and so they very quickly underwent a process of *mestizaje* (racial
interbreeding and cultural assimilation) that included forced conversion to
the Catholic faith. El Salvador became one of the most *mestizo* countries in
Latin America. Today, almost 475 years after the arrival of the first priest,
vestiges of the ancestral religion of the kingdom of Cuscatlán, its ancient
beliefs and rituals, are normally only seen during the *fiestas* (feast days) that
are celebrated at various times during the year in towns and villages.

Between 1530, when El Salvador was incorporated into the Bishopric of
Guatemala, and the mid-eighteenth century the Catholic Church consoli-
dated its power to such an extent that it developed into a state within a state.
The wearing of a religious habit came to signify status and comfort, and in
due course the sons of the local elite chose the priesthood as a career. Apart
from secular priests, who were responsible to the church hierarchy, monks
from various orders (especially Franciscans, Dominicans and Mercedarians)
arrived in considerable numbers from Spain. Priests and monks acted as
administrators of the *pueblos de indios* on behalf of Spain. They received a
state salary and tribute from the Indians, who were also required to work as
their servants and laborers.

A very lucrative institution for the priests and monks was the *cofradía*.
Following a medieval Spanish tradition, a brotherhood was established in
each Indian township. Each *cofradía* bore the name of a particular saint and
was obliged to pay the priest or monk for such religious activities as masses,
funerals and processions. The *cofradía* proved such a bonanza that it eventually led to serious friction between the powerful religious orders and the
church hierarchy, the latter resenting the diminution of a plentiful source of
revenue. Another profitable option for the priests and monks was the *capel-
lanía* (a kind of spiritual mortgage levied against a deceased person's property,
the interest being invested to fund masses for his/her soul). Although there
were undoubtedly some good, decent men of God who took seriously their
evangelical mission, the anticlericalism evident throughout El Salvador's history can be traced back to the cynical exploitation of the Indians and poor
mestizos by priests and monks during the colonial era.

The Catholic Church's invidious reputation notwithstanding, *criollo*
priests became national heroes during the struggle for independence against
Spain. The ideals of the French Revolution and the American Revolution
were spread from the pulpit by learned, liberal-minded priests such as Father
José Matías Delgado. In 1811, in defiance of the church hierarchy, whose
interests were closely tied to Spain, Delgado led the first patriotic uprising
in El Salvador. From 1821, when Central America finally attained inde-

pendence, through 1841, when El Salvador became a separate nation, to the advent of the Coffee Republic in the 1870s, church-state relations were in a constant state of friction as a result of the clash between liberals and conservatives, who fought for control of the fledgling republic's destiny during this particularly turbulent period. The conservatives regarded the Catholic Church, with its five vicarages and fifty-three parishes, as the spiritual basis of a well-ordered society. In return for the church's political backing, the conservatives were willing to support its economic privileges, such as the control of the *cofradías*. The liberals, who identified the church with colonial privilege and exploitation, sought to impose upon it the sovereignty of the state, curbing its prerogatives and introducing laws that recognized religious tolerance, civil marriage, divorce and secular education. The liberals also resented the influence and prestige of the religious orders, and in 1872 they went so far as to expel the Jesuits for meddling in the country's political affairs. A group of Capuchin monks accused of subversion were also expelled.

As the political pendulum swung violently between conservatives and liberals, the power and influence of the church waxed and waned. In 1823, at the behest of the conservatives, Pope Leo XII himself intervened to quash the appointment of the liberal hero of independence, José Matías Delgado, as bishop of El Salvador. In 1843 Pope Gregory XVI appointed a proconservative bishop, Monsignor Jorge Viteri y Ungo, who ultimately fell out with both conservatives and liberals and had to be transferred to Nicaragua. Relations between church and state became particularly explosive during the presidency of the liberal Gerardo Barrios, who signed a decree in 1861 that required the clergy to swear obedience to the constitution. Claiming that God was above the constitution, Bishop Tomás Pineda y Zaldaña accused President Barrios of anticlericalism. Pineda y Zaldaña and dozens of priests sought refuge in Guatemala, where they participated in the plot that brought Barrios down and led to his execution. Although a concordat with the Vatican was signed in 1862, relations between the state and the church continued to erupt periodically until the late 1870s, by which time the principles of a liberal, secular state had become firmly entrenched. Under the circumstances the church hierarchy decided upon a pragmatic policy, aligning itself firmly with the Fourteen Families of the Coffee Republic and the forces of law and order. Parish priests were directed to urge the *campesinos* who labored on the semifeudal plantations to accept their lot submissively, using the argument that their Christian suffering in this world would be rewarded in heaven. Newspapers from the late nineteenth and early twentieth centuries show dignified church elders photographed side by side with presidents, ministers and other dignitaries, who seem pleased to be depicted as God-fearing rulers.

In the 1910s and 1920s international events helped to forge an even tighter alliance between the Cross and the Sword. Both religious and political leaders closed ranks to shield El Salvador from the antibourgeois, anticlerical forces unleashed by the Russian Revolution (1917) and, nearer home, the Mexican Revolution (1911–20). In particular, the massacre of priests and nuns in Mexico by the so-called *anticristeros* perturbed the Salvadorean church. As trade unions and left-wing parties stepped up their demands for reforms during these years, the archbishop of San Salvador, Monsignor Belloso y Sánchez, issued a public letter to all priests and parishioners that stated that anyone who joined any socialist system ran the risk of eternal damnation.

One of the most startling illustrations of church policy in Salvadorean history occurred during the dictatorship of "the Witch Doctor," General Martínez, a non-Catholic who believed in the occult sciences. Even though Martínez personally introduced a moral curriculum in schools that contravened Catholic doctrine, the church chose to support him because he was seen as a better option than the "godless communists" who opposed his regime. Indeed, there is disturbing evidence that some priests turned a blind eye to the Great Slaughter of 30,000 peasants in 1932 on the grounds that the end justified the means. To such clerics, Martínez was saving El Salvador from the same fate as Mexico and Russia. Among the records of the tragic events of 1932 there is a photograph of a flushed, smiling priest standing next to a stout colonel as a peasant leader, Francisco Díaz, is about to be executed.[2] To the church's credit, however, when Martínez unleashed a new reign of terror in 1944 in a last-ditch attempt to save his regime, many priests and the archbishop himself condemned him and supported the national strike that brought about his downfall.

During the period of military governments from 1944 to the 1960s the church reverted to its traditional role of supporting the status quo. However, some progressive Catholics, including Archbishop Luis Chávez y González (1939–77), promoted a progressive movement known as Social Christianity. Although it stressed the importance of working within the existing political system, Social Christianity did demonstrate that there were Salvadorean Catholics, both priests and lay people, who understood the need for significant social and economic reforms to improve the lot of the poor and the underprivileged. Archbishop Chávez y González himself backed peasant cooperatives, a move that aroused the suspicion of some plantation owners, who saw in such an initiative the seeds of communism.

In fact, by 1960 the winds of change had entered El Salvador from other parts of Latin America. In the capital, student leaders and union activists were beginning to publicly discuss revolution as a political option against the corrupt regime of President Lemus. In mid-1960 the church leaders mobilized an organization known as Caballeros de Cristo Rey (Knights of Christ the King) in support of the increasingly repressive Lemus. This alienated students and workers. The image of the church was tainted further in 1967 when the bishop of San Vicente, Monsignor Aparicio, threatened to excommunicate the entire leadership of the Renovating Action Party (PAR) and any church members who supported their plan because they endorsed "communist" land reform. The bishop's equation of land reform with communism, when at the time over 60 percent of the productive land was in the hands of 2 percent of the population and up to 50 percent of the rural population was unemployed, demonstrates the extent to which many church leaders were out of touch with Salvadorean reality.[3]

THE RISE AND FALL OF CHRISTIAN DEMOCRACY

While the church hierarchy, with rare exceptions, was slow to react to the dire need for reform, prominent members of the Catholic laity proved more enlightened. In November 1960 a group of university-educated, upper-middle-class professionals, led by the civil engineer José Napoleón Duarte and the lawyers Abraham Rodríguez and Roberto Lara Velado, founded the Christian Democratic Party (PDC), which was to play a major role in Salvadorean politics until the end of the civil war in 1992. Drawing its ideology from the moral and social doctrines of three popes—Leo XIII (1878–1903), Pius XI (1922–39) and John XXIII (1958–63)—the Christian Democrats formulated an alternative to communism that they called "democracy in liberty." This was a comprehensive program of practical, sometimes far-reaching reforms. However, there was a proviso that no reform contravene fundamental Catholic doctrine. The agenda included free elections, collaboration between capital and labor, equitable redistribution of land among all sectors of society, modern education, national literacy, a nutritious diet for every citizen, sanitary housing, cheap access to health care, welfare for the aged, an acknowledgment of the status of women, protection of the family unit and regional cooperation within Latin America without pressure from the United States or the Soviet Union.

In theory it was difficult for any patriotic Salvadorean, the vast majority of whom were Catholic in name if not in practice, to cavil with this generous vision of social harmony and economic justice. For almost a quarter of a century after its foundation the Christian Democrats enjoyed considerable popularity and success. Why then did they ultimately fail to the extent that by the end of the century they were a near irrelevancy in Salvadorean politics?

On the one hand, because of its very vagueness and abstraction the Christian Democratic Party's agenda was attacked by the military and the oligarchy as too close to communism. For instance, its support of land reform earned it the nickname of *melón* (watermelon) because its detractors said that it was green on the outside but red on the inside. On the other hand, the party's insistence on its Catholic heritage, its appeals to papal doctrine and its quotations from the Scriptures played into the hands of socialists and communists, who claimed that Christian Democracy was really a front for the Catholic Church. Moreover, its emphasis on regional collaboration with like-minded parties in Venezuela, Chile and other Latin American nations left it open to the charge that it was unpatriotic. Finally, once it became a major player in national politics with President Duarte at the helm of the country's fortunes, the Christian Democratic Party found its lofty ideals and heady rhetoric overtaken by the brutal reality of El Salvador, which apart from its chronic injustices had become a pawn in the game between the superpowers during the Cold War.[4]

THE CATHOLIC REVOLUTION IN EL SALVADOR

As the Christian Democrats struggled to find acceptable Catholic solutions to the tragic scenario unfolding in El Salvador a sector within the church took the lead in what, in hindsight, might be termed the Catholic Revolution.[5] The catalyst for this profound transformation was the Vatican itself. First, a visionary pope, John XXIII, issued two encyclicals (in 1961 and 1963) that underlined every person's inalienable right to a decent standard of living, an education and political participation. Secondly, the Ecumenical Council of the Catholic Church, known as Vatican II (1962–65), opened the eyes and the conscience of the Catholic Church to the harsh reality of life in the third world. Emboldened by these events a number of Latin American bishops attending Vatican II argued for a "church of the poor" that was prepared to accept its social responsibilities for the hungry and oppressed. The winds of change sweeping through the Catholic establishment were fanned further by the Second Conference of Latin American Bishops (CELAM), which was held in Medellín, Colombia, in 1968. At the conference the new pope, Paul VI, pledged to preside over a church that responded not only to the spiritual, but also to the material, needs of the underprivileged. Most significantly, in its final document CELAM struck a political note by denouncing institutionalized violence and the international imperialism of money. It was also at Medellín that a new Catholic battle cry was coined: "the option of the poor," which provided the basis for a revolutionary theory of social and political action known as liberation theology.

The founders of liberation theology included Father Jon Sobrino, a Spanish-born Jesuit who had firsthand experience of the damage that the historic alliance of the Cross and the Sword had done in El Salvador. Liberation theologians combined the words of the Scriptures with the message of Karl Marx to draw up a persuasive agenda that justified the participation of Catholics in the struggle for liberation of the poor and the oppressed. For example, God's deliverance of the Jews from the tyranny of pharaoh (Exod. 3:7–8) was viewed as an anticipation of the Marxist liberation of the suffering masses from the yoke of capitalism. Likewise, the message proclaimed by liberation theology was compared to the "good news" that declared the "captives' release" in the Bible (Luke 4:18–19). At its most extreme this Marxist interpretation of the Scriptures led to cases such as that of the guerrilla-priest Camilo Torres, who died fighting against the army in Colombia.

Liberation theology struck a responsive chord in El Salvador, where the degree of injustice and repression was among the worst in Latin America. Throughout the twenty-four years between CELAM and the end of the civil war in 1992 most of the country's five bishops regularly expressed alarm, sometimes verging on hysteria, about liberation theology. However, the three archbishops who presided over the Salvadorean church during this era responded to its fundamental message with varying degrees of enthusiasm. Monsignor Luis Chávez y González welcomed its commitment to the poor and its call for social action to improve their lot. In the last ten years of Chávez y González's term the church split into two camps. The traditional church, consisting of the majority of the Catholic hierarchy, opposed what became known as the People's Church, which was made up of the majority of the country's 400 priests, dozens of whom shared the privations of the *campesinos* and the urban poor.

The main pillar of the People's Church was the *comunidad cristiana de base* (Christian base community), a small grassroots unit that ranged from ten individuals to up to fifty families. A priest would lead the group and use Bible classes as an exercise in *concienciación* (social and political consciousness raising). In due course the priest was replaced by a specially trained layperson known as a *delegado de la palabra* (catechist or delegate of the word), who in turn was replaced by a *dirigente natural* (a leader arising from within the local community). The ultimate aim of the leaders of the base communities was to develop a *campesino pensante* (a thinking peasant who could reach his/her own conclusions about the situation in El Salvador). As a consequence thousands of men and women became increasingly involved in social and political activities, which ranged from membership in peasant cooperatives and trade unions to participation in strikes for higher wages and the invasion of coffee plantations to draw attention to the urgent need for land reform. By the early 1970s there were approximately 60,000 Christian base communities in the country.[6] In time they provided a significant proportion of the leadership and membership of such radical organizations as the Popular Revolutionary Bloc (BPR) and the United Popular Action Front (FAPU), which in turn affiliated with the Marxist-Leninist FMLN-FDR that declared war on the Salvadorean government in 1980.

As expected, the military regime and the oligarchy were not slow to react to the impact of liberation theology and the spread of militant base communities. The first assassination of a priest in January 1972 heralded two decades of brutal repression against the People's Church.[7] A notorious incident occurred in 1977 when Father Rutilio Grande, a charismatic Jesuit who had established a network of community bases in Aguilares, was murdered by a right-wing death-squad that operated under the slogan "Be a patriot, kill a priest!" Two months later 350 to 400 peasants who were involved in a campaign for land reform in Aguilares were massacred, and all the priests who had been collaborating with Father Rutilio Grande were expelled from the country.

Monseñor Romero

Upon the retirement of Monsignor Chávez y González, Oscar Arnulfo Romero became archbishop of San Salvador in February 1977. A cleric of conservative background, he was a handpicked candidate whom the Vatican, the government, the oligarchy and his fellow bishops expected to move rapidly to curb the spread and influence of the People's Church, which was also called the Popular Church. By the time of his assassination he had become the legendary "monseñor Romero, la voz de los sin voz" (Monsignor Romero, the voice of the voiceless). His voice was heard in his weekly broadcasts far beyond his country's frontiers, as far away as Venezuela, Argentina and Mexico. Not long after his death a campaign began to have him canonized, and he soon became popularly known as Saint Oscar Arnulfo. What brought about such a remarkable transformation?[8]

No sooner had Romero become archbishop than his good friend, Father Rutilio Grande, was viciously murdered in Aguilares. Immediately afterward a concerted campaign of persecution against the priests and peasants who were involved in the Christian base communities shook Romero. The period from February to May 1977 proved particularly savage. His personal anguish soon turned to public anger and indignation at what, by 1979, had become an orgy of violence. He led the international chorus of outrage against the military's massacre of dozens of workers and peasants who were attending a rally in front of the cathedral on International Workers' Day (May 1), 1979. In one of the quirks of the country's history the archbishop found himself pitted against his namesake, President Carlos Humberto Romero, a colonel who had promised to rid El Salvador of troublesome priests. When President Romero unleashed a reign of terror, Monsignor Romero became a national symbol of resistance. He used the gospel to justify "liberation principles" and "political participation" against repression and injustice. The archbishop issued a series of pastoral letters and delivered regular homilies that endorsed the "preferential option of the poor," which infuriated the military regime and antagonized the majority of the country's bishops.

In February 1979 Archbishop Romero participated in the Third Conference of Latin American Bishops in Puebla, Mexico, which could well have been referring to El Salvador when it acknowledged "the situation of inhuman poverty in which millions of Latin Americans live, with starvation wages, unemployment, and underemployment, malnutrition, infant mortality, lack of adequate housing, health problems, and labour unrest."[9] As his thinking evolved in the face of the Salvadorean crisis, Monsignor Romero reached the controversial conclusion that Christian teaching could approve a just war against oppression, an argument that endorsed liberation theology's call for a popular revolution against the army and the oligarchy.

On Sunday, March 23, 1980, Archbishop Romero delivered his most controversial sermon. He literally gave his blessing to a mutiny by the rank and file of the Salvadorean army, police and National Guard against the government, allowing them to break God's commandment of "thou shalt not kill." The very next day the ministry of this "turbulent priest" was cut short by a sniper acting on the orders of Major Roberto D'Aubuisson, who was the rabidly anticommunist commander of El Salvador's death squads. It was indicative of the split within the Catholic Church that the majority of the Catholic hierarchy, including four of the five bishops, boycotted his funeral. More than 100,000 mourners attended his funeral. However, at the cermony the armed forces murdered dozens of mourners in what has become known as the Massacre in the Cathedral.

Although to the very end Monsignor Romero maintained that he was not a political figure and that the church's opposition against injustice was not that of a political party, his legacy transcended religion. His legion of followers elevated him to the status of a martyr, comparing him to Saint Thomas à Beckett, the archbishop of Canterbury who was murdered in 1170 for refusing to submit to King Henry II's political demands. He has also been compared to Saint Stanislaus (1030–79), the patron saint of Poland and Pope John Paul II's favorite saint, who was also viciously murdered for opposing a tyrant. Indeed, Romero has even been compared to Jesus Christ. In the words of Jon Sobrino, "Archbishop Romero was a Christ of our time, and, like Christ, a sacrament of God."[10] Romero's message inspired thousands of God-fearing men and women, including numerous priests and nuns, to join or support the guerrilla movement during the civil war that followed his assassination. In retrospect this man of peace, who read in the Scriptures a justification for a legitimate war against tyranny, is one of the most significant political figures in the history of El Salvador.

THE CHURCH SINCE ARCHBISHOP ROMERO

Concerned about the politicization of the Catholic Church in El Salvador, the pope did not immediately name a successor to Romero, appointing instead Arturo Rivera y Damas as apostolic administrator. Rivera y Damas, who had been the only bishop to consistently support Romero's unwavering commitment to human rights, was eventually anointed bishop in March 1983. His term as administrator and bishop (1980–95) was noteworthy for the conciliatory role that he played in bringing about a dialogue and a negotiated peace between the government and the guerrillas during the civil war. Alarmed by the split within the church, he cautiously sought to open the other bishops' eyes to the need for the social and economic reforms that the Popular Church advocated. At the same time he attempted to rein in the more radical elements within the Christian base communities. In his eyes, moral persuasion and spiritual ministry, not politics, were the church's business.

Upon Rivera y Damas's death the pope appointed the Spanish-born Fernández Sáenz Lacalle as the new archbishop. Sáenz Lacalle came to the job with a reputation as an archconservative who was identified with the army and the upper class. In 1993 he had been named spiritual head of the armed forces and given the honorary rank of colonel. He was also associated with Opus Dei, a wealthy, influential, right-wing Catholic organization of priests and lay people, founded in Spain, that has a strong membership among El Salvador's professional classes. Since he became archbishop Sáenz Lacalle has been promoted to the rank of brigadier general, an honorary position that nevertheless includes a handsome salary and considerable benefits. He has maintained his close links with Opus Dei, whose profile within the church has increased markedly in El Salvador at the expense of the Christian community bases. Sáenz Lacalle has also been criticized for his failure to consult with his parish priests and leaders of the Catholic community over the appointment of new bishops. Nevertheless, apart from the occasional skirmish, under Sáenz Lacalle relations between the hierarchy and the Catholic rank and file have been surprisingly amicable. This is due largely to the fact that the formerly large, influential Popular Church is now but a shadow of itself. On the other hand, Sáenz Lacalle has proved an unexpectedly accessible archbishop, holding weekly press conferences and going out regularly into the community to experience firsthand his parishioners' concerns. He now also schedules formal meetings with community leaders on a regular basis.[11] Although he is dismissive of liberation theology, he accepts that a united church can also be pluralistic, and he allows for various tendencies and personal options among Catholics. He has stressed on more than one occasion that the "option of the poor" is integral to the church's mission, and that the poor have a right to think and speak for themselves.

Although Sáenz Lacalle regards the church as apolitical, he has not been averse to engaging in debate over social issues with political ramifications, such as the rising crime rate among the country's youth, the need for honesty in public life and the importance of keeping prices down for essential public services such as public transportation and electricity. His deputy, Monsignor Gregorio Rosa Chávez, has been even more outspoken, arguing that the ten-year-old ARENA government should demonstrate more humanity by putting the needs of the poor ahead of the interests of impresarios and multinationals. Rosa Chávez has also been a staunch defender of Monsignor Romero's legacy, which lives on through the renewed vigor and more enlightened way in which the church pursues its social responsibilities. Since the end of the war much of the work that the Christian community bases formerly did has been undertaken by a social secretariat within the archbishop's office, which employs funds received from international agencies in North America, Europe, Japan and Australia to administer programs in health, education, road building, nutrition and agriculture throughout the country. Significantly, the church actively encourages self-help and development projects by nongovernment organizations, be they Catholic or otherwise, on the grounds that all sectors of society have the responsibility to work together and to listen to different opinions as they strive to build a new El Salvador from the wreckage of the past.

PROTESTANTS AND EVANGELICALS

Although freedom of worship has been a constitutional right since 1883, and the Catholic Church has not always been held in high esteem as an institution, until the last fifteen years the vast majority of Salvadoreans have been Catholics in faith if not in practice. In 1900 there was only one non-Catholic denomination in the country, which had a membership of thirty-two. As late as 1985 approximately 87 percent of Salvadoreans were baptized, married and died as Catholics. By 1996, when the first Protestant denomination in El Salvador, the Central American Mission (CAM), celebrated its centennial, the panorama had altered dramatically. According to a survey conducted by the Jesuit University, out of a population of 6 million, Salvadoreans claiming to be Catholics had fallen to 56.7 percent, with only around 32 percent actually practicing their religion. At the same time the proportion of practicing Protestants had risen to approximately 18 percent. A further breakdown of figures by Protestant organizations laid claim to another 17 percent of Salvadoreans who attended Protestant worship on an informal basis. If accurate, this would mean that in 1996, 35 percent of the population—over 2 million Salvadoreans—had some degree of meaningful involvement with Protestantism.[12]

Such figures can confuse as much as enlighten, and the numerous surveys, polls, interpretations and counterinterpretations by Catholics and Protestants suggest that a propaganda war is being waged. However, what is undeniable is that Protestantism has made profound, visible inroads in El Salvador. The ubiquitous presence of temples throughout the republic, which range from monumental complexes that cover entire blocks in the capital to humble adobe shacks with the name of Jehovah or Jesus plastered on the walls, confirms this trend. One source claims that there are over 5,000 Protestant churches in El Salvador, which signifies between two and three for every square mile.[13]

What is the history of Protestantism in El Salvador, and why has it penetrated so deeply and rapidly in a nation once considered so thoroughly Catholic? Until the late 1970s, when the country began its inexorable decline into civil war, the history of Protestantism in El Salvador was quite unremarkable. From the arrival of the first missionary, Samuel A. Purdie, in June 1896 to the outbreak of World War II, a number of Protestant denominations established operations in the country. The principal ones were the Central American Mission, the Apostles and Prophets, the Assemblies of God, the Baptists and the Church of God. The Baptists were particularly strong west of the Lempa River, and the Central American Mission was strong to the east. The denominations were fundamentalist in character, divided between Evangelicals, who give primacy to the teaching of the Scriptures, and the Pentecostals, who stress the charismatic influence of the Holy Spirit. However, in the national consciousness the Protestants (both Evangelicals and Pentecostals) soon became known as *los evangélicos* (the evangelicals), a label that has endured.

Until recently the evangelicals were popularly regarded as a small group of eccentrics who concentrated their missionary work in the countryside, where they were occasionally exposed to the taunts and even the violence of Catholics. Village priests resented their intrusion, and some would go so far as to call the police to arrest the "heretics." As late as 1961 an elderly pastor of the Central American Mission, Roy McNaught, was almost killed in a riot in the town of Santo Tomás. However, the most dramatic episode of persecution occurred during the Great Slaughter of 1932, when Indians who had converted to the Protestant faith were accused of being communists and summarily executed. Such was the fate of Pedro Bonito, the Pipil pastor of Nahuizalco, one of the centers of the insurrection in 1932. Some U.S. pastors were damned by association with the Indians and were lucky to escape with their lives. In spite of their zealous ministry, which included the foundation of Bible institutes and Sunday schools for children and adults, by 1940 the evangelicals had managed to convert a mere 0.5 percent of the population.

The years between 1940 and 1980 witnessed a gradual consolidation of the evangelical movement in El Salvador. Other denominations arrived, including the Nazarenes, the Prince of Peace and the Christian Mission of Elim. An important development was the rise to prominence of a number of Salvadorean-born leaders, most of them trained in the United States. With financial assistance from their churches in the United States, these Salvadorean pastors laid the foundations for expansion through Bible schools, youth campaigns, conventions, crusades and bookshops. Their potential congregation grew considerably through the 1960s and 1970s with a multiplication of evangelical radio stations. A Pentecostal pastor from the Assemblies of God, the American Pablo Finkenbinder, became one of the first people in El Salvador to use cinema as a medium of popular education. He produced six films on biblical topics between 1961 and 1966. The denominations also began to obtain legal status from the government, thus ensuring constitutional protection and the permanent ownership of any land or buildings purchased.

With an increasingly sophisticated leadership the evangelical churches gradually succeeded in gaining a foothold in San Salvador, where they found a receptive audience among sectors of the upper and middle classes, who appreciated the upbeat, American style of pastors who reminded them of televangelists like Jimmy Swaggart and Pat Robertson. In 1970 the Baptists founded a church in the middle-class Colonia Miramonte. By 1980, on the eve of the civil war, the capital was dotted with well-appointed evangelical centers where doctors, lawyers, businessmen, members of the military and other professionals went to worship. Mindful of the importance of attracting the sons and daughters of their members, the evangelicals conducted enthusiastic crusades among university students. They became increasingly involved in education. In response to the criticism that their emphasis on Bible studies and on the personal dimension of religion demonstrated a lack of social consciousness, the major evangelical denominations adopted a higher profile with regards to social welfare and humanitarian aid. By 1980 there were up to forty evangelical denominations with a practicing membership of over 200,000. Up to 300,000 other people attended worship on a casual basis. By this stage the evangelicals had become the alternative religion in El Salvador.

However, it was during the civil war and afterward that the evangelical movement experienced a veritable boom. Between 1980 and 1996 the baptized membership grew fivefold (from 200,000 to 1 million). Up to another million people attended evangelical churches. There are currently over 120 denominations. The largest ones, such as the Assemblies of God, the Central American Mission and the Baptists, are now in a position to send missionaries to other Latin American countries, Europe and even as far away as Australia.[14] In the 1980s, with the National University shut down for long periods and the Jesuit University under duress, two evangelical universities were opened, the Evangelical University of El Salvador and the Christian University of the Assemblies of God. A number of theological seminaries and biblical institutes were also founded, as were dozens of schools, kindergartens and even creches.

What is the explanation for this evangelical success story? One reason is a practical one. After many years of division, or at best lukewarm cooperation, in 1986 the majority of the denominations in El Salvador came together under an umbrella association, CONESAL (Evangelical Confraternity of El Salvador). Since then CONESAL has run congresses, crusades and campaigns for social and humanitarian aid. During the war and postwar reconstruction it cooperated with interdenominational, international organizations such as World Vision, World Relief and the 700 Club. Another practical explanation for the expansion of evangelism is the saturation campaign on radio. At any hour of the day or night the booming voice of a preacher may be heard on any one of the more than twenty stations on the dial. Moreover, since the mid-1980s a television channel, Canal 25, has been devoted exclusively to evangelical programs. Dynamic preachers like Brother Toby share the airwaves with other Salvadorean, Central American and U.S. preachers. It is almost impossible for a Salvadorean, irrespective of social class, political persuasion or religious affiliation, not to be exposed at some time to the show-business flair of the evangelicals on the electronic media. For the benefit of literate Salvadoreans, articles or columns with evangelical messages regularly appear in the newspapers. A chain of bookshops trading under the name of Josuá supplies evangelical literature throughout the country.

There are also profound sociopolitical reasons for the evangelical challenge to the Catholic Church. Firstly, the personal pain and distress caused by the civil war drove thousands of Salvadoreans to seek refuge in a religious movement that promoted a new kind of hope and reconciliation. The evangelical denominations themselves are not sure how best to explain the explosion in their membership during the war, conceding that people's motives ranged from escapism to selfishness to genuine spiritual need. However, a motivating factor for many people—particularly the anticommunist middle and upper classes—was the apparent apolitical character of the evangelical movement. Disillusioned, and in some cases frightened, by the Marxist message of liberation theology and the pro-guerrilla sympathies of the Popular Church, many among the oligarchy and the professional classes joined the evangelical movement. In fact, the evangelicals were not as apolitical as they seemed, for many of the pastors were staunchly pro-United States and anticommunist. Be this as it may, their congregation extended beyond the upper and middle classes to the urban poor and the exploited peasantry. The evangelicals found particularly strong support among working-class wives and mothers, such as market vendors and domestic servants, who are often the principal providers in a country where de facto marriages and absentee fathers abound. For many poor women the pastor became a spiritual father figure, and the humble temple became an oasis of security and fellowship in a cynical world.

To what extent the evangelical movement exploits the naiveté and vulnerability of good, simple people whose deep-seated spirituality is one of the few remaining vestiges of their pre-Columbian heritage is a moot point. In a different guise and with different words the evangelical pastor may well be replacing the Catholic priest, who replaced the ancestral Pipil witch doctor. Nevertheless, the fact remains that Salvadoreans from all walks of life now have their choice of religions, and neither the Catholic Church nor the evangelical denominations can afford to take their spiritual constituencies for granted.

NOTES

1. The metaphor of the Cross and the Sword was coined by Alan Riding in "The Cross and the Sword in Latin America." In Marvin E. Gettleman, ed., *El*

Salvador: Central America in the New Cold War (New York: Grove Press, 1981), 189–98.

2. Rafael Menjívar, *El Salvador: el eslabón más pequeño* (San José, Costa Rica: EDUCA, 1980), 40.

3. Richard A. Haggerty, ed., *El Salvador: A Country Study* (Washington, DC: Library of Congress, 1990), 63–64.

4. For an assessment of the Christian Democratic Party's rise and fall see Stephen Webre, "The Politics of Salvadorean Christian Democracy." In Marvin E. Gettleman, ed., *El Salvador: Central America in the New Cold War* (New York: Grove Press, 1981), 89–101.

5. For a sensitive study of the Catholic Church in Latin America during this era see Penny Lernoux, *Cry of the People* (New York: Doubleday, 1980).

6. Juan Ramón Vega, *Las comunidades de base en América Central* (San Salvador: Ediciones del Arzobispado, 1998), 112.

7. A concise account of the repression against the People's Church is included in Edward Stourton, *Absolute Truth:The Catholic Church in the World Today* (London: Viking, 1998), 102–19.

8. Many books have been written about Monseñor Romero. A particularly moving account of his life and mission is found in Plácido Erdozaín, *Archbishop Romero, Martyr of Salvador* (Maryknoll, NY: Orbis Books, 1981).

9. Lernoux, *Cry of the People*, 439.

10. Quoted in Stourton, *Absolute Truth*, 110.

11. In an attempt to promote its image and improve relations within the community the archdiocese of San Salvador has established a homepage: *http://www.callereal.org/menu8.htm*.

12. The statistics come from Francisco Schmidt, Julio Ernesto Contreras and Luis Alberto Gómez Chávez, *Cien años de presencia evangélica en El Salvador. 1896–1996* (San Salvador: CONESAL, 1996), 137–38. This is the best source of information on the history of the evangelical movement in El Salvador.

13. Ibid., 140.

14. A list of denominations up to 1996 is provided in ibid., 144–47.

4

Education

UNFORTUNATELY, the history of education in El Salvador has been one of neglect. An authoritative source described the situation in 1998 as "woefully inadequate in its coverage and quality." Following some recent reforms the description was amended in 1999 to "generally inadequate."[1] Although statistics are erratic, perhaps the most notable educational achievement since independence has been the increase in the literacy rate from 26.2 percent of the adult population in 1930 to 83.55 percent in 1998.[2] However, such statistics have to be interpreted cautiously, since literacy in a developing country does not necessarily mean being able to read and write, but rather it means being able to read and write one's name and perhaps decipher a few words and phrases.

It is also difficult to speak of education in national terms since until very recently the system ignored or bypassed the rural zones. Historically, the plantation owners have viewed the *campesinos* and their children as a source of cheap labor. The landowners, who have always had an overwhelming influence upon government policy, have preferred an uneducated workforce because educated *campesinos* could start thinking for themselves and begin asking difficult questions regarding wages and conditions. Consequently, the education system has been heavily biased in favor of the urban areas, particularly San Salvador and the larger departmental capitals. Thus, an ambitious reform program in 1968 hardly touched tens of thousands of children in the countryside. A few statistics serve to outline the unfair scenario.[3] In 1980 75 percent of the urban population were literate, and 90 percent of urban school-age children attended primary school. In the rural areas only 60 percent were literate, and less than 67 percent of children attended primary school. The city-rural imbalance was even starker with respect to secondary education. In the 1970s almost 62 percent of urban students reached the ninth grade, while less than 6 percent of rural students did so. Only 1 percent of the country's total enrollment at the upper-secondary level (grades 10 through 12) came from rural zones. The situation in the countryside was aggravated by a crippling shortage of school teachers, abysmally few secondary schools, an illiteracy rate that was twice as high for women as for men and an extremely high dropout rate, especially for girls, who were forced by circumstances to seek employment as fieldworkers or domestic servants, or who had to stay home and help care for their siblings.

The civil war turned a dramatic situation into a catastrophic one. Public education was virtually wiped out in the rural war zones in the departments of Morazán and Chalatenango. In those devastated areas that the guerrillas controlled, it was only thanks to a rudimentary program of "popular education," run by volunteer teachers with limited education themselves, that children were able to receive basic schooling.[4]

After the signing of the peace accords in 1992 the government concentrated its efforts on postwar reconstruction (housing, roads, dams, bridges) and the restoration of essential services (water, electricity, health). Consequently, it was not until 1995 that the National Commission of Education, Science and Development formally addressed the crisis in education. Since then a sweeping reform program has been undertaken with the support of AID (U.S. Agency for International Development) and with loans from the World Bank and the Inter-American Development Bank. The education system has been revamped. It is now divided into three sectors: *primaria* (primary, grades 1 through 6), *básica* (middle school, grades 7 through 9) and *secundaria* (secondary, grades 10 through 12).

Public education is free, and school uniforms are optional. However, the vast majority of rural schools still offer only primary education. Logically enough, the reforms have focussed on the primary sector. A textbook-loan plan is now in place, and a television and radio educational network is in operation. The Ministry of Education produces *Cipotes* (which means "children" in ancient Nahuatl), a series of texts for grades 1 through 6 in the four main areas: language, health and environment, mathematics and social science. A plan called EDUCO (Education with Community Participation) is meant to encourage parents and community leaders to become involved in matters that affect their children's education, including the selection of teachers and the financial management of the schools. Another plan, Escuelas Saludables (Healthy Schools), is designed to ensure that every child receives a proper diet and access to medical facilities. In 1999, according to government statistics, 3,593 out of the country's 4,000 primary schools benefited from this project.[5]

The current reforms have also addressed secondary education. Projects are now in place to upgrade and adequately equip the nation's 240 high schools. The system is divided into academic and technical programs. The Ministry of Education has set the goal of substantially increasing the very low 18–20 percent the students who progress from first grade to *bachillerato* (high-school graduation). Books of higher quality are being produced, and students are being encouraged to think for themselves and interpret facts, a long overdue initiative in a country where rote learning and authoritarian pedagogy have been the norm. Controversially, teacher training, which has been historically an underresourced and neglected enterprise, particularly at the secondary-education level, has been transferred to the universities, which are themselves facing overdue reforms. Ironically, the country now faces the prospect of a glut of teachers. An extra 11,000 teachers are expected by 2003.[6] Unfortunately, unless prompt action is taken the majority of these prospective teachers are likely to specialize in subjects for which there is no demand.

Apart from public education, El Salvador possesses a collection of independent schools. The majority are mixed gender and are located in the capital or major cities. Catholic orders run most of them. Historically, the best of these Catholic schools, such as Liceo Salvadoreño, Externado San José, Santa Cecilia and Sagrado Corazón have offered a full education for the children of the elite and professional classes. A second layer of Catholic schools provides an education for children from less-affluent backgrounds. A third layer, such as Polígono Industrial Don Bosco, caters to children in the poor urban zones, where the evangelical churches also run a number of schools.

In the last quarter century, and particularly since the beginning of the civil war, a cluster of private, nondenominational schools have risen to prominence in San Salvador. Expensive, well-equipped, and staffed by highly trained teachers, these schools have become extremely popular with parents from the oligarchy and the professional classes. The curriculum is designed so that by the end of primary school students are fluent in a foreign language. English is obviously the most popular language. The results are certainly impressive, as children continue to speak in English in the schoolyard and after classes. Apart from their high standards such schools provide an alternative for parents who are disenchanted with the way that politics infiltrated the Catholic schools during the war years.

The second major law that the newly independent Republic of El Salvador passed was the creation of the government-funded University of El Salvador

(UES). It was not until almost 125 years later, in 1965, that a second university was founded, the Jesuit Central American University José Simeón Cañas (UCA). Located in San Salvador, both universities have played significant roles in the nation's history in an educational, intellectual sense and also—often quite dramatically—in the political sphere. The reason for their political involvement is related to their institutional charters. Whereas a university traditionally has a three-pronged mission—to teach, to research and to transmit cultural values—in a developing society such as El Salvador UES and UCA felt obliged to pursue a higher "civilizing" mission.[7]

Throughout the nineteenth century and until the end of the Coffee Republic in the 1920s, the civilizing missions of UES were building a nation and forging a national identity. From the dictatorship of General Martínez to the end of the last civil war the dire circumstances afflicting the country expanded the university's sense of mission. Students and teachers became increasingly involved in political affairs. UES participated in the opposition movements that brought down General Martínez in 1944 and Colonel José María Lemus in 1960. In 1968, during the Central American Universities' Congress in San Salvador, UES representatives advocated joining the social forces that were fighting to change the repressive socioeconomic structures that stifled the country's development.

In 1980, inspired by Fidel Castro's brand of Marxism and encouraged by the Sandinistas' success in Nicaragua, university activists aligned themselves with the FMLN-FDR coalition that had declared war on the junta that was in power in El Salvador. Indeed, many of the FMLN-FDR commanders had been students or teachers at UES. Two commanders, Fabio Castillo and José Napoleón Rodríguez Ruiz, had been rectors. Not surprisingly, throughout the war UES was a hotbed of antigovernment agitation. Guerrilla commandos hid on the campus, utilized it as a munitions depot and employed it as a logistical center. In retaliation the government cut the university's funds and sent in the army, which occupied the campus between June 1980 and May 1984. The army ransacked buildings, destroyed the library and laboratories and persecuted students and teachers. The rector, Félix Antonio Ulloa, was assassinated by a death squad in October 1980. He was the second rector to suffer that fate in three years.

Forced to drastically reduce its operations, UES continued to function from rented premises with economic assistance from European governments and universities. At one stage UES was an educational shell. Its student body collapsed from over 30,000 in 1980 to under 6,000 in 1982. Upon reopening in 1984 it staged a remarkable recovery. Its student population increased to just under 30,000 by the mid-1980s.[8] However, by that point many of its best teachers had been killed or had gone into exile, its infrastructure had been decimated, and its academic standards had dropped alarmingly. Its diminished circumstances did not prevent the university from again becoming a hotbed of unrest, so much so that the FMLN chose it as the springboard for their so-called "Final offensive" in November 1989. In the fierce fighting the air force bombarded the campus, which the army again occupied until June 1990.

UES continued to operate during the civil war, which bears testimony to what has been described as its "tremendous institutional survival instinct."[9] Since the peace agreements it has gradually rebuilt its material resources and reestablished its academic credentials. It now boasts fifteen faculties, three of them servicing provincial areas, and it has introduced masters degrees in sixteen areas of study. As a public university its students are representative of all sectors of Salvadorean society. A large percentage come from working-class and lower-middle-class families. With a modernized curriculum, a new library, a revamped administration and an active office of international relations UES is valiantly endeavoring to reconcile its social mission as "the people's university" with the universal ideal of academic excellence.

In 1965, in response to the left-wing politics of students and teachers at UES, the government of President Julio Adalberto Rivera passed a decree that legalized private universities. That very same year the Jesuits founded UCA with the financial backing of the elite, who expected it to provide a politically acceptable, intellectually rigorous, Catholic alternative to UES. While living up to their reputation for intellectual excellence, the Jesuits surprised, then shocked, their well-heeled supporters by propagating liberation theology, promoting the Christian community bases and sympathizing, in some individual cases even affiliating, with the FMLN-FDR during the war.

To many of the wealthy, influential parents who paid handsome fees to send their sons and daughters to UCA, the Jesuits were nothing less than traitors. Spanish-born Jesuits, in particular, aroused the fury of the military hard-liners. Father Ignacio Ellacuría and Father Jon Sobrino, both of whom had taken Salvadorean nationality, were denounced as alien meddlers in Salvadorean affairs. Ellacuría, who became rector of UCA in 1979, professed the triumph of a "civilisation of poverty" in a socialist utopia, and his support of a negotiated peace to the armed conflict infuriated the hawks in the military high command. Sobrino was the eloquent voice of liberation theology in El Salvador. One of the most brutal episodes of the war happened on the evening of November 15, 1989, when 250 soldiers invaded the UCA campus and executed Ellacuría, five other prominent Jesuits, their cook and her daughter. Sobrino was spared the same fate because he was in Thailand lecturing on Christology.[10]

Under Sobrino, who became rector upon Ellacuría's death, UCA has continued to consolidate its reputation as one of Latin America's leading universities in many areas, particularly in theology, business administration, health sciences and ecology. It has 8,000 students, its own radio station, a video-production center and an outstanding publishing house. One of its journal publications, *ECA* (Central American Studies), is essential reading for any student of El Salvador. UCA has a sliding tuition structure that ranges from approximately US$1,800 to US$380 per year, thus allowing a wider cross section of society to enroll in the country's most prestigious university. Apart from fees, UCA receives donations from international sources in the Catholic world, and the Inter-American Development Bank has provided substantial loans both for buildings and for staff to improve their qualifications abroad. However, there has been some criticism that UCA is becoming too technocratic, which is evidenced by the fact that with the ending of its *carrera* (major) in literature, it is no longer possible for a student to specialize in this area in El Salvador.

Between 1977 and 1980 four new private universities were founded, all of them with very respectable academic credentials. They were José Matías Delgado, Albert Einstein, Universidad Politécnica, and Alberto Masferrer. In the 1980s UES was shut so often that a five-year degree became a ten-year saga, and UCA was under duress. So vested interests took advantage of the situation to open a series of alternative institutions. As a consequence there was a boom in private universities, and more than thirty new ones were created by 1990. Including UES, UCA and the government-funded Military University that was created in 1988, a staggering forty universities existed in 1999. This is thirty-two more than the average for the rest of Central America! Not surprisingly, grave problems soon came to light regarding academic standards and facilities. At least one institution was accused of awarding diplomas to nondeserving students.

Following the passing of the Law of Higher Education in November 1995, well-defined standards were prescribed for all universities. These laws included a minimum of five career tracks (four professional and one technical), an adequate infrastructure, a minimum of one professor for every thirty-five students, a minimum of one full-time professor for every sixty-five part-time teachers and one major research project per university. This law has reduced the number of universities to less than thirty, and there is the likelihood of a further reduction.

There are currently over 75,000 students enrolled in universities in El

Salvador. Almost 70 percent are in the private sector. No university is yet in a position to offer doctorates, although international grants and agreements provide scholarships for the best students to pursue higher studies abroad, mainly in Spain and the United States. In spite of the endeavors to open tertiary education to a wider cross section of society, only a privileged 3 percent of the population enroll in university, and a mere 1 percent complete their degree.[11] Nevertheless, the commitment and dedication with which the leading universities are pursuing their mission augur well for the future.

NOTES

1. See *Country Profile. Guatemala, El Salvador, 1997–1998* (London: Economist Intelligence Unit, 1997), 86; and *Country Profile. Guatemala, El Salvador, 1999–2000* (London: Economist Intelligence Unit, 1999), 46.

2. The statistics have been drawn from *La historia de la reforma y la reforma de la historia: La reforma en marcha de El Salvador* (San Salvador: Ministerio de El Salvador, 1999).

3. These statistic are provided by Richard A. Haggerty, ed., *El Salvador: A Country Study* (Washington, DC: Library of Congress, 1990), 73.

4. For an account of the experiment in popular education, see Kevin Murray and Tom Barry, *Inside El Salvador* (Albuquerque: Resources Center Press, 1995), 124–26.

5. See *La historia de la reforma y la reforma de la historia*, 13.

6. See Yesenia Accevedo, "Futuros maestros sin oferta laboral," *La Prensa Gráfica*, June 22, 1999, 7.

7. For an informative account of the interaction between universities and politics in El Salvador see Yvon Grenier, *Universities, Intellectuals and Political Transition in El Salvador*, CDAS Discussion Paper No. 71 (Montreal: McGill University, 1992).

8. Ibid., 19.

9. Murray and Barry, *Inside El Salvador*, 123.

10. Edward Stourton, *Absolute Truth: The Catholic Church in the World Today* (London: Viking, 1998), 109–10.

11. The status of higher education in El Salvador is analyzed in Helga Cuéllar, "El potencial de la ley de educación superior a partir de su proceso de creación y adopción," *ECA* 589–90 (November–December 1997), 1169–87.

Izalco volcano. Courtesy of *El Diario de Hoy*.

Archaeological ruins, San Andrés. Courtesy of *El Diario de Hoy*.

Tortilla vendor selling her wares door-to-door, Colonia Escalón.

Typical village scene.

Typical middle-class living room.

La Dalia arcade, San Salvador. Courtesy of *El Diario de Hoy*.

Selling fish, La Libertad.

Typical provincial scene.

Typical scene in the village of Citala, in the department of Chalatenango.
Courtesy of *El Diario de Hoy.*

Well-dressed children in mall, San Salvador.

Patio in Suchitoto.

Boy at well and water pump, Suchitoto.

Beach scene, private country club, western region.

Panoramic view of Don Rúa church, the biggest church in San Salvador.
The San Salvador volcano is in the background. Courtesy of *El Diario de Hoy*.

"Old Chapeltique" church, the oldest church in the eastern city of San Miguel. Courtesy of *El Diario de Hoy.*

Holy Week procession in Sonsonate. Courtesy of *El Diario de Hoy.*

Bolívar Park, San Salvador. Courtesy of *El Diario de Hoy.*

Movie house in provincial town.

The writer Manlio Argueta.

Dr. David Escobar Galindo, leading contemporary author.
Courtesy of *El Diario de Hoy*.

Hat weavers. Courtesy of *El Diario de Hoy.*

Typical craft store, Panchimalco.

High-rise buildings in El Salvador.

City Hall, San Salvador. Courtesy of *El Diario de Hoy*.

Salvadorean tapestry.

Salvadorean clay miniatures.

5

Traditional Culture and Popular Entertainment

TRADITIONAL CULTURE

EL SALVADOR'S long-standing marginalization in the Spanish-speaking world explains why its wonderfully varied colorful traditional culture—a mixture of indigenous traditions and Spanish customs—is so little known outside its borders. Whereas Mexican enchiladas, the Argentinian tango, the Peruvian poncho, the Brazilian samba, and Cuban Havanas (cigars) have become part of the English language, very few foreigners or even fellow Latin Americans are likely to identify equivalents from El Salvador. In fact, the country's peripheral status has contributed to the preservation of what Salvadoreans call *cultura típica* (typical culture) in a wide range of human activities that extend from the most fundamental, such as language and food, to the more specialized, such as pottery and dance.

Nevertheless, since the end of World War II the two biggest neighbors, Mexico and the United States, have exerted an ever increasing influence upon the culture and customs of Salvadoreans of all ages and social classes. This is most notable with regards to cinema, television, radio and commercial propaganda. Moreover, the tens of thousands of legal and illegal migrants who have been to Mexico and the United States, both during and since the last civil war, have affected the lifestyle, morality and way of thinking of the 6 million Salvadoreans who live in the country. Consequently, it is now as common to eat Mexican tacos and enchiladas in a restaurant as it is to hear a middle-class lady announce that she is going to a "baby shower." In certain affluent households, Halloween and even Thanksgiving are celebrated in the most American tradition. In shopping malls in the capital, "hi," "thank you" and the U.S. dollar are used almost as much as "hola," "gracias" and the Salvadorean *colón*. Batman, Walt Disney, Coke, Pepsi, hamburgers, rap and pop compete with Mexican *telenovelas* (television soap operas) and the shrill strains of mariachis for the loyalty of Salvadoreans.

Yet Salvadoreans do not seem to be unduly alarmed by the potential dilution of their typical culture by these foreign influences. On the one hand, there seems to be an unspoken consensus that what is happening is part of the universal trend of globalization, which is not perceived as entirely a bad thing for a country that has been as marginalized as El Salvador. On the other hand, as Carlos Cañas, one of El Salvador's outstanding young intellectuals has explained, "You only need to scratch the surface to realise that underneath the foreign veneer adopted by many Salvadoreans beats the heart and mind of a true *guanaco*."[1] The *guanaco*, a slow-witted, cud-chewing animal that is related to the llama, is the symbol foisted upon Salvadoreans by their not always friendly Central American neighbors. Salvadoreans, however, retort with what has become their battle cry: "Soy guanaco, y a mucha honra!" (I am a *guanaco*, and proud to be one!). Consequently, the *guanaco* has become synonymous with the typical culture and customs that distinguish Salvadoreans from the rest of the world.

SALVADOREAN SPANISH AND THE PRE-HISPANIC HERITAGE

The great Nicaraguan poet Rubén Darío (1867–1916) maintained that all the fundamental differences between the United States and the countries below the Río Grande are explained by the fact that they speak different languages. Linguists commonly believe that the language that a particular culture speaks is a manifestation of its collective identity. In the case of El Salvador, *la lengua salvadoreña*, its distinctive brand of Spanish, provides penetrating insights into the way that Salvadoreans think, feel and behave. It describes the way that they view the world in all its multiple facets, visible and invisible, objective and subjective, material and spiritual, magical and real. In this regard, the language spoken in El Salvador today reflects the attitude of the citizens' pre-Hispanic ancestors, who believed that to exist a person had to speak.[2]

Although Salvadoreans are notoriously disinclined toward showing off, which helps to explain the lack of a national tradition in the performing arts, they are lively, inventive speakers whose language is characterized by a style that has been compared to that of a snake charmer. An anthropological explanation for this vibrant oral tradition is that it was bequeathed to Salvadoreans by their ancestors, the Pipiles, Lencas, Ulúas, Pokomames and Chortis, who inhabited the country when the Spaniards arrived in 1524. Archaeological evidence suggests that while the priests and princes of these ancient tribes possessed a rudimentary form of hieroglyphic script, the common people could only communicate orally. As a consequence, the spoken word acquired an overwhelming significance in daily life. The sounds, rhythms and patterns of words, as well as their symbolic significance, mattered as much as their literal meaning did. This ancestral fondness for the spoken word is reflected in modern Salvadoreans' untiring capacity for telling stories and jokes, which can make the unwary visitor's head spin and his body ache with laughter. Certainly even the non-Spanish speaker can detect the pleasure as the words roll off languorously and melodiously from the tongues of *guanacos*.

Many of the country's toponyms (place names) have retained their native terms, which apart from their poetic quality bear testimony to the beliefs and customs of ancient Salvadoreans. A few examples are typical: Acelhuate (River of Nymphs and Lilacs), Nacascolo (Place of the Twisted Ear), Guasapa (Place of the Laughing Falcon), Jucuarán (Hill of the Warring Ants), Tushán (Mother Serpent), Chumtrum (Land of Ghosts), Poy (Evil Spirit), Chorit (Edge of the Field of Corn). The *conquistadores* may have slaughtered the Indians and dismantled their religion, but they could not altogether wipe out their language, which lives on proudly and stubbornly next to Spanish in the names of towns and villages, such as Santiago Texacuangos (Saint James of the Hill of High Stones), San Pedro Nonualco (Saint Peter Among the People of Strange Tongue) and San Juan Tapezontes (Saint John in the Narrow Gap in the Hill).

By contrast with other countries, such as Paraguay, Guatemala and Bolivia, where large sections of the population speak the native languages, in some cases with more fluency than Spanish, Nahuat, the principal Indian language, has almost disappeared as a medium of communication in El Salvador. Yet in a very curious way all Salvadoreans retain a collective memory of Nahuat. It is almost impossible to have an everyday conversation without having recourse to the lexicon (words) or phonemes (sounds) that were in existence in pre-Columbian times. Salvadorean speech, be it in the bedroom, kitchen, government, shopping mall or coffee plantation, resounds with the echoes of Nahuat, the ancestral language of the kingdom of Cuscatlán. Spanish-speaking visitors have to learn a whole new botanical, zoological and domestic vocabulary if they are to fully appreciate the country's popular culture and customs. Certainly no Spaniard, Argentinian, Chilean or Venezuelan can be expected to arrive and know the meaning of such everyday words as *masa-*

cuata (a type of snake), *tecolote* (owl), *güisquil* (choko), *chirimol* (a sauce made up of chile, chopped onion and tomato), *chingaste* (coffee sediment, by extension any waste matter), *comal* (pot), *shuco* (dark corn, by extension dirty), *cipote* (child), *huishte* (broken glass), *bayunco* (in bad taste), *chiche* (female breast) and *chompipe* (turkey).

When a Salvadorean, particularly one from the rural areas, forms a string of typical words into a sentence, pronouncing them in the eccentric fashion of his Nahuat-speaking ancestors, more than one foreign professor of Spanish has been left mystified. Indeed, it is not uncommon for *costumbrista* (typically Salvadorean) works, such as Salarrué's celebrated *Clay Stories* (see Chapter 6), to have a glossary of terms. In only four or five other Latin American countries (i.e., Guatemala, Peru, Paraguay, Ecuador and Bolivia), is popular speech influenced to the same extent as in El Salvador by the Indian heritage.

TRADITIONAL MYTHS

The oral culture has spawned a folkloric tradition of storytelling among Salvadoreans of all social classes. An illiterate grandmother in a remote hamlet in Chalatenango will tell her grandchildren variants of the same stories that her counterpart in an elite suburb of the capital tells her grandchildren. The most persuasive storytellers belong to a special breed of Salvadoreans who keep alive a collection of traditional myths that have been handed down from generation to generation since before the arrival of the *conquistadores*. Not surprisingly, the most celebrated storytellers hail from towns with a strong indigenous tradition, such as Panchimalco and Santiago Nonualco. While the popular myths are of ethnographic value because they provide insights into ancestral beliefs and customs, they are also significant because they trace certain psychological and spiritual correspondences between modern and ancient Salvadoreans. The majority of these myths are characterized by magical realism, that peculiarly Latin American worldview in which reason and superstition, the physical and the spiritual, the visible and the invisible, this world and the next coexist in natural harmony. Even Salvadoreans who are educated in universities in the United States sometimes will not enter a particular room in their parents' home because it was haunted during their childhood! And wherever they may settle, Salvadorean migrants and exiles take with them tales of witches, devils, monsters, midnight apparitions and wandering souls.

Of the repertoire of traditional myths, three stand out: el Cadejo, la Cihuanaba, and el Cipitío.[3] El Cadejo is a monstrous dog with eyes as bright as embers that haunts the countryside, usually at night. It confuses its victims with its piercing whistle, which the farther away it sounds, the closer it is, and vice versa. A black Cadejo is said to prey upon men, while a white one stalks women; another version associates the former with good and the latter with evil. A person who sees a Cadejo will fall ill, go mad or even die. Used as a cautionary tale against drunks, philanderers, crooks, wayward women and disrespectful children, the tale of el Cadejo typifies the didactic character of such myths. Another typical aspect of this myth is its association with *nahualismo* (totemism), which harks back to the pre-Hispanic belief, also common among North American Indians, that each individual has an animal totem or guardian. There are numerous other myths that involve animals in El Salvador, among them that of the *mujer-chancha* (a woman who turns into a pig), the *hombre-puma* (a man who becomes a puma) and the *brujos-micos* (witch doctors who transform themselves into monkeys). In an anthropological sense the persistence of such zoomorphic (animal) myths may be interpreted as a symptom of a collective unconscious, an ancestral memory that links El Salvador to the Nahuat kingdom of Cuscatlán.

It is a common experience for a visitor to meet Salvadoreans claiming to have had an encounter with la Cihuanaba, or who claim to know someone who has seen her. Salarrué, the country's favorite writer gave her literary status in a short story, *la Ziguanaba* (an alternative spelling). In Nahuat the word means "the crying woman," which turns la Cihuanaba into the local version of la Llorona, the mythical crying female of Mexican lore. The Salvadorean basis of the myth is an ancient tale of a beautiful Indian princess who committed adultery, a crime for which the gods punished her by transforming her into a monstrous female who was doomed to spend eternity washing clothes by riverbanks under the light of the moon. When men see la Cihuanaba, she appears to be a winsome maiden who is naked to the waist, but upon being approached she becomes a hideous, cackling hag with a tangle of long hair and drooping breasts that she beats against the water. Should a man dare to touch her, her skin turns into banana leaves or cornhusks. Fevers, lunacy or death await the fellow unlucky enough to meet la Cihuanaba, who sometimes will transform herself into the beautiful princess she once was to tempt solitary horsemen to let her ride with them. Mounted behind them, she reverts to la Cihuanaba, tearing the flesh off their backs with her huge fingernails. la Cihuanaba's curse may be staved off by making the sign of the cross and uttering the incantation "María pata de gallina" (Mary chicken legs), by carrying a dagger, by biting a machete or by smoking a cigar.

The myth of la Cihuanaba invites interpretations that provide insights into gender relations in El Salvador. There is an obvious warning against adultery—the unfaithful princess wanders the countryside in the desperate hope that she may find a miraculous river to wash away the stain upon her honor. The implicit message is that a woman can never be trusted—irrespective of beauty or status she may betray her husband at any moment. It is tempting to perceive in the tale a reflection of the notorious Salvadorean *machismo* (male chauvinism). According to a long-suffering female character in *Milagro de la paz* (The miracle of peace), a recent novel by Manlio Argueta, an ancestral law dictates that "men are bad when they are with a woman."[4] This judgment seems to be confirmed by the number of women in El Salvador who seek help in what are known vulgarly as *las casas de las penqueadas* (refuges for women who have been "worked over" by their husbands). From a feminist perspective, however, maybe when la Cihuanaba taunts, scratches or drives men mad, she is symbolically exacting revenge on behalf of her Salvadorean sisters.

La Cihuanaba's illegitimate son is reputedly el Cipitío, whose name is derived from Xipec-totec, the Nahuat name for a god of fruit and vegetation who is associated with fertility. Known affectionately as *el Cipi* (the little Cipitío), he is a short, fat, nocturnal Romeo who roams the countryside in an enormous hat in pursuit of female companions. He only eats ash, wallowing in the smoldering heaps that are left in the mills after the sugarcane has been crushed. An impish spirit, he plays "catch me if you can" with irate husbands, boyfriends and fathers. He confuses them with his footprints, since his feet are backward. Numerous Salvadoreans swear to have seen el Cipitío or at least his distinctive footprints. When men tell the story, it is possible to detect a certain sympathy for this amorous rogue. Interestingly, women have a soft spot for him, probably because he appeals to their maternal instinct—as a punishment for his mother's sin he is doomed to be seven years old forever.

LEGENDS AND HEROES

Although most Salvadorean myths have pre-Columbian antecedents, its legends are woven around people who carried out bold deeds during the colonial or republican eras. In some respects these legendary figures are reminiscent of heroes like Robin Hood and Zorro, or they resemble antiheroes like the English highwayman Ben Turpin and the Australian bushranger Ned Kelly.

The rise and fall of Anastasio Aquino, the Indian chieftain who led a bloody uprising against the new republican government in 1833, has certainly stirred the popular imagination. After anointing himself the king of the Nonualcos by placing on his head a crown of gold and emeralds, which was snatched from a statue of St. Joseph, Aquino reigned briefly over a sovereign Indian state. Betrayed by a henchman, he was captured and executed, and his Indian troops were subjugated. The real Aquino was an explosive character who combined a thirst for political justice and a pride in his Indian heritage with a huge ego, ruthlessness and lust. However, no sooner had he died than he was turned into a national symbol of liberation against tyranny. An abundance of plays, poems, songs and paintings have been inspired by him, and during the recent civil war the FMLN guerrillas named a battalion in his honor.

El Salvador's Robin Hood is certainly el Partideño, a nineteenth-century hero whose name means "cattle driver," a reference to his original vocation. El Partideño became an outlaw when a wealthy man raped his bride. He slew the culprit and swore lifelong revenge against the rich and powerful. He became a rustler, and it is said that he hoarded loot in a secret cave. More than one Salvadorean claims to know its whereabouts.[5] However, el Partideño had a second personality—that of a defender of the poor and underprivileged. He shared food and money with them, and he protected them against tyrants and thieves. He soon became a folk hero, and magical powers were attributed to him. It was said that to escape his pursuers he would change into an animal or a bunch of bananas. While one version of the legend maintains that he was captured and hanged in Santa Ana, another alleges that he escaped to Honduras. Irrespective of his destiny, the spirit of el Partideño lives on in El Salvador, and artists and writers turn to him for inspiration. Indeed, in his famous play, *Ursino* (1887), Francisco Gavidia portrays him as a national messiah.

In the popular Salvadorean imagination one scoundrel stands out above all others: Pedro Urdimales (his punning name means "Peter the Trickster"). Whether Pedro existed or not is a moot point, but colonial history and literature are full of rascals like him who fled from Spain to the New World with nothing but their wits to live on. Salvadorean lore overflows with stories about Pedro, who was the scourge of all authority. He was particularly fond of tricking the king, whose daughters he seduced on more than one occasion. Priests were also the butt of his jokes, which are often quite crude if not unprintable. Almost 500 years later Pedro lives on in the oral tradition, having outlived all his enemies, victims and lovers. The reasons for his longevity are not difficult to identify. Firstly, through his exploits the common people can exact vicarious revenge upon their masters, from the royal family to presidents, bishops and *gringos* (a derogatory term for English-speaking foreigners). When Pedro, laughing and victorious, escapes unscathed from their clutches, the people identify with him. Secondly, Pedro is incorrigibly chauvinistic, and in this sense he appeals to the deep-seated Salvadorean *machismo*. Tales of Pedro's seduction of a princess or of a silly old woman's daughter may not be politically correct, but for that matter neither is the typical Salvadorean male.

In total contrast to Pedro Urdimales stands the latest addition to the pantheon of legendary heroes: Monseñor Oscar Arnulfo Romero, the archbishop whose assassination in 1980 presaged the outbreak of the last civil war. Stories of miracles by San Romero (Saint Romero) abound. There are shrines to him throughout the country, and he is glorified in numerous posters, murals, novels and plays. Legends are a combination of truth and fiction, and most contain a heavier dose of the latter than of the former. However, in the case of Monseñor Romero it is difficult to determine where the truth ends and the fiction begins.

TRADITIONAL MEDICINES AND SORCERY

Although the provision of medical services has improved considerably in El Salvador, many rural people live in scattered settlements where access to doctors and hospitals is difficult if not impossible. However, even more Salvadoreans would die, particularly children and the aged, if it were not for the traditional medical knowledge that has been handed down from father to son and from mother to daughter since pre-Hispanic times. In the countryside and in urban areas with heavy concentrations of rural migrants, family elders often employ folk remedies to treat health problems that range from piles to warts to syphilis. When the problem is serious enough, the specialized knowledge of the local *sobador* (bone mender) or *curandero* (healer) will be sought.

One indispensable study catalogs some forty examples of Salvadorean flora with medicinal properties, many of them with untranslatable names.[6] One example will suffice to give an indication of the extraordinary powers that such products have. Just about every part of the *marañón* (cashew tree) is supposed to cure or prevent a disease. The shell prevents tooth decay. Oil from the tree destroys warts and callouses. The bark may be used as an astringent. The tincture from the bark can be applied to skin infections. The almond of the fruit is used for emulsions. As if all this were not enough the almond is also used to make mouthwatering candy and syrup, and the gum from the bark makes an ideal furniture varnish.

El Salvador is a superstitious country. Traditional Catholic notions of heaven and hell, angels and demons, good and evil, have fused with Indian beliefs in the supernatural and sorcery. Particularly in towns with a strong indigenous tradition, such as Panchimalco and Izalco, *brujos* (witch doctors or medicine men) can be hired to cast curses or to remove spells. In fact, it is not unknown for a *capitalino* (city slicker) who is smitten by love or betrayed by a business partner to travel to an outlying town or village to consult with a *brujo*. Some *brujos* are said to command such magical powers that they can make toads materialize in the stomach of a victim. Unless the victim seeks an antidote from another *brujo*, the animal will keep growing, causing unbearable agony and even death. In some cases the *brujo* performs prayers and incantations, although it is just as common for him to prescribe a particular ritual that must be followed to the letter by the *devoto* (the petitioner).

One of the most common maladies that requires the services of a *brujo* is *mal de ojo* (the evil eye), which is said to strike babies following an encounter with a malevolent adult. The *brujo* is likely to prescribe that the infected baby wear a bracelet made from multicolored beads, to which is attached a large seed known as *ojo de venado* (eye of a deer). Superstitious parents are also on the lookout for *el empacho*, a malaise that causes vomiting, diarrhea and a sunken skull in babies. Said to be brought on by an ill wind, it requires the *brujo* to "blow" the ill wind away by hanging the baby upside down and hitting it on the soles of the feet until the skull straightens itself out.

Desperate men suffering from *mal de amores* (love sickness) will sometimes visit an *entendido* or *entendida* (a witch doctor or witch expert in matters of the heart), who after diagnosing the problem will prescribe an appropriate remedy. One of the more common antidotes against *mal de amores* is to stand at a crossroads (the emphasis is on the "cross") at midnight, tie a long, red ribbon around a leg and recite a magical incantation. Another popular antidote is *la oración del puro* (the prayer of the cigar), which consists of an incantation that is recited while smoking a cigar that has been "blessed" previously by the witch or witch doctor. If the supplicant has faith, he will win the girl. Otherwise he will suffer from a broken heart.

As in other Latin American countries, fewer and fewer people believe the ancestral knowledge or practice magic in El Salvador. However, it is still possible to find *campesinos* revered for their age-old wisdom. *Cabañuelas* (the science of interpreting the movement of celestial bodies) is supposed to allow these sages to predict unusual weather, drought, floods and hurricanes. Some also specialize in interpreting the behavior of animals. For example, if *zompopos* (bull ants) build nests that resemble miniature volcanoes, it is claimed that a rainy winter is sure to follow. It is supposed to be a warning against heavy storms and cyclones if a species of bird known as *chiltota* builds low-hanging nests.

One of the most superstitious regions in the country is the eastern department of San Miguel, where the winds of April and May are feared because they make people invisible. To protect themselves against unseen visitors, locals will place a bucket of saltwater by the front doors of their homes. The superstition is that any threatening spirit will dissolve in the water.

TRADITIONAL FEAST DAYS, MUSIC, DANCES

Hardly a day goes by in El Salvador without the celebration of a *fiesta* (feast), which are Catholic in name but with a heavy secular—not to say pagan—component. Most are *fiestas patronales* (in honor of the patron saint of a particular locality) or national holidays, such as Easter or the *fiestas agostinas* (August feasts). In some places *cofradías*, brotherhoods that date back to the Indian townships that flourished during the colonial era, are in charge of organizing the festivities. Although there are individual variations, most feast days follow a similar pattern. The people are awakened by an *alborada* (reveille), which is a cacophony of flutes, drums, cock crows, church bells and firecrackers. This is followed by prayers, sermons, masses, baptisms and confirmations. The *fiesta* culminates in a procession of the faithful, who accompany their patron saint through the streets of the town. A particularly charming tradition called *los Cumpas* (the Buddies) occurs in Jayaque and San Pedro, when an image of one patron saint visits the image of another saint in the neighboring town.

A colorful repertoire of activities complements the religious agenda. This turns the affair into a carnival of street markets, stalls selling typical foods and popular entertainment, which may include acrobats, clowns, rodeos and even bullfighting with cows and young bulls. In certain towns a traditional type of verbal jousting known as *bombas* is celebrated in streets, squares and even inside the local churches. If the participants—individuals or groups accompanied by musicians—are quick witted, the *bombas* can be very amusing, featuring sexual innuendo and veiled scandal about local dignitaries.

Music and dancing are indispensable components of the festivities. Some performances recall pre-Hispanic fertility rites, while others are reminiscent of the ceremonies that invoked the favors of the gods in time of war or during the harvest season. The famous *Baile del Tunco de Monte* (*Cuyan-Cuyamet* in Nahuat, meaning the Dance of the Mountain Pig), and the *Baile del Tigre y del Venado* (Dance of the Tiger and the Deer) are obviously linked to *nahuatismo* (totemism). The protagonists wear appropriate animal masks and skins. *Jeu Jeu* (an untranslatable war cry repeated over and over again) is typical of Izalco. If performed in the traditional manner, it consists of proud warriors in feathers who brandish bows and arrows as they call upon the gods to bring rain for their crops. In the eastern region of the country a popular dance is *Los Emplumados* (Men in Feathers), which involves dancers moving in circles to the rhythm of *maracas* (pairs of rattles held in the hands) and *cascabeles* (bells tied to the feet).

There are almost 100 traditional dances extant in El Salvador, mainly in the central and western districts. Most, however, are seldom practiced and are in danger of dying. The fate of traditional music is even more precarious, and it is only thanks to a few cultural institutions and a handful of folk groups that Salvadoreans have a chance to hear the instruments of their indigenous ancestors. Perhaps the outstanding folk group is Talticpac, founded in 1987 for the purpose of researching, preserving and promoting pre-Hispanic music. Talticpac has recorded for posterity such traditional songs as "Tumijmiktuk," "Ne-Tal Chunga," "Mushta" and "Metzti," which range from the deeply melancholic to the wistfully joyous cadences that typify pre-Columbian music.

The principal pre-Columbian instruments that Talticpac has preserved include flutes and whistles made from a variety of materials, such as clay, reeds, hollow twigs and cane. The pitch of the flute's note is determined by the length and diameter of the instrument.[7] The *huestete*, the most primitive kind of drum, consists of a vertical cylinder of clay or wood that is supported on three legs. It has a skin of animal hide and is played by hand or with sticks. The *tepunahuaste*, a horizontal drum of various sizes that is fashioned from hollowed wood, has both ends covered with parchment and openings cut in the upper surface. It is played using rubber-headed sticks. The *tortuga* is made from the carapace of a turtle. It is played with sticks and produces the distinctive high-pitched sound of a small drum. The *tarasca* consists of "tapping sticks" that are made from animal jawbones, which are tapped together to produce basic rhythms. Unique to El Salvador, the *caramba* can best be described as a stringed percussion instrument. It has a curved, wooden shaft with an open gourd attached and a metal string that is stretched between the ends. The string is struck with a stick as the opening in the gourd is partially covered. The primitive *marimba* employs a single keyboard with wooden legs over long gourds. This instrument, which can still be found in the western region, can be small enough to be played while suspended around the neck. *Chinchines* are similar to the better-known *maracas*, hollow gourds filled with pebbles, which are shaken violently. An unusual instrument is the *tarro con maíz* (a vessel with corn seeds), which, when inverted simulates the sound of running water. These pre-Columbian instruments are principally five toned. It was not until the arrival of the Spaniards that a sixth and seventh tone were added with the addition of guitars, trumpets and the two-keyboard *marimba*.

Most traditional dances and music are a combination of indigenous and Spanish influences, with the latter superimposed upon the former. The Spaniards brought with them their own customs and traditions, which they adapted to local needs and conditions, usually with an eye to converting the natives. The most famous works that date back to the colonial period are the *Historias de Moros y Cristianos* (Historical tales of Christians and Moors), which are also known as *Historiantes* (Tellers of historical tales). These are essentially pageants that provide fanciful interpretations of the Reconquista, the period between 711 and 1492 when Christian Spain waged a war of reconquest against the invading Moors. However, some of the pieces, such as *Carlos V y el Renegado Corinto* (Charles V and Corinth the Renegade), amplify the historical boundaries and encompas the struggle for world supremacy between God and Allah. Needless to say, each *Historia* concludes with the resounding triumph of the Christians over the infidels. Characters in colorful costumes sing, dance and act out scenes of dramatic words and gestures. Since the original versions are long and the pseudohistorical dialogue is quite stilted, the modern performances are abbreviated, for the benefit of both the public and the actors.[8] A highlight is the wooden masks that are decorated to represent pious Christians and dastardly Moors, although a *gracioso* (fool) dressed in rags may wear the mask of a rat, monkey or other unattractive animal.

On the surface the *Historias* do not seem to have much relevance to El Salvador's pre-Hispanic past. Yet it is curious to find that they are most popular in localities with a robust indigenous tradition, such as Izalco and Nahuizalco. The best actors are usually the most ethnically Indian. Because they are semiliterate, they learn their lines by listening to the *maishtro* (the director) read their parts. Could it be that these descendants of Pipiles and other native tribes identify with the dark-skinned Moors who, like them, lost the battle against the Spaniards? Maybe one way of exacting revenge against their former colonial masters is by hamming it up in what are essentially burlesque representations of Spanish history. Although it is possible to speculate about such underlying social or historical interpretations, it is important to remember that the events that are associated with the *fiestas* are ultimately about popular enjoyment and entertainment. The supreme symbol of their popularity is *el torito pinto* (the painted bull), which local artisans make of paper and wood. Borne by a sturdy young man, *el torito pinto* is loaded with *buscaniguas*, firecrackers that pop loudly at the feet of onlookers, who jump out of the bull's way. To an outsider this ritual may seem rather childish. However, it is a reminder that after all the grimness of its recent history, there is still a capacity for innocent fun in Salvadorean life.

Nevertheless, the ostensible motive for the majority of feast days is religious. The citizenry—Indian, *mestizo* and European—are supposed to honor a saint, venerate the Virgin Mary or worship God, usually in the guise of his son, Jesus Christ. The Catholic trappings are quite glaring. For instance, La Fiesta de las Palmas (The Feast of the Palms) in Panchimalco is highlighted by a multicolored procession of flower-strewn coconut palms in whose midst is borne the Virgin Mary, the guardian of this town, which is one of the most ethnically Indian in El Salvador. El Salvador del Mundo (Christ the Savior), after whom the country is named, is worshiped on August 6, when a historic wooden image is paraded along the streets of the capital before massive crowds. In a ceremony known as *la bajada* (the descent), the holy image, shrouded in purple, is lowered inside a wooden shell, only to emerge a few minutes later in radiant white. Legend has it that if the image of Christ falls during *la bajada*, a natural or political catastrophe will soon befall the country.

El Día de la Cruz (The Day of the Cross), celebrated on May 3, is a national holiday. Towns, villages and private homes erect wooden crosses that are covered with every variety of tropical fruit and surrounded with *cortinas* (curtains) of rice paper. The ritual of adoration of the cross includes eating the fruit, which has been "blessed" by contact with the holy wood. In this way, as in the sacrament of the Eucharist, the worshippers can commune directly with Christ. As Christian as this ritual may appear, it has curious associations with El Salvador's pre-Hispanic past. The tree from which the crosses are made is traditionally the *ajiote*, which in Nahuat means "the tree whose skin can be removed." It is the symbol of a god called Xipe-Topec, "our lord whose skin can be removed." High priests of the ancient kingdom of Cuscatlán would don the skin of a flayed captive in homage to Xipe-Topec, a god of regeneration who was comparable to the resurrected Christ, giver of new life. Such associations illuminate the subtle manner in which indigenous beliefs and traditions continue to permeate even the most Catholic rituals in El Salvador.

On El Día de los Difuntos (November 2, All Souls' Day) friends and relatives remember their loved ones. Cemeteries become veritable fairgrounds. Entire families visit shrines and tombs that are bedecked with fresh flowers. Many tombs are freshly painted, and some are even renovated.

Flower vendors, food stalls, noisy children and every conceivable type of seating arrangement fill the grounds, as if the teeming crowds had taken a collective decision to pay a visit to some old friend. To Americans or Europeans who are accustomed to treat death with tears, respect and even fear, the general impression can be quite startling. In fact, the carnival atmosphere reflects the pre-Hispanic attitude to death, particularly that of the Aztecs, cousins of the Pipiles, for whom death was an implacable, bloodstained bride. Since nobody could escape death's clutches, there was no point in fearing it. Death was embraced in a macabre dance, as immortalized by the Russian film director Sergei Eisenstein in the film *Viva Mexico!* Although not a common practice, Salvadoreans will sometimes dance a Mexican hat dance with the figure of death, which is usually somebody dressed up as a skeleton.

Semana Santa (Easter) features processions and other acts of devotion throughout the whole country. Although not nearly as extreme in the expression of their Catholic faith as some of the citizens of the Philippines and Peru, some Salvadoreans do engage in dramatic behavior on Good Friday, particularly in Sonsonate, where images of the Crucifixion are borne by hooded penitents, some of whom flog themselves. On Holy Thursday schools and cultural centers stage scenes that depict the Washing of the Feet and the Last Supper. On the following day the Trial and the Crucifixion are gravely portrayed. A picturesque custom in Santa Ana, Sonsonate and other western localities involves the decoration of entire streets with *alfombras* (carpets) that are made from a varied assortment of perishable materials—flowers, sawdust, coffee grounds, rice, salt, leaves, sand and paper—and depict scenes from the Passion of Christ. What is truly intriguing about this street art is that so much effort and imagination are expended on it. The beautiful, colorful carpets are doomed to be trampled under the feet of the faithful who accompany the holy images of Christ. Could this ritual perhaps be interpreted as a collective reminder of the fate that awaits all flesh without the redeeming power of Christ?

As in the rest of Christianity, Christmas is a joyous occasion in El Salvador. While Santa Claus and reindeers in the best North American manner are now not uncommon, the feast day retains many local traditions. The most typical are *las posadas*, when groups of children in biblical costume wander a neighborhood in search of shelter for Jesus. When they are welcomed in a designated home, they celebrate with typical refreshments, although Coke, Pepsi and pizzas are now quite popular. Also typical are *las pastorelas*, representations of the birth of Jesus, which feature carols and children dressed as shepherds. Christmas trees are popular among the middle class, but the most typical decoration consists of *nacimientos*, clay miniature-nativity sets in a variety of colors that are set up in most homes, from the wealthiest to the most humble.

TYPICAL FOOD

El Salvador's *comida típica* (typical food), known also as *comida popular* (popular food), may not be as well known as Mexican or Peruvian food is, but it is certainly one of the most creative aspects of its national culture.[9] The basic diet of the *campesino* has changed little since pre-Hispanic times. There are three staples: *tortillas* (corn patties about 6 inches in diameter and half an inch thick), *frijoles* (beans, stewed or fried) and salt. Nowadays, portions of rice, vegetables and even the odd morsel of meat or chicken add variety to this diet. During the coffee harvests *campesinos* will eat a heartier meal of *chengas*, which are bigger *tortillas* that are made from red maize and smothered with the traditional beans, salt and maybe cheese. In the countryside, the accompaniment to the *tortilla* is known as *el conqué*, which means "what do you eat it with." In the more fortunate households this can mean "with whatever you like." The *campesino* diet has influenced the eating habits of even the most sophisticated Salvadoreans, who will certainly expect to have a choice of *tortillas* or bread in even the finest restaurants.

The classic dish of typical Salvadorean cuisine is the *pupusa*, which is traditionally served in establishments known as *pupuserías*. So famous is the Salvadorean *pupusa* that a visitor to other *pupusa*-loving countries will find signs in *pupeserías* certifying that only the Salvadorean variety is served there. Since the massive arrival of Salvadoreans in the United States, *pupuserías* have sprung up in various cities, most notably Los Angeles. The *pupusa* is basically a *tortilla* with a particular type of filling. The favorite kinds are *pupusas de frijoles* (beans), *pupusas de chicharrón* (crispy pork skin), *pupusas de queso* (cheese with special herbs) and *pupusas revueltas* (a combination of the three previous ones). In some parts of the country *pupusas* are filled with diverse ingredients, including *chipilín* (an edible leaf), *pepescas* (tiny, fried fish), *ayote* (a type of pumpkin) and *camarones* (prawns). The *pupusa* must be served with *curtido*, a spicy pickle of cabbage, carrot and onion that is marinated in vinegar. The bottles of *curtido*, which can be *picante* (hot), are displayed prominently on the tables of *pupuserías*.

Maize, the sacred crop of pre-Columbian cultures in Mexico and Central America, features prominently on Salvadorean tables, irrespective of social class. *Elote* (corn on the cob) may be eaten roasted with lemon and salt or boiled with mayonnaise and chili. The most popular corn-based drink is *atol*, a pasty, milky liquid. A spicier variety is *atol shuco* (dirty or stained *atol*), which is made from a dark corn, black beans, chili and *alguashte* (a local paste). Salvadoreans suffering from a hangover swear that *atol shuco* is the ideal cure. Many popular eating places serve *chilate con nuéganos*, a watery *atol* in a large bowl that is served with mandioca or egg dumplings smothered in honey. As in ancient times, when *campesinos* have to travel some distance to their *milpa* (corn patch), they will take with them *totopostes*, hard balls of corn that they dunk in water to form a sustaining cold soup that is rich in calories. *Chicha*, an ancestral corn-based drink, is fermented in earthenware pots that are stored underground.

Another classic corn-based dish is the *tamal*, a small rectangular block of dough that is wrapped in banana leaves and cooked in large pots. The most popular *tamales* are stuffed with small chunks of chicken or pork. They can be *dulces* (sweet) or *salados* (salted). As with *pupusas*, *tamales* can come with a variety of fillings, such as cheese, banana, chili, prunes, tomatoes, beans or potatoes. An interesting variant is the *tamal* wrapped and cooked in corn husks (rather than the customary banana leaves), which is eaten with cream. Christmas and New Year usually involve a crucial decision for Salvadoreans: *pupusas* or *tamales*?

Typical Salvadorean cuisine is not devoid of French influence, as evidenced by the popular *gallo en chicha*, a local version of *coq au vin*. An extremely rich dish that consists of pieces of rooster smothered in a sweet stew of *chicha*, prunes, carrots, onion and chilies that is flavored with many spices, it is reserved for special occasions, including the traditional meal eaten after *la misa del gallo* (literally "the mass of the rooster," celebrated on Christmas Eve). Because of the time it takes to prepare—and though not admitted openly, also because of the digestive disorders it can produce—nowadays *gallo en chicha* tends to be replaced by *pan con chumpe*, delicious bread rolls filled with turkey slices and salad bathed in *salsa criolla* (a highly condimented sauce).

A curious gastronomic custom involves eating a national symbol, the *flor de izote*, a white flower comparable in sentimental value to the maple leaf in Canada or to the wattle in Australia. Salvadoreans utilize it to make soup. They also dip it in egg or dunk its buds in pickles. *Boquitas* (the equivalent to Spanish *tapas* or predinner snacks) are extremely popular. They are usually washed down with a local beer or a cool drink. One of the most popular *boquitas* is *yuca con chicharrones*, which consists of pieces of boiled mandioca with pickles and crisp pork skin. A variant is *yuca con pepesca*, mandioca with fried, freshwater fish.

The Spanish predilection for *paella*—a rice dish made in combination with a variety of ingredients, most commonly seafood, chicken or vegetables—

has influenced popular cuisine throughout Latin America, but nowhere more so than in El Salvador. There are about twenty Salvadorean rice dishes. The most basic is *casamiento* (matrimony), in which, as the name implies, boiled rice is "wedded" to red beans. An interesting local invention is *arroz con cerveza*, in which rice, vegetables and chicken are cooked in beer. Game may have almost disappeared in El Salvador, but the taste for it remains. In the absence of deer and boars, small animals like rabbits, *cusucos* (armadillos) and *garrobos* (iguanas) feature prominently in menus. Another specialty is boiled or fried iguana eggs, which must be removed from the membrane before cooking. Boiled turtle eggs are also considered a delicacy. Visitors to the seaside will invariably order *cócktel de conchas*, a cocktail of a local mollusk that is served in long glasses with a dark, piquant sauce.

Salvadoreans' reputation for being *golosos* (having a sweet tooth) is confirmed by their rich assortment of cakes, candy and confectionery. At any time of the day they will eat *pan dulce* (sweet bread), which includes the perennial favorite, *semita*, a rectangular slice that is filled with pineapple jelly. Other popular types of *pan dulce* are *quesadilla* (rice bread), *teperechas* (flat bread decorated with multicolored grains of sugar), *maríaluisa* (egg-based cake), *torta de yema* (soft bread sprinkled with poppy seeds), *marquesote* (a kind of sponge cake) and *suspiros* (crispy sponge slices). The mouthwatering array of confectionery extends from the rustic *dulce atado* (boiled molasses wrapped in corn husks) to marsipan that is charmingly shaped and colored to resemble every type of fruit. *Melcocha* and *alfeñique* belong to the class of toffee confectionery that has been spun, twisted or rolled in the same traditional manner for hundreds of years. Certain families in Santa Ana and San Vicente are famous for their confectionery, which includes *dulce de toronja* (candied grapefruit skin), *dulce de tamarindo* (sugar-coated balls made from the fruit of the tamarind tree), *dulce de camote* (yam candy shaped like little volcanoes) and *conserva de coco* (dessicated coconut). A feature of many fairs and festivals are the famous *dulces pintados*, which are hard, brittle candy that is molded and painted to represent flowers and people. When Salvadoreans cannot make up their mind, it is customary to purchase a *canasta de dulces*, a little basket with an assortment of typical confectionery. Instead of ice cream, many people prefer *minuta*, crushed ice that is flavored with a choice of syrups, which is sold traditionally by street vendors from their colorful *carretones* (carts).

No survey of what a typical Salvadorean eats and drinks could be complete without a reference to *refrescos* or *frescos* (cool tropical drinks). The most popular is probably *horchata*, which is made from the seed of a native gourd and is flavored with cocoa and perhaps milk. *Horchata* is commonly drunk at children's parties and during *novenas*, a Catholic devotion that consists of special prayers over nine consecutive days. Other popular drinks are made from the tamarind seed, cashew pulp, mango, coconut and guava. The most unusual is *fresco de ensalada*, which is prepared from a combination of lettuce, cashew pulp and pineapple. The most typical alcoholic drinks are the local beer and a cheap liquor, which is favored by *campesinos* and sold in cheap bars, called *aguardiente* (burning water).

CRAFTS

Because of their marginalization from the main tourist routes Salvadorean crafts are still not very well known outside the country. Yet the locals are immensely proud of them. It is not unusual to hear a well-traveled Salvadorean claim "Somos los mejores artesanos del mundo" (We are the best craftsmen in the world).[10] An exaggeration perhaps, but there is no doubt that Salvadoreans deserve the description given to them by one of their greatest poets, Roque Dalton, in his "Poema de Amor" (Poem of Love): "los hacelotodo, los vendelotodo" (the makers of everything, the sellers of everything).

Handmade wooden products range from the simplest, almost shapeless, tiny dolls to the highly sophisticated *marimbas*, guitars, religious statues, reliefs and ritual masks. Numerous toys are fashioned from wood, including cars, trucks, spinning tops, yo-yos and *volatines*, flexible figures that are sometimes used for religious festivals. One of the favorite toys is the *capirucho*, a sort of wooden hat or hood that is attached by a string to a stick. Wood is also used to make both fashionable rustic furniture for terraces and bars and all manner of artifacts and souvenirs for tourists, such as brightly painted fruit and small caskets with rural scenes that are painted in a typical Salvadorean style.

Textiles, traditionally handwoven by women, are made on small or large hand looms. The typical designs are in prime colors and have an embossed texture. These small hand looms are used to make narrow articles, such as belts and straps, while larger hand looms can produce scarfs and place mats. Cotton has now replaced the traditional fabric, wool, and the introduction of foot looms has allowed much larger pieces of cloth to be woven. Traditional handwoven hammocks, which were originally made from cactus fibers, require a large laurel-wood needle. However, cotton, nylon and other synthetics are now commonly utilized to make hammocks in textile mills for the export market. Other textile crafts include cushions, tapestries and embroideries with rustic designs and three-dimensional, stuffed, brightly colored cloth dolls and animals, such as fish, turtles, butterflies and parrots.

Weaving includes three important groups: matting, sombreros and baskets. Matting, which is used for sleeping or floor coverings, is woven from palm leaves by using the same techniques as the ancient Mayas did. Palm leaves are also the primary material for sombreros, brooms, brushes and soft baskets. Bamboo, reeds, willow and vines are all used to make a variety of receptacles, including baskets of all shapes and sizes for bread, shopping, linen, garbage and storage. Brooms and brushes are also made from sorghum fibers. Although some of these products are also made for the tourist market, they are basically utilitarian items.

The best known of the papercraft are the *piñatas*. These are elaborately decorated figures of animals or caricatures of famous people that are made from crepe paper. Filled with candy, chocolate and trinkets, they are hung from the ceiling and children break them open with sticks or bats at birthday parties. *Huevos chimbo*, brightly painted eggs filled with confetti, are used in many religious festivals. Flowers of crepe paper bunched together in the shape of baskets, crowns, crosses and garlands are very popular on November 2 (All Souls' Day). Stonework, on the other hand, is indispensable for everyday life. For example, it is used for manufacturing the grindstones, mortar and pestles that crush *maize* and seeds into flour.

Much of the metalwork is used for practical purposes, such as for making machetes, jugs, vessels, saucepans, bowls and plates. However, miniatures of these items, including milk jugs, water cans and bowls that are decorated with folk art, are made in the villages for the tourist trade. What may be labeled neoartisan articles are fashioned from metal as decorative pieces for homes, offices or churches. These include candlesticks, candelabras and figurines.

Clay, so important to everyday life in El Salvador, is glorified by Salarrué in his collection of short stories, *Cuentos de barro* (Clay stories), which he dedicates to the celebrated *alfareros* (potters) of the little town of Ilobasco. Clay articles for domestic use include the *comal*, the indispensable dish for making *tortillas* and *pupusas*. Traditional ceramics glazed with vegetable and mineral dyes are used for kitchenware. Gaudily painted clay miniatures, popular items for the tourist market, are shaped into fruit, native animals, tiny houses, buses full of people, animals and food. There are also *sorpresas* (surprises), miniature scenes set on a base and covered with a lid of various shapes, such as huts, trees, chickens or eggs. The lid is lifted and the surprise is revealed. It could be a nativity set, a domestic scene or what really causes tourists to raise their eyebrows, a graphic scene of a copulating couple in any position imaginable. El Salvador is a very modest country. Public nudity is frowned upon, so this is indeed a *sorpresa*!

An unusual craft in El Salvador involves the use of seeds and beans to make necklaces and bracelets, which combine different shapes and colors. Seeds are also utilized by painters of miniatures, some of whom are so talented as to be worthy of the label of "artist." One of the techniques involves cutting in half a *copinol* (local seed) and painting a rural scene on the flat surface. Gourds known as *tecomates*, traditionally used by the *campesinos* as water receptacles, may also be painted with typical scenes of volcanoes and native flora and fauna. The gourd can also be filled with pebbles and used as an musical instrument called a *chinchín*.

Leather, tortoiseshell, corn, wax and string are some of the other miscellaneous materials that Salvadorean craftsmen and women use. Their handiwork is certainly as attractive as any other facet of their country's traditional culture.

As the postwar process of reconstruction and reconciliation transforms the political and economic face of El Salvador the benefits of modernization and globalization are reaching a greater proportion of the population. It is also important, however, that the country's cultural guardians protect and promote the typical *guanaco* heritage, which impresses as much for its variety as for its distinctiveness and creativity.

POPULAR ENTERTAINMENT

Popular entertainment is very much an urban, middle-class affair. It is limited to San Salvador, Santa Ana, San Miguel and other major towns. After radio and television, by far the most popular form of entertainment and the one most affordable to the largest sector of the population, is cinema. In descending order, films from the United States, Mexico, Argentina and Spain dominate the market. All the major American screen heroes have big appeal, especially among the youth. There is no local film industry. On the other hand, there are a few popular music groups that play principally salsa, cumbia, merengue and rock. There is also a small recording industry. Young Salvadoreans, particularly those in the growing number of discos in the upper-class suburbs of San Salvador, enjoy dancing to their local idols (Baby Swing, Los Cocodrilos, Adrenalina and others), but they prefer the latest hits from the United States and England. Another extremely popular strand of music is Mexican. *Mariachi* musicians such as Pedro Infante, Jorge Negrete, and Fernando and Vicente Fernández enjoy a great following. Tex-Mex, tango and every kind of music from Spain also appeal to local tastes. There has been no really big Salvadorean star on an international scale, although the balladeer Alvaro Torres has a following among Salvadoreans in the United States.

For the tiny cultural elite, the National Symphonic Orchestra performs regularly in the capital, and various cultural centers stage recitals throughout the year.[11] There is a limited amount of serious theater. From time to time a ballet or modern dance is performed, which delights the minority of aficionados. The major embassies host occasional cultural events, such as poetry recitals and film evenings.

In the absence of the serious outlets that are found in the larger, more sophisticated Latin American capitals, such as Mexico City and Buenos Aires, the most common form of entertainment among the cultured minority is reading or the traditional *tertulia* (long, pleasant conversations held after a sumptuous meal), when serious political, social or cultural topics are discussed, often against a background of classical music.[12] While San Salvador, in particular, has an impressive array of restaurants that serve national and international cuisine, most well-to-do Salvadoreans prefer to eat and entertain at home. Their sons and daughters, on the other hand, have an increasing preference for American-style food, particularly pizzas and hamburgers.

Although El Salvador is a great sports-watching society, it does not have an outstanding sporting tradition or reputation. Soccer (as in the rest of Latin America and Spain, known as *fútbol*) is played passionately among schoolboys and youths. The semiprofessional national league is followed avidly everywhere. However, only once in its history (1982) has the national team qualified for the World Cup. The team does well at regional (Central American and Caribbean) championships, but it seldom reaches the finals. Only one Salvadorean soccer player has made an impact at an international level, the mythical Mágico Gónzalez, who in the 1980s became a celebrated figure in Spain. The other major sport is basketball, which is played enthusiastically at the high-school level and is the subject of a highly competitive national intercollegiate competition.

El Salvador's lack of success in the sporting arena can be attributed to three principal factors: its troubled political history, which has led to a diversion of resources to more urgent areas, a dearth of satisfactory training and sporting facilities and the inadequate diet of the majority of the people. However, with the program of postwar reconstruction that includes a focus on a healthy diet and physical education for schoolchildren, there have been positive signs that a competitive sporting culture is emerging in El Salvador under the auspices of the National Institute of Sport. The Sub-17 (the national soccer team made up of teenagers) has performed with distinction in regional Central American tournaments. In the 1998 Central American and Caribbean Track and Field Championships, El Salvador won a historic high of thirty-three medals in a diverse range of events, including tae kwon do, weight lifting, table tennis, shooting, archery, cycling and swimming.

NOTES

1. Interview conducted with Carlos Cañas by the author in San Salvador on January 20, 1998.

2. Pedro Geoffroy Rivas, *La lengua salvadoreña* (San Salvador: Dirección de Publicaciones del Ministerio de Educación, 1978), Nota Editorial, 5–6.

3. These and other myths, which most Salvadoreans know, were first heard by the author during his childhood in El Salvador. Rafael Rodríguez Díaz, a professor of literature at the Universidad Centroamericana José Simeón Cañas (UCA), is currently collecting them for a proposed work on the traditional culture of El Salvador. The author is grateful to him for the many hours that were spent discussing and analyzing various aspects of Salvadorean culture.

4. Manilo Argueta, *Milagro de la Paz* (San Salvador: Adelina Editores, 1994), 25.

5. During a recent trip to El Salvador by the author, a taxi driver in Santa Ana offered to take him to the location of el Partideño's treasure—for a fee of $US100.

6. Lilly de Jongh Osborne, *Four Keys to El Salvador* (New York: Funk & Wagnalls Company, 1956), 125–34.

7. See ibid., 101–6, for an excellent account of traditional Indian music.

8. The full, traditional versions of some *historias* are contained in Adolfo Herrera Vega, *Expresión literaria de nuestra vieja raza* (San Salvador: Ministerio de Educación, 1961).

9. Two excellent books on Salvadorean cooking are Vilma G. de Escobar, *Comida típica*, 4th ed. (San Salvador: Industrias Unisola, 1998); and Anamaría Membreño de Melhado, ed., *Secretos de nuestra cocina* (San Salvador: Compañía Hotelera El Salvador, 1998). The author is particularly indebted to Anamaría Membreño de Melhado for inviting him to taste some of the recipes in her book.

10. For an illustrated book of Salvadorean crafts see Vilma Maribel Henríquez, Ch., Federico Trujillo and Isabel R. de Bettaglio, *El Salvador: su riqueza artesanal* (San Salvador: Banco Agrícola Commercial, 1997).

11. Most cultural centers are located in the capital. However, there are important centers in other towns. One of the most active is presided over by the legendary Alejandro Cotto in Suchitoto.

12. In the course of researching this book the author was invited to attend many such *tertulias*.

6

Literature and the Media

PRE-HISPANIC LITERATURE

SINCE a nation's literature is an expression of its distinctive, particular consciousness it follows that there could not have been Salvadorean literature until the creation of the independent Republic of El Salvador in 1841. Nevertheless, there was literary activity in the area before El Salvador became a nation. Indeed, scholarly research has shown that as far back as the pre-Hispanic period some of the indigenous languages possessed identifiable systems of pictographic, hieroglyphic or ideographic scripts. Ethnologists and folklorists have pinpointed some possible echoes of these ancient languages, particularly Nahuat and Pipil, in the oral literature of Salvadorean peasants.[1] For instance, traces of ancestral songs can be discerned in Salvadorean folklore, and tales that involve animals and legends with supernatural themes have their roots in pre-Columbian traditions. However, much work remains to be done on the possible Amerindian influence upon Salvadorean literature.

COLONIAL LITERATURE

Because of the strict censorship that the Spanish Crown imposed upon "pagan" or "profane" literature, and because of the isolation from the principal cultural centers in Peru and Mexico, there was a dearth of literary activity in Central America during the colonial era. Not all of the literature written during these years in the territory that was to become El Salvador has survived, and information about its authors is usually nonexistent or unreliable. A few Spanish officials, administrators and priests engaged in literary activity while on duty in El Salvador. Most prominent among them were the poet Juan de Mestaza, the lord mayor of Sonsonate between 1585 and 1589, and Diego Sáenz de Ovecuri, who wrote a pious work in praise of St. Thomas of Aquinas in 1669. Details of Salvadorean-born writers are sketchy, but it is known that the Jesuit Antonio Arias, who was born in Santa Ana in the late sixteenth century, wrote an extravagant theological treatise. Another Jesuit, Bartolomé Cañas, who was born in San Vicente, published a religious tome in Italy in 1767.

Although the modern printing press arrived in 1660 or 1661, apart from pious literature there were very few books that were published in the provinces of San Salvador and Sonsonate. There is evidence, which some scholars dispute, that approximately twenty years earlier a rudimentary press had been devised for self-publishing purposes by a Franciscan, Juan de Dios del Cid, who printed a fascinating tome entitled *El puntero. Apuntado con apuntes breves* in 1641. The prosaic translation of the punning Spanish title is *The Indigo-Dye Master. Annotated with Brief Notes*. Although not without its literary charm, this practical guide for the production of the precious commodity that was the mainstay of the Salvadorean economy during most of the colonial era is of greater interest to the student of history than to the student of literature.

On the other hand, a literary scholar cannot help but be fascinated by the most celebrated work written in El Salvador between the Spanish Conquest and independence: *Carta de relación* (Letter recounting events), which was composed by none other than Pedro de Alvarado, the ruthless *conquistador* who entered El Salvador in 1524. Sent by Alvarado by way of military dispatches to Hernán Cortés in Mexico, the letter is an invaluable historical document and a unique example of what scholars now designate as testimonial literature. Written in graphic, robust, often ungrammatical Spanish, the letter affords a fine insight into the disingenuous motives of the *conquistador*. This letter has inspired a number of novelists and poets. Among them was Manlio Argueta, who incorporated long excerpts from Alvarado into *El valle de las hamacas* (The valley of the hammocks, 1970) and from which he derived the title for *Cuzcatlán donde bate la mar del Sur* (Cuzcatlán, Where the Southern sea beats, 1986). Indeed, a case could be made for designating the rough-hewn, barbaric Pedro de Alvarado as the first writer that El Salvador produced.

LITERATURE SINCE INDEPENDENCE

Since independence two outstanding features have characterized Salvadorean literature: small clusters of writers who stand out like beacons among their contemporaries and the tragic connection between literature and politics. As one surveys the panorama from the formation of the Federal Central American Republic in 1824 to the creation of an independent Salvadorean nation in 1841 to the present, it is apparent that El Salvador's literary canon does not possess many significant schools or movements.

Moreover, the thesis that in history centuries are not to be measured in years but by epochs is eminently applicable to the history of Salvadorean literature since independence. There is a very long period of literary activity that helps to form a national consciousness until the Great Slaughter of 1932. There follows a very short period from 1932 to the signing of the peace accords in 1992 when literature reflected the political turbulence of these six decades. Since then there has been a renaissance of hopeful, vibrant literature as writers who stayed in El Salvador have joined those who went into exile to express a new dawn of political reconciliation.

A general survey of the literary history of El Salvador yields one other important insight, which relates to the observation that the novel is essentially a bourgeois genre. Since El Salvador has always been a feudal, semifeudal or third-world country it has produced very few novelists or novels of substance or merit. Due to economic exigencies writers have simply not been able to afford the time that great novels require to be researched and written. Publishing houses have not had the resources to print large tomes, and the vast majority of the literate education have not had the money to buy, or the time to read, novels. Consequently, poetry has been the principal genre. There have also been important contributions in areas such as the short story, literary journalism, literary criticism and, to a lesser extent, the theater.[2]

The Long Nineteenth Century

In the years immediately following the war of independence, one poet in particular spoke with what may be considered a Salvadorean voice: Miguel Alvarez Castro (1795–1856). He wrote verses in a pastoral or patriotic manner. His best-known works were "Al ciudadano José del Valle" (Ode to José del Valle, citizen) and "A la muerte del Coronel Pierzon" (Upon the death of Colonel Pierzon). The other important poet of this early period was José Batres Montúfar (1809–44), who has been dubbed the "Salvadorean Leopardi" because of his propensity for verses that could express both heroic sentiments and deep anguish. His lyrical poetry in the madrigal or elegiac manner identifies Montúfar as one of the principal transitional figures between neoclassicism and Romanticism in Central America. In 1845 Montúfar wrote a collection of evocative short stories and verses about life, courtship and intrigue in the colonial era, *Tradiciones de Guatemala* (Guatemalan traditions).

Literary life in the 1870s was dominated by the florid, grandiloquent Spanish poet from Santander, Fernando Velarde, who spent ten years in El Salvador. Velarde's sonorous *Cánticos del nuevo mundo* (Songs from the new world) ignited the imagination of a young generation of writers in 1860. Under Velarde's tutelage, Salvadorean Romantics sang of self, love and country in poetry that reflected the currents of passion, pantheism and liberty that were flowing from Europe. The Romantic who did most to forge a national consciousness was Juan José Cañas (1826–1918), who penned the stirring words of the national anthem as his country was beginning to grow in confidence during the era of the Coffee Republic. Franciso Galindo (1850–96) was another Romantic figure of renown. His splendid thoughts and wondrous words earned praise from the celebrated Rubén Darío, the father of modern Spanish poetry. Antonia Galindo (1858–93), El Salvador's first woman poet to make an impact, wrote touching verses that combined personal sensibility with universal sympathy. Her poem "A mi madre" (To my mother) is regularly anthologized in a country where the figure of the mother is idolized and the woman is identified with the nation.

A significant aspect of El Salvador's literary history is that its distinguished tradition in literary journalism dates back to the Coffee Republic, when leading writers wrote criticism and commentaries in the cultural pages of the country's newspapers. During this period Joaquín Méndez (1868–1942) founded La Juventud (Youth), a society of literary and scientific inquiry that published *La Juventud Salvadoreña* (Salvadorean Youth), a journal that reached its peak in the 1890s. El Salvador's strengthening cultural consciousness in the second half of the nineteenth century was confirmed by the foundation in 1870 of the National Library, which by century's end was well stocked with modern scientific and literary publications. The establishment of the Academy of Language in 1876 and the creation of the Academy of Science and Literature in 1888 also provided active forums for debate by an emerging intelligentsia. For a brief period the Academy of Science and Literature published the monthly journal *Repertorio salvadoreño* (Salvadorean Repertoire), which published poems and articles by the country's leading intellectuals. It also attracted contributions from international luminaries such as Ricardo Palma (Peru), Julián del Casal (Cuba) and Rubén Darío

(Nicaragua). Another important literary journal of the period was *La Quincena* (The Fortnightly), which was edited by the poet Vicente Acosta (1867–1908).

Modernismo (Latin American modernism) is identified in El Salvador with one of the country's true literary giants, Francisco Gavidia (1864–1955), who introduced the master himself, Rubén Darío, to the rhythms of the French alexandrine. A prodigious writer, Gavidia spent eighty years of his life writing poetry, drama, philology, essays and fiction. However, he excelled as a modernist and epic poet, and some of his compositions are of the highest quality. His translation of "Stella," a poem by Victor Hugo, is particularly noteworthy. Other important poems by Gavidia are "La Ofrenda del bramán" (The brahman's offering), "La defensa de Pan" (In defense of Pan), and "Sotéer o tierra de preseas" (The saviour or land of precious things). Undoubtedly, Gavidia could be extremely exotic, but he was also capable of a genuine, committed response to his time and place in history. He could sing with as much aplomb of swans, fauns and princesses as he did of the Amerindian *zenzontle* (a native bird), the Indian maiden Xochitl or the Christ of Esquipulas whom Salvadoreans worshipped. His poems move effortlessly from the classic figures of Apollo, Orpheus and Euridice to national heroes like Francisco Morazán and José Matías Delgado. Gavidia had an overriding interest in national themes, and he gave them literary expression with a view to fostering a Salvadorean consciousness. Two of his dramatic works, *La princesa Cavek* (Princess Cavek, 1913) and *Cuento de marinos* (Seafarer's tale, 1947) are truly Salvadorean pieces in that they strive to transmit pride in the nation's heritage. In a 1947 masterly collection of short fiction, *Cuentos y narraciones* (Stories and tales), he skillfully blends personal memory and national history. The founder of modern Salvadorean literature, his own epitaph appears in the final verses of "Turris Babel" when he wrote "¡Poeta! / Tú de nuevo edifica, / No la torre . . . el idioma!" (Poet! Your task is to rebuild not the tower . . . but language).

Inspired by Gavidia's example a small but impressive nucleus of writers, mainly poets, helped to forge the modern Salvadorean literary tradition. Two gifted Romantics, José Calixto Mixco (1880–1901) and Armando Rodríguez Portillo (1880–1905), stand out. Their poetic melancholy presaged their early deaths by suicide. Another follower of Darío was Carlos Bustamante (1890–1952), who began his career by writing sonorous verses that were redolent of *modernista* color and panache. In the early years of the twentieth century the foundation of a modern Salvadorean theater was also established. J. Emilio Aragón (1887–1938) and José Llerena (1895–1943) were the most important playwrights.

Only one other figure ranks alongside Gavidia in talent and stature: Alberto Masferrer (1868–1932), who exerted a profound, lasting influence through a series of beautifully written and persuasive treatises on moral and philosophical topics. Masferrer applied an eccentric mixture of Christianity, mysticism, theosophy and parapsychology in his dissection of Salvadorean reality. His main publications included *Las siete cuerdas de la lira* (The seven strings of the lyre, 1926), *El dinero maldito* (Wretched money, 1927) and *El mínimum vital* (Life's minimum, 1929). He dabbled in poetry and theater, and he also wrote a novel, *Una vida en el cine* (A life in the cinema, 1922), which had a feminist theme. In 1926 he founded a newspaper, *Patria* (Homeland), that included a section entitled "Vivir" (Living) for the purpose of showcasing up-and-coming writers. Masferrer was also an erudite and acute literary critic who encouraged the imitation of the French masters, but he also warned that European models should be read creatively and critically in the search for an original Salvadorean voice. In this regard he anticipated the ideals of the famous Cuban writer Alejo Carpentier (1904–80), who believed that an independent identity for Latin America could be found via its European heritage. Masferrer was a committed intellectual who lent his name and prestige to the candidacy of the reformist Arturo Araujo in the presidential election of 1930. When Araujo was overthrown in December 1931 Masferrer's fate was sealed. He ended his life as a sad, brokenhearted man two years later during the brutal regime of Maximiliano Hernández Martínez, who was the antithesis of everything that Masferrer stood for intellectually and politically.

As *modernismo*'s star waned a new movement took its place in El Salvador: *costumbrismo*, a literature of manners and customs. Its leading exponents in prose were Arturo Ambrogi (1875–1936) and José María Peralta Lagos (1873–1944). Ambrogi was a youthful prodigy who began his career as an obsessive Modernist. He was nicknamed "la señorita azul" (the blue miss) after Rubén Darío's famous collection *Azul.* In due course he discovered a genuine, celebrated voice as the verbal painter of El Salvador's rural life and spirit. His most famous book, *El libro del trópico* (The book of the tropics, 1917), is a series of short stories and vignettes in which he captures the colors and shapes of the Salvadorean countryside with impressionistic strokes. His style combines formal craftmanship with an authentic feel for the nuances and registers of Salvadorean Spanish. On occasions he manages to enter the consciousness of his humble folk and to penetrate the depths of their hearts, as in the case of "Bruno," a touching tale of a peasant's love for a woman who is promised to another. Not only does Ambrogi endow his *campesinos* with an emotional dignity that sometimes rises to grandeur, but he also raises the uneducated idiom of peasants to the level of poetry. The most popular Salvadorean writer of his day, Ambrogi's reputation was further enhanced by the publication of a travel book, *Sensaciones de Japón y China* (Impressions of Japan and China, 1915).

José María Peralta Lagos was a graduate from military school who rose to the rank of general and became the minister of defense during the presidency of Manuel Enrique Araujo. However, he forged a second career under the alias of T. P. Mechín as the author of two famous books, *Burla burlando* (Mocking the mocked, 1923), and *Brochazos* (Brushstrokes, 1925), a festive description of Salvadorean customs and types. He also wrote a short novel, *Doctor Gonorreitigorrea* (1926), a satire of Salvadorean provincial life, and the play *Candidato* (The candidate, 1931), a political spoof on the presidential campaign of 1930. His humor made him the most popular writer of his time.

Ambrogi and Peralta Lagos had their poetic counterpart in Alfredo Espino (1900–28), a tragic figure long regarded as El Salvador's national bard. Following his death by suicide, his father, the poet Alfonso Espino, published his son's work under the title *Jícaras tristes* (Cups of sadness, 1930). With an impressive command of traditional meters (endecasyllables, octosyllables and alexandrines), the younger Espino conveyed a gentle, nostalgic love of country that was shadowed by personal intimations of mortality. Espino sang the natural wonders of Cuzcatlán, as conveyed by the titles of some of his best-loved compositions: "Vientos de octubre" (October winds), "El nido" (The nest), "Los pericos pasan" (The parakeets fly past), "Arbol de fuego" (The tree of fire), "Bajo el tamarindo" (Under the tamarind tree) and "Cañal en Flor" (The canefield in bloom). Inspired by what he called his "Indian muse . . . crowned with the plumes of the quetzal," Espino's poetry has become compulsory reading in Salvadorean schools.[3] It brings tears to the eyes of Salvadorean expatriates and exiles.

The Short Twentieth Century

According to the acclaimed Peruvian novelist Mario Vargas Llosa, times of profound political convulsion and moral disturbance often provide a stimulus for literary creativity. This is precisely what occurred in El Salvador from approximately 1932, when President Martínez ordered the slaughter of about 4 percent of the country's population to save El Salvador from an alleged communist insurrection, to 1992, when the peace accords ended over ten years of a fratricidal war that claimed the lives of over 70,000 people.

In the fifteen years or so following Martínez's Great Slaughter a constellation of intellectuals offered passive resistance to the military-oligarchical regime that was in power. Among these intellectuals was Salarrué (the pseudonym of Salvador Salazar Arrué), who lived from 1899 to 1975.[4] Seeking refuge in esoteric spirituality from the political turmoil of the 1920s, the young Salarrué began his literary career with *El Cristo negro* (The black Christ, 1926), a theosophic parable that was based on the legend of the Christ of Esquipulas, one of El Salvador's most revered icons. Although he remained a theosophist all his life, Salarrué found fame both at home and abroad as a writer of regionalist short stories. His very first collection, *Cuentos de barro* (Stories of clay, 1933), became a Salvadorean classic due to the incomparable manner in which he utilized the sounds and rhythms of the rural folk's Spanish to represent the external trappings of their lives and the inner workings of their minds. A master of narrative technique, Salarrué also gave his stories an air of magic and superstition that anticipated the magical realism of subsequent generations. He used his fine ear for the spoken registers of Salvadorean Spanish to compose another classic, *Cuentos de cipotes* (Kid's stories, 1945), a highly original collection of stories about children for both children and adults. Narrated in a charmingly eccentric style, the extremely brief stories, many of them vignettes barely half a page long, sought to emulate the inventive, sometimes incomprehensible voice of Salvadorean *cipotes* (street kids or urchins) talking to each other. A special edition that the Ministry of Education published in 1974 and reprinted in 1976 is today a collector's item. It contains delightful illustrations by Maya Salarrué, the author's daughter. Salarrué was himself a talented artist with a penchant for surrealist and expressionist compositions which his contemporaries described as psychedelic. Strangely enough in a country full of poets, Salarrué hardly had time to put together one book of poetry before his death. *Mundo nomasito* (My little world, 1975), is a deceptively ingenuous folksy anthology which, upon closer examination reveals hidden depths.

Salarrué can be credited with ushering in a literary renaissance. Many contemporary writers of different styles and tendencies came to the fore in his wake. Claudia Lars (a pseudonym for Carmen Brannon, 1899–1974) is considered El Salvador's finest woman poet. Her outstanding lyrical voice is comparable to the Chilean Gabriela Mistral, who won the Nobel Prize for Literature in 1945. Lars's most highly regarded collections are *Estrellas en el pozo* (Stars in the well, 1934), *Romances del norte y sur* (Ballads of the north and south, 1947) and *Sonetos* (Sonnets, 1947). Like Salarrué, Lars wrote until the end of her life. Even as her country plunged into the nightmare of civil strife she kept her eyes firmly on the universal scheme of things. For instance, in *Nuestro pulsante mundo* (Our pulsating world, 1969), she responds with fascination to pop music and to the conquest of space.

Another significant poetic voice of the time was Vicente Rosales y Rosales (1894–1980), who mused on a varied range of cosmic, mythological and mystic themes. His outstanding collection was one with a flamboyant title, *Eutorpologio politonal* (Polytonal eutorpologium, 1938), in which he applied a personal vision of comparative theory and music to versification. In the 1940's Lydia Valiente (1900–76) made a name for herself as a writer of poetry that expressed her proletarian ideals. Serafín Quiteño (1899–1952) produced one memorable anthology, *Corasón con S* (Heart written with an S, 1941), which conveys heartfelt emotions.

Among novelists two names stand out in the Salarrué generation: Alberto Rivas Bonilla (1891–1985) and Miguel Angel Espino (1902–68). One of El Salvador's best-loved books is Bonilla's *Andanzas y malandanzas* (Adventures and misadventures, 1936), a picaresque tale of the trials and tribulations of canine life in El Salvador. Whether it is an allegory of existence in the dehumanizing climate of the time is a moot point. Espino, brother of the poet Alfredo, is remembered for two novels, *Trenes* (Trains, 1940) and *Hombres contra la muerte* (Men against death, 1947). A fictional autobiography, *Trenes* is particularly interesting for two reasons: it is an ode to woman in her multiple personalities (virgin, mother, courtesan, goddess) and an experimental work that presaged the self-conscious Latin American novels of the post-boom period (1980s and 1990s). On the other hand, *Hombres contra la muerte* is a novel of the jungle that was inspired by the Colombian José Eustasio Rivera's classic *La vorágine* (The vortex, 1924). Powerful in content and lyrical in style, *Hombres contra la muerte* denounces the exploitation of forest workers in what is now Belize.

An influential intellectual figure also stands out in the Salarrué generation: Alberto Guerra-Trigueros (1898–1950), who was born in Nicaragua but was Salvadorean by nationality and allegiance. A disciple of Alberto Masferrer, in 1928 he became owner and director of the newspaper *Patria*, which became his forum for denouncing imperialism in Central America, in particular dictatorship in El Salvador. He was committed to a humanistic philosophy in art and literature, which he explained in his essay "El libro, el hombre y la cultura" (The book, the man and the culture, 1948). He was also a talented poet whose principal collection, *Surtidor de estrellas* (Fountain of stars, 1929) puts into practice some of the poetic ideals (simplicity, humility, existentialism) that he advocated in another important essay, "Poesía versus arte" (Poetry versus art, 1942). More than anybody else, Guerra-Trigueros paved the way for the subsequent group of committed writers who rose to prominence following the Revolution of 1948 (see Chapter 1).

Another period of the authoritarian rule that has characterized Salvadorean history led to a new literary movement. Disenchanted intellectuals were moved to express their anger and defiance through poetry. Their principal medium in a country where poetry has always been held in high esteem, their voice was heard beyond the confines of literary circles. The general tone was one of patriotism, irreverence and rebellion. They composed iconoclastic verses that denounced social injustice and the cynicism of the Salvadorean establishment. In some cases their verses reached El Salvador from exile. Pedro Geoffroy Rivas (1908–79) wrote his antibourgeois lament, "Vida, pasión y muerte del anti-hombre" (Life, passion and death of anti-man) while in jail in Mexico in the 1930s. One of the verses of this poem, which has become the anthem for committed writers in El Salvador, provided the title for the celebrated novel by Roque Dalton, "*Pobrecito poeta que era yo*" (What a dud poet I was, 1976). "Monólogo en dos preguntas" (Monologue in the form of two questions, 1954) by Antonio Gamero (1917–74), in which the poet is lionized as the singer of proletarian ideals, and the provocatively titled *10 sonetos para mil y más obreros* (10 sonnets for a thousand workers and more, 1950) by Oswaldo Escobar Velado (1919–61) both conveyed the overriding sense of commitment that was in much of the poetry of this period.

However, not all Salvadorean intellectuals were politicized. Some of the most notable figures of the period refused to permit politics to "contaminate" their creative work. The principal representative of this school of thought was Raúl Contreras (1896–1973), a fine poet who had made a name for himself in 1925 with *La princesa está triste* (The princess is sad), a play in verse adapted from the famous poem by Rubén Darío. In the 1940s and 1950s, under the pseudonym Lydia Nogales, he crafted some of the most alluring verses in the history of Salvadorean literature. Such was the impact of Contreras's invention of Lydia Nogales that by the 1950s the Salvadoran literary establishment had been split into two camps: the pro-nogalistas, who preached truth and beauty beyond the corrupting influence of politics, and the anti-nogalistas, who clamored for an aesthetic that was built upon the music of hammers, saws and hoes. This division has persisted in El Salvador to this day. Creative writers react in one way or the other to the succession of juntas, dictators and civil strife that have torn the country apart.

An outstanding writer who chose to stand outside the political fray but still intensely suffered his country's agony was Hugo Lindo (1917–85). A poet and a novelist, Lindo set a personal mission for himself: to maintain the beauty of Latin America's literary heritage in El Salvador. He wrote finely honed poetry with metaphysical overtones, moving effortlessly from the natural to the spiritual. Toward the end of his life he published *Resonancia de Vivaldi* (Sounds of Vivaldi, 1976), in which he created with impressive verbal skill the color and magic of the Italian musician's *Four Seasons*. With original illustrations by Carlos Cañas, one of El Salvador's outstanding painters, this book is one of the most beautifully presented in the history of Salvadorean literature. A collection of Lindo's poetry, *Sólo la voz/Only the Voice* (1984), was published in a bilingual edition by Elizabeth Gamble Miller. Lindo was also an accomplished novelist. His major work in this genre was *¡Justicia, señor gobernador!* (Give us justice, Mr. Governor, 1960), a fine psychological portrayal of a judge who, in the course of presiding over a trial of a child murderer, reviews his country's social and economic inequalities. The judge scandalizes his compatriots when he finds God guilty of the crime and all other crimes in the country. Lindo was also the pioneer of science fiction in El Salvador, as seen in his collection of short stories, *Guaro y champán* (Liquor and champagne, 1947). He explored the boundaries of science fiction in *Espejos paralelos* (Parallel mirrors, 1974).

Hugo Lindo was also a distinguished literary critic and anthologizer whose articles and books introduced students to the discriminating reading and lucid commentary of Central American authors. His outstanding contributions in this area were the two-volume sets *Antología del cuento centroamericano* (Anthology of Central American short stories, 1949–50), and *Obras escogidas de Salarrué* (The select works of Salarrué, 1969–70).

There have been very few professional literary critics in the country. The most prolific, far-ranging critic was Luis Gallegos Valdés (1917–90), whose *Panorama de la literature salvadoreña* (Panorama of Salvadorean literature, 1981), offered a personal, perceptive commentary from pre-Hispanic times to the 1970s. This volume places Salvadorean writers within the context of Central and Latin American literature. It is indispensable to any serious student or researcher. Another important literary critic belongs to this distinguished generation: Matilde Elena López (b. 1922), a specialist on Alberto Masferrer and on the analysis of poetry. In 1997 she became the first woman to occupy a seat in the National Academy of Language of El Salvador.

Since the 1950s there have been very few literary intellectuals in El Salvador who have been able to escape the philosophical influence of Jean Paul Sartre's existentialism or the political influence of Fidel Castro's revolution in Cuba. As a consequence, there have been successive generations of committed writers, but their commitment has ranged from the purely verbal to the spiritual to the ideological to the political, and in some notorious cases, to the militant. The embodiment of commitment with one's place and time in history was Italo López Vallecillos (1932–86), a figure revered in contemporary circles for his incorruptible morality and his immense contribution to Salvadorean and Central American thought and letters. He was the director of two important publishing enterprises, EDUCA and UCA, both of which sought to disseminate quality writing and to promulgate progressive ideas, including liberation theology. A fine creative writer in his own right, López Vallecillos utilized his favorite genre, poetry, to explore existential dilemmas. As a playwright his outstanding work is *Las manos vencidas* (Losing hands, 1964), a provocative variation upon Sartre's *Les mains sales* in which he presents an even-handed dialectic between a group of Marxist true believers and a group of skeptical existentialists.

Revolutionary commitment in a Marxist sense in El Salvador is identified with Roque Dalton (1935–75), a rare and precocious literary talent for whom the poet's pen was as militant an expression of the armed struggle as revolutionary Che Guevara's rifle. In one of Dalton's best-known books, *Taberna y otros lugares* (In a tavern and other places, 1969), he explored the indivisible link between poetry and politics, which he summarized with disarming clarity in "Arte Poética 1974": "Poetry,/forgive me for having helped you to understand/that you are not made solely of words." Dalton was a master of collage, a technique he exploited to create the illusion that it was possible to erase the boundaries between life and art. In his celebrated *Las historias prohibidas del Pulgarcito* (The forbidden stories of Tom Thumb, 1975), he tells the untold story of El Salvador's history through a mix of poetry, songs, letters, journalistic reports and chronicles of the Spanish Conquest. He was also a promising novelist who left behind two important works. In *Miguel Mármol* (1972), which is in hindsight a revolutionary kind of storytelling that presaged the testimonial narratives that became popular not long after his death, Dalton used an interview with the legendary Miguel Mármol, a survivor of the 1932 communist uprising, as a pretext to narrate, interpret and debate the history of his embattled country. In *Pobrecito poeta que era yo* he composed a stylistic and verbal extravaganza in which the reader, not knowing whether to laugh or cry, perceives the lunacy and despair of a man who is seeking to find justification for being a writer in a country like El Salvador: "What a joke! It's horribly absurd to be a Salvadorean writer." Apart from Francisco Gavidia, no writer has left such an indelible mark, morally and creatively, as Roque Dalton. His tragic death at the hands of fellow communists brought to a premature end the life of one the most talented, funniest writers Latin America has produced. His legendary *jodarria* (a Salvadorean term meaning ridicule) has been often imitated but never equaled.[5]

Roque Dalton's generation included other writers of merit and sensibility. One of the most talented was Roberto Armijo (1937–97), who was El Salvador's unofficial literary ambassador in Europe during his long exile in Paris from 1970 to the day he died.[6] As a poet his work fell neatly into two categories: up to the 1960s, when he earned fame as the poet of El Salvador's forgotten province of Chalatenango, and his European poems of exile, many of them unpublished and only recently anthologized under the title of *Poemas europeos* (European poems, 1997). In the latter collection Armijo combined memories of El Salvador with a subtle European aesthetic as he probed the paradox of an existence based ultimately on words. Armijo also wrote a major play, *Jugando a la gallina ciega* (Blind man's buff, 1970), which combined elements of the grotesque and of horror with considerable dramatic impact.

Another important figure of this generation is Roberto Cea (b. 1939). He is a prolific, versatile writer of novels, plays, short stories, poetry and literary criticism. He also performs the important task of promoting Salvadorean literature and art as the director of his own publishing house, Canoa Editores.[7] It is as a poet, however, that Cea has gained a reputation that has transcended his own national boundaries. His works range from the mythical and the magical in *Todo el códice* (The entire codex, 1968), to the erotic in *Mester de picardía* (The picaroon's craft, 1977), to the political and historical in *Los herederos de de Farabundo* (Farabundo's heirs, 1981). In the midst of all this dazzling experimentation Cea, a veteran of Salvadorean literature, still seems to be struggling to find a true, authentic poetic voice with which to express the maelstrom of Salvadorean reality.

Alfonso Quijada Urías (b. 1940) is a poet who earned Dalton's admiration for *Estados sobrenaturales y otros poemas* (Supernatural states and other poems, 1971), in which he explores the fears and neuroses of being alive in Central America in the 1960s. Two other iconoclastic writers of Dalton's time were the dramatists Walter Bénecke (1930–80) and Alvaro Menéndez Leal (1931–2000), alias Menén Desleal, which is a pun on *leal/desleal* (loyal/disloyal). Bénecke, who was assassinated on the eve of the civil war, is remembered for *Funeral Home* (1959), a bleak depiction of alienation in an absurd world that in retrospect may be interpreted as a parable of times to come in El Salvador, when the country was turned into a morgue. Menéndez Leal, who also writes fantastic fiction, is the author of *Luz negra* (Black light), which since its publication in 1966 has become the most widely performed and translated play by a Salvadorean, with over thirty editions and 100,000 copies printed. An absurdist work that shows the influence of the Irish dramatist Samuel Beckett, its principal characters are two severed heads with Germanic names (Goter and Moter) who spend most of the time engaged in grim conversation with each other in the very gallows where the execution occurred. The gory anguish of the scene again proved prophetic.

In spite of its rich vein of literary talent, apart from Roque Dalton only two modern writers have succeeded in consistently transcending the borders of El Salvador: Claribel Alegría (b. 1924) and Manlio Argueta (b. 1935). Not insignificantly, their most important works have been published outside the country. Alegría, born in Nicaragua of a Nicaraguan father and a Salvadorean mother, lived in El Salvador until the age of nineteen. Following a long period in the United States, France, Mexico and Mallorca she returned to live in Nicaragua after the Sandinista revolution. She calls Nicaragua her *matria* (motherland), while acknowledging El Salvador as her *patria* (fatherland). A profound Salvadorean consciousness characterizes her work, which includes over thirty books, including novels, short stories, poetry collections, testimonial writings and anthologies of work by other Central American writers.[8] She is also the admirable translator of Robert Grave's poetry into Spanish. Some of her best-known work has been translated into English by her husband and longtime collaborator, Darwin Flakoll (1923–95). Her most memorable poems—subjective, sensuous, lyrical compositions that convey an increasingly paradoxical sense of stupor and indignation in the face of cruelty and ugliness—are contained in *Anillo de silencio*, (Ring of silence, 1948), *Vigilias* (Vigils, 1953), *Acuario* (Aquarium, 1955), *Huésped de mi tiempo* (Guest of my time, 1961), and *Sobrevivo* (I survive, 1978). Her work shows the influence of poet Juan Ramón Jiménez and poet Emily Dickinson. In a later work, *La mujer del rió Sumpul* (The woman of the Sumpul River, 1987), she experiments with testimonial poetry by recreating the voices of the victims and witnesses of a particularly brutal massacre.

Claribel Alegría's best prose has been written under the stimulus of Fidel Castro's triumph and is set against the background of revolutionary activity and military repression in Central America. It combines childhood memory, oral testimony and technical experimentation to portray the terror, anguish and courage of the victims of the civil strife in El Salvador from the Great Slaughter to the civil war of the 1980s. *Cenizas de Izalco* (Ashes of Izalco, co-authored by Darwin Flakoll, 1966), a novel of superb crafmanship, combines personal and historical stories that fill the reader with pity and terror. It is Alegría's poignant portrayal of the female condition in a harrowing man-made world, and of a female consciousness that strives to give voice to the voiceless sectors of Central American society, particularly its women, that has earned her a reputation as one of Latin America's outstanding feminist writers. Paradoxically, this gifted writer has a higher reputation internationally than in her own country.

The other acclaimed international Salvadorean writer of the modern period, Manlio Argueta, originally made his mark as a poet of political commitment alongside Roque Dalton and other members of the so-called Círculo Literario Universitario de la Generación de 1956 (University Literary Circle of the Generation of 1956). In "Quien que es no es romántico" (Who is there who isn't a romantic, 1975) Argueta penned a moving elegy in which, as he remembers Dalton, he conveys the fusion of the political and poetic ideals that galvanized him and his colleagues. Following Dalton's death Argueta went into exile in Costa Rica, where he remained until the mid-1990s, when he returned to El Salvador to work at the National University.

However, it is as a novelist that Argueta has excelled, evolving from the sophisticated, occasionally self-indulgent spokesman of the dissident intellectual elite of urban San Salvador to the mature, disciplined craftsman of testimonial fiction that records the collective voice of El Salvador's long-suffering peasantry.[9] Argueta's first novel, *El valle de las hamacas* (The valley of the hammocks, 1970), is full of structural and stylistic pyrotechnics. Infused with a spirit of nausea and bad faith, the novel depicts El Salvador as "el culo del mundo" (the asshole of the world) in desperate need of redemption. *Caperucita en la zona roja* (Little Red Riding Hood in the red zone, 1977), arguably Argueta's most cryptic and challenging novel, is a homage to Dalton, who is portrayed as a complex, flawed, but good human with a love of life and a commitment to social justice whose flame was prematurely extinguished by murderers who betrayed the ideals of both revolution and poetry. This compelling novel, which is structured as a collage of monologues, conversations, speeches, sermons, songs and fables, succeeds in conveying Dalton's celebrated *jodarria*.

Although not as ambitious as his other novels, *Un día en la vida* (One day of life, 1980) cemented Argueta's international reputation. The English translation became a best-seller in both the United States and Great Britain and was reviewed as far away as Australia and New Zealand. Published just as the civil war of the 1980s was erupting, this novel can now be interpreted as a prophecy of the bloodbath that was soon to follow.

In *Cuzcatlán donde bate la mar del sur* (Cuzcatlán, where the southern sea beats, 1986), Argueta applies previous devices and motifs to narrate a syncopated history of Cuzcatlán, the indigenous name for El Salvador, while at the same time penning a stirring homage to the women of El Salvador, who are depicted as the sun around whom the satellite of hope in this poor country revolves. In the midst of the political massacres and volcanic eruptions, the spirit of the Salvadorean woman is symbolized by the *metate*, the volcanic stone that has been utilized since time immemorial to make the tortilla, the peasants' principal food. The antithetical symbol to the *metate* is the helicopter, a dark agent of evil sent by a foreign power to scorch the earth and destroy the peasants' spirit. Through this dramatic juxtaposition of symbols—the natural against the artificial, the national against the foreign, primordial lava against the military-industrial complex—Argueta denounced the forces of imperialism in Central America.

During the civil war, literary activity in El Salvador was seriously curtailed. The country's two best-known writers (Alegría and Argueta) were in exile, and a number of promising talents lost their lives in the conflict. Among the poets who were killed were Alfonso Hernández, José María Cuéllar, Rigoberto Góngora and Jaime Suárez, all of whom were affiliated with a literary circle known as La Cebolla Púrpura (The Purple Onion), which aspired to Roque Dalton's ideal of poetry at the service of revolution. Most of the literary magazines where poets and short-story writers had been able to publish their work, such as *La Pájara Pinta*, *Universidad* and *Vida Univesitaria*, were shut down. The magazines of the Jesuit University, *Abra* and *Taller de Letras*, were published lovingly but irregularly by a team of teachers and student scholars, who were headed by the critic Rafael Rodíguez Díaz. These magazines offered a tenuous alternative for young writers, who worked under increasingly precarious conditions. It was in the pages of *Taller de Letras* that the talents of a young playwright, Roberto Gustaves, came to light. None of his plays were performed, however, as very little serious theater was staged in El Salvador during those years. The National Theatre in the beleaguered capital preferred to offer escapist fare, usually featuring television stars.

One of the few revolutionary poets of genuine quality to fight and survive the civil war, Miguel Huezo Mixco (b. 1954), stated that "la guerra no fue un período muy fértil para la invención literaria" (the war was not a fertile period for literary creativity).[10] To be sure, a vast quantity of literature, particularly poetry, was produced during the years of combat. Most of it was impromptu and testimonial in character. It came from the men, women and in some cases children who fought in the ranks of the FMLN. A combatant, no matter how talented, had little time to polish or revise his/her text. Accordingly, with rare exceptions the war literature that the guerrillas wrote is essentially of a historical, sociological or anthropological interest. The works provided a personal record of the fighters' lives and often gave moving insights into their motives, ideals, dreams, frustrations and existential angst. For example, one cannot help but be moved by Virginia Peña Mendoza, a guerrilla who wrote these verses a few months before she fell in combat in 1986: "and the only thing one knows is that one wants to live." Perhaps it is not great poetry, but as Huezo Mixco observes, its authors envisaged those texts to be not so much literary masterpieces as another weapon in a climate of militancy, faith and solidarity.[11]

Among the writers who chose to remain in El Salvador during the war years and who survived, physically and creatively, one person undoubtedly stands out: David Escobar Galindo (b. 1943), a poet, novelist, dramatist, short-story writer, journalist and literary critic. A precocious talent with a preference for classical versificaion, Escobar Galindo has produced poetry of the highest quality since 1963, when he was still a student. His best collections, *Duelo ceremonial por la violencia* (Ceremonial wake for violence, 1971), *Trenos por la violencia* (Lament for violence, 1977), *Sonetos penitenciales* (Penitential sonnets, 1982) and *Oración en la guerra* (Prayer in war, 1989), treat the theme of violence from the point of view of an anguished humanist. In "Penitential Sonnet I" Escobar Galindo writes that "Igual que en el soneto de Quevedo / miré los muros de la patria mía, / y en lugar de la justa simetría / sólo hay desorden crápula, remedo" (Just like Quevedo in his famous sonnet / I beheld the walls of my dear country / and where there should be glorious symmetry / saw only chaos, dissipation and parody). In *Después de medianoche* (After midnight, 1981), a one-act play, Escobar Galindo represents the topsy-turvy reality of daily violence in which nothing makes sense anymore. His short novel *La estrella cautiva* (The captive star, 1985) is a subtle study of psychological agony and erotic intrigue that is set against the background of political mayhem in the city of San Salvador. An intriguing combination of literary conservatism and experimentalism, Escobar Galindo has always been interested in emulating the formal rigor of the classics while seeking to expand the boundaries of his chosen genres. This is exemplified by the bilingual edition of *Fábulas/Fables* (1985). In this collection of 233 fables he explores the possibilities of an ancient genre by eschewing verse in favor of direct, often colloquial prose, giving many of them a Salvadorean flavor. Escobar Galindo never took up arms and never openly sided with either side during the war, but he emerged as a committed poetic witness of the tragedy that was enacted in his homeland.

Literature since 1992

Since the end of the civil war in 1992 there has been evidence of a literary renaissance in El Salvador. Much of the work comes from writers who publish abroad, mainly in the United States but also in Canada, Europe and such far-flung countries as Australia. It is perhaps too early to speak of an aesthetic of peace replacing the literature of war. However, left-wing writers who were formerly in exile have now returned to live and work with others who were identified with the governments of President Duarte (Christian Democrat) or President Cristiani (ARENA). A clear indication that the process of reconciliation was firmly in place occurred in San Salvador on February 21, 1996. On that day both an international congress in honor of Roque Dalton, the literary icon of the revolutionary left, was inaugurated and a memorial for Roberto D'Aubuisson, the hero of the die-hard right, was held. Guests traveled peacefully for the twenty minutes that it took to go from one event to the other, aware of the deep symbolism of the occasion.

The positive profile and continuing creativity of its two famous resident writers, David Escobar Galindo and Manlio Argueta (Claribel Alegría lives in Nicaragua), has been a considerable boon to the status of postwar literature in El Salvador. Since his participation in the peace negotiations in 1992 Escobar Galindo has become El Salvador's most admired public intellectual. He combines his role as rector of José Matías Delgado University with that of an assiduous writer. He has continued to write a popular series of weekly short stories, *Historias sin cuento* (Stories without a story), which was initiated in 1988 in *La Prensa Gráfica*, one of the two major newspapers. Focusing on the joys and sorrows of daily life in the towns and villages of El Salvador, these stories are written in the elegant, controlled style of a superb craftsman who aims to write for a wide audience that is irrespective of class or ideology. His aim is essentially to bring quality literature in digestible form to literate readers who very seldom have the time, inclination or money to buy and read books. He has begun to devote more time and effort to journalism, writing another weekly column that is entitled *Quinta columna* (The fifth column), in which he reviews or comments upon events and people of relevance to Salvadorean affairs. *En el subsuelo de los volcanes* (In the subsoil of the volcanoes, 1997), a collection of the first fifty columns, is highlighted by five pieces in which, with equal doses of candor and gratitude, he reviews the contribution to the peace process of the Cristiani administration, the FMLN, the Salvadorean military, the United States, Spain, Venezuela, Mexico, Colombia and the Salvadorean people.

Since the end of the war testimonial literature by former combatants from both sides, but particularly by former guerrillas, has continued to flourish in the form of war memoirs, journals, novels, poetry and short stories. The most remarkable and moving example of this style of writing is *El venado y el colibrí* (The deer and the hummingbird, 1996), a collaborative venture by Escobar Galindo and Eduardo Sancho. Friends during their youth, the two men's lives took radically different paths. Sancho became an FMLN commandant who was involved in the kidnapping of Escobar Galindo's father, a well-known landowner from Santa Ana. Composed during the war and postwar, the poems in this collection, by design or by coincidence, reverberate with common sounds, colors and images that revolve around two ancient Indian totems, the deer (a symbol of protection and hope) and the hummingbird (a symbol of creation and renewal). Beyond the clear literary quality of its content the book symbolizes the spirit of reconciliation that has descended upon El Salvador since 1992. As Escobar Galindo writes in one of his sonnets, "Filtro solar" (Solar potion), Salvadoreans have at last rediscovered a magic word: "¡Hermano!" (Brother!).

Since his return to El Salvador, Manlio Argueta has gradually reestablished his national profile and reputation. He became one of the most influential advocates for "la necesaria cultura de la paz" (the necessary culture for peace).[12] He has published two new novels, *Milagro de la paz* (The miracle of peace, 1994) and *El siglo de o(g)ro*, (The century of the golden ogre, with an untranslatable pun on "gold" and "ogre," 1997). In these novels Argueta modifies his previous testimonial style, adding an autobiographical dimension that is reminiscent of Mario Vargas Llosa. In this regard it is significant that *El siglo de o(g)ro* has the following subtitle: *bio-novela-circular* (circular bio-novel). Both novels are finely wrought literary artifacts. However, they also constitute a significant political statement, which is that the carnage of war is over, and writers can at last return to their natural domains of dreams, art and the freedom of the imagination. Unfortunately, given the precarious state of literary publishing in El Salvador, neither *Milagro de la paz* nor *El siglo de o(g)ro* has had any significant resonance outside the country. The few copies to reach the United States or Europe are in the hands of university professors, students or expatriates. The fate of these two novels reflects the marginalization that even internationally acclaimed writers such as Argueta have to endure.

The novel is the most expensive, time-consuming genre. In El Salvador, commercial publishers are few and even the most successful writers have other full-time jobs. Despite these problems a younger generation of Salvadorean novelists is emerging. One of the most promising talents in this genre is Horacio Castellanos Moya (b. 1957). His latest novel, *Asco* (Nausea, 1997), has become popular for its virulent attack against every aspect of Salvadorean culture and customs. The targets range from the national beer, described as "pigswill," to its doctors, denounced as "savages," to its art and literature, stigmatized as "illiterate." Written as a parody of Thomas Bernhard, the Austrian writer celebrated for his dark vision of life, Castellanos's novel reflects the disenchantment of a Salvadorean expatriate forced to return home temporarily while the country is still recovering from the material and cultural effects of the civil war. The novel's diatribe against the country says as much about the neurotic, obsessive narrator as it does about the target of his bile. Its restrained, erudite reception speaks admirably of the new intellectual maturity evident in El Salvador.

Salvadorean writers of different generations and diverse styles, such as Jacinta Escudos, Rafael Menjívar, Melitón Barba, Carlos Castro, Jorge Kattán Zabla, Mario Bencastro, Ricardo Lindo, Armando Molina, Walter Raudales and Martivón Galindo continue to produce novels and short fiction of quality. Raudales's novel, *Amor de jade* (Love of jade, 1996), stands out as an intriguing postmodern exercise. Its roots are deep in Amerindian mythology. It also asks questions about the nature of words, art and sexuality. It is one of the few Salvadorean novels written by a man that has a convincing and well-rounded female protagonist, a seductress upon whose body is inscribed the peace agreement of 1992. Another novel worthy of special mention is Ricardo Lindo's *Tierra* (Land, 1996), which is a veritable concert of voices from El Salvador's indigenous and Hispanic pasts.

It is in poetry, however, that Salvadoreans at home and abroad continue to be most fertile. Established names such as David Escobar Galindo, Claribel Alegría and Roberto Armijo have produced some outstanding collections. The best of the younger poets have turned inward, ontologically rather than selfishly, to probe the paradoxes of existence and the mysteries of literature in a society that is in a state of flux.

One of the outstanding poetic talents is Roger Lindo (b. 1955), a longtime resident of Los Angeles whose work appears regularly in national anthologies and literary magazines. In his poems life is depicted as an equivocal experience of beauty and pain, of pleasure and anguish, in a masochistic world. Jacinta Escudos (b. 1960), who lives in Nicaragua, writes a mordant, self-flagellating kind of poetry that is from the perspective of a woman stung by love and lust. Another poet who has made a mark is Carmen González Huguet (b. 1963), whose poetry features social commentary from a feminine perspective. Two young poets noted for their formal precision and awareness of their place in literary tradition are Ernesto Flores and Luis Alvarenga, who were both born in 1969. Not all poets, however, have turned their back on the angry legacy of the war years. Augusto Morel and Armando Salazar, who were both born in 1961, write poetry that conveys the sound and the fury of former combatants.

Miguel Huezo Mixco, whose poetic voice is one of the most resonant in contemporary El Salvador, has lamented that many poets were killed during the war for no other reason than that they were poets.[13] moreover, because of the political sympathies—and in some cases military involvement—of many poets, poetry was regarded by many as the black sheep of the arts.

Happily, today the situation has changed dramatically. El Salvador is a country where poets abound and where poetry has reclaimed its former status as the most revered literary genre. New talents are coming to the fore, and neglected figures are being rediscovered, as has happened with Berta Funes Peraza (1911–98), a gifted poet whose work has earned posthumous recognition.

The postwar literary renaissance has also witnessed the publication of literary and cultural magazines of quality, such as *Cultura, Ars, Amate, Tendencias* and *Paradoxa*. Through the National Council of Arts and Culture (CONCULTURA) the government actively supports literary activity. The universities and private foundations, such as María Escalón de Núñez, are also engaged in the promotion of literature. Books of literary criticism are appearing in the university bookshops, and professional critics such as Rafael Rodíguez Díaz, Ricardo Roque Baldovinos and Rafael Lara Martínez are analyzing Salvadorean writers objectively and dispassionately. It is not uncommon for Salvadorean writers to figure in university courses inside and outside of the country. After years of marginalization, therefore, Salvadorean literature can face the future with renewed confidence.

THE MEDIA

Newspapers, radio and television play a vital role in Salvadorean society in three fundamental ways: as information media, as molders of public opinion and as entertainment. Interestingly, whereas in first-world countries the media is often viewed with distrust, in El Salvador only the Catholic Church enjoys greater credibility than mass media. This is probably because of the prestige and power of literacy in a country with low educational levels. Almost all media are privately owned, and since the end of the war there has been minimal government interference in the dissemination or interpretation of the news. The overall quality of the print and electronic media is beginning to show the benefits of the professional training that over a dozen universities in San Salvador offer. Many journalists have an excellent command of English, and the influence of U.S. media, in style and opinion, is very noticeable.

There are currently four national daily newspapers. *La Prensa Gráfica* and *El Diario de Hoy* are morning tabloids and have the largest circulation. *El Mundo* and *Co-Latino* are afternoon tabloids with limited circulation. The two morning dailies are comparable in quality and extent of coverage to the best city dailies in Latin America. However, an excessive amount of advertising, usually up to 75 percent of their pages, mars them. Both are available on the Internet. *La Prensa Gráfica*, born of the merger in 1939 between *La Prensa* and *El Gráfico*, is owned by the influential Dutriz family, whose editorial line is pro-business, moderate on social and political issues, and supportive of the United States in foreign policy. Its philosophy—and most noticeably its quality and style of writing—are influenced by one of its chief editorial advisers and contributors, David Escobar Galindo, who is one of the country's outstanding intellectuals (see the section on literature). Accordingly, its cultural pages are truly outstanding, with particularly stimulating coverage of literary activity in the country and the rest of Latin America. Its main rival, *El Diario de Hoy*, is owned by the Altamirano family, which has always identified itself with the landed oligarchy. After espousing rabidly anticommunist, ultraright-wing views during the civil war, it has begun to tone down its outlook. Like *La Prensa Gráfica* it is pro-business, but it is more traditional in that it lends unconditional support to the coffee industry. Its cultural pages are also first class, with regular features by major international figures, including Mario Vargas Llosa, the celebrated Peruvian writer. An up-and-coming intellectual, Carlos Cañas Dinarte, has helped to improve its cultural coverage.

El Mundo, which was founded in 1967, is a small enterprise with a loyal readership among the progressive elements of society. During the war it was the only newspaper that dared to present an antimilitary line. It was instrumental in publicizing state terrorism and the violation of human rights. *Co-Latino*, the nation's oldest newspaper, was founded in 1890. It changed its title from *Diario Latino* in 1989, when its workers formed a cooperative to save it from bankruptcy. During the war it promoted an overtly FMLN line, attracting to its pages many of El Salvador's leading left-wing intellectuals. Since the peace accords it has concentrated on cultural, particularly literary, events, both in El Salvador and among the Salvadorean intellectual community in the United States.

RADIO

Since its inception in 1926, radio has become the most popular medium of news coverage, propaganda, publicity and entertainment in El Salvador. The civil war, so destructive in every other way, contributed to a boom in the radio industry. The majority of the population relied on radio for up-to-date information on the state of national affairs. The FMLN established two major clandestine stations (Radio Venceremos and Radio Farabundo Martí), while the armed forces employed Radio Cuscatlán for propaganda purposes. On more than one occasion paramilitary forces bombed the Catholic station, while guerrilla commandos occupied stations at vital stages of the war to broadcast propaganda. There are currently 163 stations, 68 AM and 95 FM, more than in any other Central American country, and a few are now available on the Internet.

The former clandestine stations have now become part of mainstream radio. They operate along capitalist lines and include paid advertisements by their former political opponents! Every possible kind of broadcast is available. Religious matters (Catholic or Protestant), current events, political debates, pop and rock music in English, sports, news and children's programs are all available. Nonprofit community radio is slowly obtaining a foothold on the overcrowded airwaves. Educated Salvadoreans point with pride to the classical music station as a measure of how far their country has advanced since the dark, joyless days of war propaganda.

TELEVISION

After a slow start in the mid-1950s the development of television in El Salvador was further retarded by the civil war. The country's electrical network suffered considerable damage. Local and international investors were unwilling to risk their money in such an insecure environment. However, since the war television has boomed. The number of sets is growing faster than the population is. There are twelve local channels, including two that are state owned. In general, the private channels offer a nonstop diet of news and current affairs, Latin American soap operas, the latest American series, sports, children's programs, musicals, variety shows, game shows and women's programs. The two government channels offer an impressive amount of educational and cultural content, much of it high quality. The affluent classes have cable television, with more than one hundred programs to choose from, including many in English or other languages.

NOTES

1. See Gloria Aracely de Gutiérrez, ed., *Tradición oral de El Salvador* (San Salvador: CONCULTURA, 1993); and Pedro Geoffroy Rivas, *La lengua salvadoreña* (San Salvador: Dirreción de Publicaciones del Ministerio de Educación, 1978).

2. There have been very few general studies of Salvadorean literature. By far the most comprehensive is Luis Gallegos Valdés, *Panorama de la literatura salvadoreña*, 3rd ed. (San Salvador: UCA, 1987). Verity Smith, ed., *Encyclopaedia of Latin American Literature* (London: Fitzroy Dearborn Publishers, 1997), contains a general survey and sections on some of the country's leading writers.

3. From "Cantemos lo nuestro" (Let us sing of our own land), *Jícaras tristes* (San Salvador: UCA, 1997), 15.

4. For a perceptive analysis of Salarrué's work see Hugo Lindo, *Obras escogidas de Salarrué, I* (San Salvador: Editorial Universitaria, 1969), vii–cxviii.

5. Roque Dalton is the Salvadorean writer who has generated the greatest critical interest, particularly outside the country. Some of the most illuminating pages on Dalton as a novelist and poet are by John Beverley and Marc Zimmerman, *Literature and Politics in the Central American Revolutions* (Austin: University of Texas Press, 1990), 122–34, 189–91.

6. See Carlos Cortés, "El Legado poético. Notas de lectura a los poemas europeos'," *Cultura* 79 (1997), 58–78.

7. For an assessment of Cea's work see Rafael Arturo Rodríguez Díaz, "Roberto Cea, un escritor en busca de su expresión poética," *Temas salvadoreños (y unos pocos foráneos)* (San Salvador: UCA, 1992), 41–51. Rodríguez Díaz's book contains an excellent collection of insightful essays on Salvadorean literature and culture.

8. For a critical assessment of Alegría's work see Sandra Boschetto-Sandoval and Marcia Phillip McGowan, *Claribel Alegría and Central American Literature* (Athens: Ohio University Center for European Studies, 1994).

9. For a compilation of critical essays on Argueta as a novelist see Roy C. Boland and Marta Caminero Santangelo, eds., *Antípodas* (Madrid/Melbourne: Vox/AHS, 1998), 81–140.

10. Miguel Huezo Mixco, *La casa en llamas* (San Salvador: Ediciones Arcoiris, 1996), 51.

11. Ibid.

12. Manlio Argueta, in his plenary address to the Conference of Central American Literature, at the Polytechnic University of El Salvador, February 21, 1996.

13. Huezo Mixco, *La casa en llamas*, 52–55.

7

Visual and Performing Arts

BEST KNOWN for its political upheavals and natural disasters, El Salvador possesses a surprisingly rich cultural history that has gone largely unnoticed outside its frontiers. The list of artists covers most forms, but it is undoubtedly in painting that Salvadoreans have excelled, which is evidenced by the numerous galleries that have flourished since the end of the civil war. Splendidly illustrated tomes dedicated to painting and to particular painters are another testimony of this trait.[1] After painting, the most notable achievements have been in music. However, until recently there has been very limited information or research on this area of endeavor. The prospective inauguration in San Salvador of the David J. Guzmán National Museum of Anthropology, which consists of seven galleries that cover the most important areas of creativity, should stimulate interest in the country's artistic heritage.

PAINTING, SCULPTURE AND OTHER VISUAL ARTS

Pre-Hispanic Painting, Ceramics and Sculpture

It is indeed significant that an anthropological museum was chosen to showcase Salvadorean art. In recent times leading commentators have identified the anonymous painters and sculptors of pre-Hispanic El Salvador (approximately 1500 B.C. to A.D. 1524) as among the most talented that the country has produced. Indeed, the ancient name for El Salvador, "Land of Precious Objects," could well refer to the magnificent works of art that have been found in such archaeological sites as Chalchuapa, Joya de Cerén and

San Andrés. Without trying to compensate for the traditional neglect of El Salvador's indigenous heritage, it is certainly possible to trace an expressive, dynamic artistic evolution from the past to the present.[2]

Any survey of Salvadorean art must begin in 1300 B.C. with the paintings in Cueva de Corinto, a cave that measures ten feet in width, three-and-a-half feet in depth, and forty feet in height, in the northeastern department of Morazán. No student of art can fail to be impressed by the quality of paintings in red, green, yellow and brown that depict human and animal shapes in various guises: men with bows and arrows, a dancer, a witch doctor and figures wearing masks of horned animals and birds. There is also a painting of a dark, red sun and a series of paintings of hands. Prehistoric art of rare quality is found elsewhere in El Salvador, most notably in the area around Lake Güija on the Guatemalan border, where rock carvings depict a range of human and animal forms of varying degrees of complexity. Full of religious symbolism and magical connotations, such art exudes a mysterious power that continues to influence contemporary artists. In this regard El Salvador possesses a long-standing, continuously evolving artistic identity.

Findings from the archaeological sites that are dispersed throughout the country show that El Salvador's ancient artists excelled in ceramics. There are beautifully decorated vases, incense burners, pots, glasses, urns and figurines of various shapes and sizes, most dating from about 1500 B.C. to about A.D. 950.[3] Quite apart from their utilitarian or ceremonial uses such ceramics reveal a fine aesthetic dimension that makes them worthy of the adjective "artistic." An outstanding example is the Batik or "negative-style" ceramic known as Usulután. This ceramic from the southeastern region used a mixture of wax and clay to produce contrasting effects in white, orange and brown. Another style of ceramic is Salúa, which is from the central region. It bears a variety of mythological and realistic designs that are painted in black and orange. Particularly striking are the polychrome (multicolored) vases known as Campana, which are characterized by geometric designs of fine, sharp lines that are painted in black and orange against a cream-beige background. Such vases remind the modern observer of the Romantic poet John Keats's reaction upon viewing an ancient Grecian urn: the beauty of art shows a truth that transcends the limitations of time and space.

For a variety of reasons (a lack of adequate material, the cost of tools, a dearth of training academies) sculpture has not become a major form of artistic expression in El Salvador. However, there is convincing evidence that in the pre-Hispanic era it was indeed an important activity. In the western region, archaeologists have discovered a series of delicately sculpted, cream-colored clay figurines known as Las Bolinas, which were named after a local plantation. Dating from approximately 500 B.C. to A.D. 250, most are modeled in the shape of voluptuous women with monumental hips, solid limbs and facial expressions that range from deadpan gravity to joyous smiles. In all likelihood they represent goddesses of fertility and reproduction, but they could also be indicative of a matriarchal society in that region of pre-Hispanic El Salvador. Their archaeological significance notwithstanding, what is most remarkable about these figurines is their artistic quality. They have finely crafted "miniskirts," elaborate headpieces with a wide range of hairstyles and a varied assortment of bracelets, necklaces and earrings.

Another striking illustration of pre-Hispanic sculpture is found in Santa Leticia, the site of a village that was established around 550 B.C. The visitor to this southwestern corner of the country is amazed to find three monumental stone sculptures, which are known locally as *gordinflones* (fat ones). It does not require a great leap of the imagination to see in these massive structures, which each weigh between seven and twelve tons, the handiwork of a pre-Columbian Fernando Botero, the celebrated sculptor whose elephantine men and women seem to float delicately on air. Significantly, Valentín Estrada (1898–1979), one of El Salvador's most accomplished sculptors, found inspiration in the works of his pre-Hispanic precursors.

Colonial Era Architecture, Painting and Sculpture

By contrast with the new-found pride with which cultured Salvadoreans now point to their pre-Columbian heritage, it has become increasingly common to dismiss the legacy of the Spaniards. In truth the limited artistic output during the colonial era fails to impress. The fundamental reason is that the twin provinces of San Salvador and Sonsonate were too far removed from the metropolitan centers of Peru and Mexico to be in a position to absorb any meaningful cultural influences. Moreover, life was hard in this marginal corner of the Spanish Empire, so the goal of material advancement took precedence over aesthetic pursuits.

The three principal art forms during the colonial era, which were architecture, painting and sculpture, pale in significance by comparison with the wonders found in other parts of Latin America.[4] Earthquakes, the bane of San Salvador, have destroyed most of the colonial buildings, including the many convents and churches that once were features of the capital. The rest of the country has been more fortunate. About thirty parish churches from colonial times still stand. The majority are small, simple, well-built structures. Their most striking characteristic is their coffered ceilings done in *mudéjar* style (a style developed by Moorish artists in Spain). The most attractive churches—in San Vicente, Chalchuapa, Panchimalco, Izalco, Sonsonate and Metapán—possess some typical Baroque features, such as arches, small circular windows, skylights and high ceilings. The Church of San Pedro in Metapán, which was built in 1740, is considered by many to be the most beautiful architecturally. Its whitewashed walls, high nave and red doors combine to give the impression of a doll's house. The cathedral in Santa Ana, on the other hand, possesses a splendid gothic facade.

Most of the paintings remaining from the colonial period are housed in the churches. As would be expected they consist mainly of dramatic representations of Catholic scenes. Many are no more than copies of Spanish or other European originals. The Church of San Pedro does contain an attractive series of paintings of saints on its central dome, while the altar in the Church of Panchimalco is decorated with fine images of the Crucifixion and the Resurrection. The sculpture in the churches is neither original nor memorable. The best are probably the statues of the apostles in their individual niches on the facade of the Church of Panchimalco and the equestrian statue of Saint James the Moorslayer atop the Church of Chalchuapa.

Independence, Painting and the Influence of Carlos Alberto Imery

Not surprisingly, it was the triumph of independence that generated the national consciousness that was necessary to develop authentic expressions of Salvadorean art. At times creativity in the arts has been extremely restricted, although painting always shined like a beacon in times of peace and war. Some of El Salvador's best painters took up other arts, such as sculpture or engraving, as a secondary activity. Interestingly, a number of architects or former students of architecture have become painters. Painting provides an outlet for artistic expression in a developing country, where the construction of houses and buildings is essentially a utilitarian enterprise.

The first major painter was Juan Francisco Wenceslao Cisneros (1823–1978), a legendary figure who left El Salvador at the age of nineteen and never returned. He studied and worked for many years in Paris and Rome before finally migrating to Cuba, where he became director of the Academy of Fine Arts in Havana. Although most of his work is found outside El Salvador, Cisneros is nevertheless lionized there as the "Salvadorean Michelangelo." A painter in the Romantic and neoclassical styles, he specialized in evocative biblical scenes, such as *Lot's Daughters*, which has an unusually sensual depiction of the female form for a pious painting. He is also famous for his portraits. One of his best-known works is *A Portrait of Don José de*

La Luz, a serene study in white, black, brown, gold and green of a scholarly man.

In 1864 President Francisco Dueñas founded the National Academy of Fine Arts in the capital. Unfortunately, this was destroyed in the earthquake of 1873. As a consequence there was relatively little artistic activity in the country in the last quarter of the nineteenth century. Only two painters, Pascasio González (1848–1917) and his disciple Marcelino Carballo (1874–1949), are worthy of particular mention. Both of them specialized in pious portraits and religious scenes. González produced a memorable and oft-reproduced portrait of the stern bishop of San Salvador, Jorge Vileri y Ungo. His *González Family* is also distinctive, with a peculiar, fairy-tale atmosphere that envelopes the figure of the father and his four children. Carballo's masterpiece is a moving self-portrait in yellow, mauve and brown entitled *The Painter at Sunset,* which depicts the artist with his back to a spectacular dusk as he contemplates his own mortality.

By the turn of the century the European movement known as modernism began to penetrate the cultural scene. The Italian painter Antonio Rovescalli was contracted to decorate the National Theatre of Santa Ana, which was completed in 1910. Between 1903 and 1907 the magazine *Quincena* was influential in the arts. It counted among its discoveries the painter Carlos Alberto Imery (1879–1949). Originally a student of Marcelino Carballo, Imery soon felt stifled by his teacher's emphasis on religious themes. He eventually left his master's studio to experiment with paintings of tropical Salvadorean scenes and of the human body. In 1904 he was awarded a presidential scholarship to Rome, where he studied and lived until 1908, when he moved to Paris to further his education. In 1911 he returned to his country. He specialized in painting but was also competent in lithography and embossing. Because of failing eyesight Imery's creative output was quite limited. His entire body of work barely reached 100 paintings. Comprising a combination of European and Salvadorean subjects, his best works demonstrate a rare ability to combine a cosmopolitan spirit with a sharp eye for Salvadorean landscapes and characters. His *Italian Peasant Girl* is reminiscent of the French master Auguste Renoir. His *Peasants, Boy and Mask* and *Landscape with Volcano* exude a charming primitivism that is suggestive of another French master, Paul Gaugin.

However, it was as a teacher that Imery left his most enduring legacy. At a time when there was hardly any formal education available for young artists he established the School of Graphic Arts, which he directed from its inception in 1901 until his death in 1949. Successive generations of painters learned their skills under his enlightened tutelage. His emphasis was on the application of modern European techniques to the interpretation of Salvadorean reality. With very limited backing Imery almost single-handedly ran a school that taught a variety of arts and crafts, including drawing, draftmanship, telegraphy, photography, lithography and photoengraving.

Paisajismo and Costumbrismo

Two of Imery's contemporaries, Miguel Ortiz Villacorta (1887–1963) and Pedro Angel Espinoza (1891–1939), helped to lay the foundations of two related styles of painting known as *paisajismo* (national landscape) and *costumbrismo* (national customs and manners). Ortiz Villacorta paid homage to Salvadorean volcanoes in such works as *San Salvador Volcano* and *Jiboa Valley*, both of which are characterized by his favored use of stark lines and resplendent sunlight. He also produced a superb series of portraits of leading national figures, including one of President Juan Lindo, which was vandalized along with other works during the security forces' invasion of the National University in 1960. Pedro Angel Espinoza painted in a relaxed, colorful style, as exemplified in *Landscape*. A man of humble origins, he delighted in depicting typical scenes, such as in his celebrated *The Owner and his Cock*, which conveys the powerful bonds between the proud owner and his gladiatorial bird.

Perhaps the outstanding painter of Salvadorean customs and manners was José Mejías Vides (1903–80). A precocious talent, Mejías Vides began his training under Carlos Alberto Imery. He continued his education in Mexico, where he came under the twin influences of the famed Mexican muralist Diego Rivera and the Japanese painter Tamiji Kitagawa. Mejías Vides is renowned for his oils and watercolors of the charming town of Panchimalco, one of the few places in El Salvador where an indigenous lifestyle may still be found. Perhaps in reaction to the Great Slaughter, Mejías Vides lovingly and imaginatively recreated the faces, bodies and customs of the *panchos* (Indians from Panchimalco), the descendants of the Pipiles in this part of the country. He took particular delight in portraying voluptuous, innocent, copper-colored women. His paintings show them in typical dress and selling fruit or half-dressed or naked as they bathe or wash clothes in the river.

Another renowned painter of *costumbrismo* was Luis Alfredo Cáceres Madrid (1908–52), who specialized in portraying indigenous women and native flora and fauna. Dubbed the "poet painter" by his contemporaries because of his use of brilliant colors to convey emotion, he defined his art as a "simple, strong, transcendental" search for the soul of El Salvador.[5] Although essentially an idealist, Cáceres Madrid was also capable of employing his canvas to transmit social messages, such as in his two related paintings *Rural School* and *School Under the Amate Tree.*

Another of Carlos Alberto Imery's students was Julia Alvarez (1908–80), the first woman to make a name for herself as an artist in El Salvador. For three consecutive years (1936–38) she won first prize in the national Friends of Art Exhibition. Her paintings of typical scenes and characters are unique in that she introduces elements from art deco and the techniques of the famous Mexican muralists. In such compositions as *The Fruit Vendors* and *The Baskets* her female Indians can be as exotic as Jennifer Lopez, or a Latin Madonna. She lived for over twenty years in the United States, where she turned to ceramics with considerable success.

Primitivismo

Primitivismo, a style that captured the public imagination, originated in El Salvador with Zelia Lardé (1901–74). She was a self-taught artist. Her paintings may be best described as childlike, with a formula of bright colors, thick lines and a startling lack of proportion that is utilized to represent topsy-turvy scenes in parks, fairs and markets. Some of her most charming work is found in the illustrations of the first edition of the classic *Cuentos de cipotes* (Kids' stories, 1945), which was written by her husband Salarrué (see Chapter 6). Her portraits are quite bewitching. A case in point is *Family*, which features a formulaic drawing of the almond-shaped eyes and a rudimentary treatment of the bodies of the dusky-skinned mother and her two daughters. Zelia Lardé's *primitivismo* lends itself to ready imitation. Markets, tourist stores and street fairs throughout the country offer cheap, colorful paintings in this style. Most are pleasing enough, but they tend to be rather repetitive and unimaginative, as if coming out of a toy factory. However, her style has also inspired some fine artists, among them her daughter, Maya Salarrué (1924–95).

José Nery Alfaro (b. 1951), another of Zelia Lardé's heirs, has put a personal imprint on Salvadorean *primitivismo* by almost exclusively painting scenes of Villa San Marcos, the township in San Salvador where he lives. Whereas both Zelia Lardé and Maya Salarrué employed broad strokes, Nery Alfaro's technique is one of fine, almost obsessive detail. His paintings of houses, streets and vegetation resemble bright postcards. The most celebrated *primitivismo* painter in El Salvador today, his work is found in galleries throughout the world.

Salarrué

One of the most original painters that El Salvador produced was Salarrué (1899–1975), whose output was so varied that it defies classification. While some of his paintings echo the *costumbrismo* of his famous writings (see Chapter 6), he experimented with various styles, including cubism, art nouveau and poster art, among others. However, his most original work consists of his startling pictorial interpretations of theosophy, the esoteric doctrine that he professed and practiced.

After studying at the Corcoran School of Art in Washington, DC between 1917 and 1920, he returned to El Salvador, where he developed the technique of "spontaneous" or "automatic" creation, whereby the painter momentarily suspended consciousness and allowed his hand to start the creative process before his personality took over. Some of his most impressive works, such as *The White Nun*, were painted in this fashion, which Salarrué defined as "astral." He believed that he could reach a higher consciousness that permitted him to see into the inner nature of objects and people. Thus *The White Nun* is a paradoxical study in white that seems to transcend space and time.

Yet Salarrué also sought out his ancestral heritage, such as in his allegorical tapestries *Death of Kukulkán* and *The Conquest*. He also painted interpretations of fantastic characters from Salvadorean folklore, such as *El Cipitío* and *La Ciguanaba* (see Chapter 5). Some of his paintings of the 1930s anticipated the hippie or psychedelic movement of the 1960s. These paintings had a predominance of darker shades of green, orange, violet and ochre in floral designs, undulating forms and seashells. His psychedelic paintings could be taken to represent intergalactic worlds, anthropomorphic clouds and mountains or elusive mermaids. His range was such that he could also paint a picture like *Still Life on the Beach*, a fine homage to the French postimpressionist Paul Cézanne. He immortalized himself in a striking *Self-Portrait*, in which he appears as a sage with film-star looks.

A friend and contemporary of Salarrué, Toño Salazar (1897–1981) was regarded as one of the country's most talented and influential artists. After completing formal studies in San Salvador in the mid-1920s, Salazar traveled to Europe, Mexico and Argentina, where he honed his superb skills as a caricaturist in prestigious newspapers and journals. By the 1940s he had forged an international reputation. He produced a series of striking caricatures of social, political and cultural celebrities, among them the Spanish painter Pablo Picasso, the Mexican muralist Diego Rivera, the French novelist Colette and the Russian composer Igor Stravinski. A committed democrat who was fiercely opposed to the political oppression that has blighted his country's history, in the 1930s and 1940s Salazar drew a collection of scathing caricatures of the fascist dictators in Europe. In 1971 the prestigious French journal *Médécin* published an issue in honor of Salazar, praising him for having raised the popular genre of caricature to the level of high art. After the Salvadorean government awarded him the National Award for Culture in 1978, Salazar set up his personal archives in his house-museum in Santa Tecla, outside San Salvador, where they now await collation and study by scholars.

Valero Lecha and the First Generation

No survey of Salvadorean painting would be complete without highlighting the contribution of another celebrated teacher, Valero Lecha (1894–1976), whose legacy surpasses even that of Carlos Alberto Imery. Imery and Lecha each ran his own academy; in 1968 the government combined these two academies into the National Center of the Arts. This ensured that the creative legacies of these two rival figures would combine to enrich the development of the arts, particularly painting, in El Salvador.

The Spanish-born Lecha arrived in the country in 1919. He spent the next twelve years as a theatrical designer before returning to Spain to study painting. Forced into exile by the outbreak of the Spanish Civil War, he settled permanently in El Salvador in 1936, where he became an art teacher. Some of the most illustrious Salvadorean painters studied under Lecha, who instilled in them a passion for the wonders of his adopted country and "its marvelous light, its extremely varied landscape, so rich in colours and shades, so fluid in its forms and dimensions."[6] Lecha also encouraged his pupils to seek inspiration in El Salvador's history, its traditions and its legends. In his opinion no other country could offer more poetic or extraordinary material for a local artist. Although essentially a realistic, almost photographic painter, Lecha was occasionally capable of flights of fancy. In *October Winds* he transported Jean Paul Rubens' fair, buxom, naked *Three Graces* from their mythological garden to a high hill in El Salvador, where they were transformed into a trio of long-haired, dusky maidens who were fully clothed from head to toe in typical dress.

In assessing Valero Lecha's legacy as a teacher, art historians highlight the first group of talented graduates from his academy, who have become known as the First Generation. One of the most distinguished members of the First Generation was Julia Díaz (1917–99), who became known as the grande dame of Salvadorean art both for her painting and for her tireless promotion of national culture. Forced by circumstances to cut short her secondary education, she studied painting for five years under Lecha, who was impressed by her talent. Lecha persuaded the government to grant her a scholarship to Europe, where she studied in Spain, Italy and France for five years. Although she was tempted to stay in the Old World, her patriotism proved too strong, and she felt compelled to return to her small country. Soon afterward, in 1954 she set up an artist's studio, which a fire destroyed. Undaunted, in 1958 she founded Galería Forma, the first art gallery in El Salvador. With a drive and energy that have become legendary, she encouraged local artists, sought out patrons and strove to raise the cultural consciousness of the public. In 1983 Julia Díaz's long-held dream became reality when her Galería Forma was turned into Museo Forma, by far the best and most comprehensive museum of art in El Salvador. An indication of its breadth and quality is that it will form the basis of the proposed Museum of Contemporary Art of El Salvador.

Another talented pupil of Valero Lecha was Raúl Elías Reyes (1918–97), who made a considerable contribution to the history of Salvadorean art as painter, teacher and critic. After continuing his education in Mexico, he spent seven years in Europe, where he studied in Paris and developed a special interest in Paul Cézanne's geometrical experimentations with space. Nostalgic for the natural light and exuberance of the tropics, he returned to El Salvador in 1950. He then engaged in what may be described as an orgy of violent colors, so much so that in some of his paintings, such as in *Landscape*, even night is depicted as luminous and vibrant. From the vantage point of his home in the mountains of Los Planes de Renderos outside the capital, he repeatedly, almost obsessively created and recreated the natural and urban scenes around him in such works as *Forests, Tropics, Summer Landscape*, and *Blue Hills*. His urban paintings are particularly interesting in that they contrast geometric patterns with the undulating shapes of mountains and hills.

One of the most talented members of the First Generation was Mario Araujo Rajo (1919–70). He was from humble, rural Usulután, and he experienced a troubled childhood that scarred him for life. Fortunate enough to win a scholarship to Valero Lecha's academy, after graduating he was forced to give up painting to make a living as a graphic designer. Not surprisingly, he excelled at this trade, and many of the tourist posters and promotional calenders from the 1940s and 1950s bear his imprint. In 1955 his good friend Julia Díaz persuaded him to return to his artistic vocation, so he created a series of vibrant, colorful paintings of typical scenes, such as *Christmas, Izalco* and *Fireworks*. Critics, however, agree that his best work are the mysterious watercolors of dark, brooding skies that reflect his troubled psyche. Disenchanted with El Salvador, a country that is not always kind to artists or intellectuals, he traveled throughout South America. He lived and painted in Chile and then in Venezuela, where he died in self-imposed exile at the age of fifty-one.

Another artist in exile was Noé Canjura (1924–70), a member of the First Generation who has become an almost mythical figure in El Salvador—the barefoot goatherd from the village of Apopa who went on to become a successful artist in Paris. His paintings were imbued with a social conscience and laden with religious symbolism, as in *Indian Christ* and *Christ of Maize*, both of which were heavily influenced by the Mexican muralists. In 1949 a government scholarship permitted him to study for five years at the National School of Fine Arts in Paris. Although he returned to his country only twice in his twenty-one remaining years of life, the memory of the dramatic colors and of the tropical light of El Salvador infiltrated much his work. Some of his best-known paintings, on the other hand, such as *Cartridges* and *Daisies*, are dreamlike compositions of blurred lines and colors that have earned Canjura the description of a poetic realist.

Perhaps the most unusual of Valero Lecha's students was Rosa Mena Valenzuela (b. 1924), who during her long life has hardly varied the style or content of her paintings. Reacting very early against the realistic precepts of her master, Mena Valenzuela experimented with surrealism until she found her personal style in expressionism by concentrating on emotions rather than on external reality. From a very early stage she was fascinated by self-portraits. Over the years she produced haunting images of herself that ranged from stylized poses to twisted caricatures that are reminiscent of the grotesque creations of the Spanish painter Francisco Goya. Following studies in Europe and Asia she developed what she has called a "mystical expressionism," which is inspired by the flowing lines of arabesques and early Christian icons and frescoes. One of her most evocative works in this style is *Mystical Scene*, a blurred composition in soft, mixed tones that is criss-crossed by gentle lines and scratches that give the impression of being viewed through a veil.

The Independents

At the same time that the First Generation was establishing its reputation in the 1940s and 1950s another group of painters who had studied with Carlos Alberto Imery was also making its mark. In the Salvadorean context the two great masters were considered rivals. Lecha insisted upon a respect for European tradition and the importance of formal techniques, while Imery was prepared to encourage experimentation and free expression. The differences between the the two masters were more of spirit and nuance than of substance, as their respective origins and outlooks reflected. Lecha was a European with a personal affinity with El Salvador, while Imery was a Salvadorean with a personal admiration for European tradition. To the modern observer there does not seem to be very much separating the paintings of the First Generation from those of the Independents.

Carlos Cañas (b. 1924) is not only the greatest member of the Independents, but according to most critics he is a living classic who is the embodiment of just about every previous artistic influence in El Salvador. He has also been called the most important influence upon younger artists in the country. His style can be realistic, lyrical, magical, abstract or surrealistic. His mood can range from joyous to tragic. He covers the entire spectrum of colors. His techniques vary from oils and watercolors to an incorporation of blood, mud, sand and sawdust.

After his initial training with Imery he won a national scholarship to Spain, where he became imbued with the avant-garde, particularly with a style known as synthetic cubism. Upon returning to his country he studied pre-Columbian history and ideas, which were to exert a considerable influence upon his *Maya Series*. Cañas also developed a personal artistic theory. He argued that an artist must be guided by three fundamental principles: sincerity, ability and a commitment to one's place in time and history. In retrospect, his own work may be interpreted as a sincere commitment to Salvadorean reality.

In two important groups of paintings Cañas interpreted two crucial events in his country's history: the teacher's strike of 1968 and the military invasion of the National University in 1972. One of his most celebrated creations is the famous mural that he painted in 1972 in the National Theatre, in which he incorporated numerous scenes and details from previous paintings and drawings to project an idyllic vision of El Salvador. Sadly, subsequent events belied his optimism. Cañas is also a respected teacher and researcher who specializes in art history and criticism.

Although he may not be the most innovative of the Independents, Camilo Minero (b. 1917) is probably the member of this movement who has lived his life most in accordance with his social and political convictions. Unusual among Salvadorean painters in that he writes extensively about the significance of art and the mission of the artist, Minero is at heart a Romantic. His ideal is that of the Romantic poet John Keats: beauty in art is truth. He has encouraged Salvadorean and other Central American artists to not be slavish imitators of foreign models and to strive for authenticity by responding imaginatively to the reality around them. In some of his most dramatic paintings he utilized thick brush strokes and angular profiles to portray wide-eyed children, who are sad but have a glint of hope for the future, as they play typical Salvadorean games. A particularly striking painting is *Girl in Her Garden*, in which a bare-breasted peasant steps resolutely forward as a field of gigantic sunflowers lights up her path. After suffering years of persecution, imprisonment and exile, Minero returned to El Salvador in 1993.

Another gifted member of the Independents is Luis Angel Salinas (b. 1929). Like many of his contemporaries he has experimented with a variety of styles. However, three principal features characterize most of his work: indigenous culture, Mexican muralism and surrealism. One of his best-known works is *Worker*, a heroic representation of a muscular peasant bearing a crosslike slab of stone. It is painted in the style of a small mural. His muralistic paintings are unusual in that they contain surrealistic touches, with trees that resemble torsos, hills that turn into breasts, and landscapes with human faces.

Contemporary Trends and Influences

A panoramic survey of the artistic scene in El Salvador since 1950 reveals that painting has continued to dominate. A few painters also excel in other forms, such as sculpture. Although it is difficult to identify a contemporary group or movement of painters that is comparable to the First Generation or the Independents, a number of salient features may be discerned. Upon returning to the country after periods of study or work abroad, many painters reveal the influence of major contemporary trends in Europe and North America. It is also noticeable, however, that most painters have striven to absorb or interpret the traditions established by their national masters, making *costumbrismo* and *primitivismo* the most influential styles. Additionally, many painters reflected the impact of the increasingly agitated social and political climate that led to civil war in 1980.

In El Salvador the term avant garde is identified with Mauricio Aguilar (1917–78), a solitary genius who spent many years in Paris, Rome and New York. Upon returning to El Salvador he literally shut himself in his studio, sealing it off from the sunlight as if he were a bat in search of cave. Because of his obsession with artificial light Aguilar may be compared with the Italian Renaissance painter Caravaggio, who was famous for his dramatic experiments with chiaroscuro (the use of dark and light only). Aguilar painted hundreds of compositions in this style, which gives the impression that the painter has an insight into a secret world that is imperceptible to the viewer. Aguilar devised a mixed technique by combining unconventional materials, such as sand and soil, with oil-based paints. The result was that his works acquired a rough texture and a quirky, three-dimensional quality.

The avant garde tradition that Aguilar initiated flourished through the work of a cluster of younger artists. Perhaps Víctor Manuel Rodríguez Preza (b. 1936) most clearly marked the beginning of a new period in El Salvador. Although not a full-time painter, his abstract paintings display a masterly control of color and a keen eye for line and space that captivate the viewer. He has also composed surrealist works that project dreamlike visions that are reminiscent of Salvador Dalí, as in *Gentleman of the Night*, where a cartoon-like owl with an alligator's tail is embraced by a naked woman whose hair seems to be turning into an angel's wings. He has been adventurous in stretching the boundaries of *costumbrismo*, as in *Without a Title*, where an androidlike face stares at the viewer from behind the waist of an eyeless woman who is stroking a huge snail which is held in a clawlike hand, while another face looks on.

In El Salvador there has always been a debate over the problematic relationship between tradition and modernity. No artist provides a more fascinating case study in this regard than Ernesto San Avilés (1932–91). As a student at the Valero Lecha Academy he learned respect for tradition, while further studies in Madrid, Rome and Paris taught him what modernity could offer to a daring artist. He soon realized that a modern artist could look beyond nature and reality as depicted by traditional European masters and go on to develop a truly original vision. After his close analysis of painters, which ranged from the Italian Sandro Botticcelli of the fifteenth century to Aduanero Rousseau of the nineteenth century, he devised a style that was known as hyperrealism, which is characterized by a precise attention to detail and shapes. However, San Avilés also shrouded objects and figures in religious mystery. Indeed, many of his paintings, such as *Annunciation, The Virgin Mary* and a series that portrayed Christ in various guises, have biblical connotations. He was fascinated by flies as a symbol of mortality, and in one of his more controversial paintings he shocked viewers by showing one feeding on the wound in Christ's side.

A particularly talented avant-garde artist was Benjamín Cañas (1933–87). He was a professional architect and a sculptor, but above all he was a painter of dazzling imaginative scope. He devised a personal, abstract style that was known as aesthetic nudism before moving on to a mischievous kind of surrealism that was inhabited by monsters, saints, fabulous creatures and figures drawn from such literary classics as Franz Kafka's *Metamorphosis* and Miguel de Cervantes's *Don Quixote de la Mancha*. Like many other innovators Cañas believed that before artists could start breaking new ground, they had to learn the lessons of the traditional masters. Accordingly, some of his most striking works consist of surrealistic interpretations of the fifteenth-century Flemish painters. This is exemplified by *Last Breakfast*, a multidimensional portrait in contrasting shades of three weird figures who could be the Virgin Mary, Jesus and Joan of Arc. Another of his suggestive compositions is *Don Quixote and Dulcinea*, a surrealistic fantasy that depicts the saintly looking Man of La Mancha in an erotic pose with his seminaked beloved, while the squire Sancho Panza, dressed like a mafioso, strikes a phallic pose with a key.

Although not coherent enough to be described as a school or movement, social expressionism was popularized in the 1970s and 1980s by a talented group of painters who were associated with the National Center of the Arts. A dramatic representation of figures to express social concerns or psychological anguish characterized this style. The painter credited with the introduction of social expressionism in the country was Antonio García Ponce (b. 1938). He spent part of his youth in Mexico, where the harsh reality of life in the lower echelons of society moved him. Upon his return to El Salvador he set out to capture on canvas the dirt, poverty and degradation of existence among the urban poor and disaffected.

Miguel Angel Polanco (b. 1935) utilized social expressionism to convey the stifling character of religion, such as in his painting *Procession*, in which women dressed in drab devotional garb wear a haunted look. In other paintings Polanco turned his attention to the sadness of being young in a country like El Salvador. For example, in *Untitled* two adolescents, perhaps a brother and sister from a middle-class family, stare into space as if contemplating an uncertain future.

Undoubtedly one of the most committed social expressionists is Armando Solís (b. 1940), whose vivid, crowded paintings seem to jump out of their frames at the viewer. Although very much an artist committed to his time and place in history, Solís derives inspiration from the pre-Hispanic art of El Salvador's past. He claims that his purpose is to create *mestizo* art that reflects the dual (Spanish and Indian) nature of El Salvador. A particularly expressive painting in this *mestizo* style is *Infinite Heads*, in which a series of colorful pre-Hispanic faces seem to float inside a colonial frame of arches and windows. Solís uses such faces and masks to express a wide range of emotions, from the fierce protectiveness of a mother clinging to her child in *Maternity* to the schizophrenic horror of *Ghost*. He endeavors to express the pain of oppression and the desire of liberation of Salvadoreans. Solís is also known for his engravings of animals (for example, *Bats* and *Porcupine*) that seem to be struggling to escape from their constricting frames.

Two other names stand out among the social expressionists: Bernardo

Crespín (b. 1949) and César Menéndez (b. 1954). An eccentric figure who studied in Paris and has spent time in a psychiatric asylum, Crespín's work reflects both his personal demons and his feeling for the poor and the oppressed. His evocative *Self-Portrait* projects a quirky vision that is reminiscent of Vincent Van Gogh, the Dutch master with whom Crespín identifies. While Van Gogh cut off his ear, in his self-portrait Crespín cuts off his brain, which hovers in the shape of a cone with wings over the artist, who is encased in a blue straitjacket. Another painting, *City in a Wrap*, features an urban underworld that is inhabited by rocks with eyes and flying canoes that could be buzzards, while boats are stranded on an orange desert. César Menéndez, the youngest of the social expressionists to make his mark in the 1970s and 1980s, spent a year in New York in 1982 to perfect his study of abstract techniques. His paintings of anguished females, who howl or shout their pain to the world, remind the viewer of *The Scream*, the famous work by the Norwegian expressionist Edvard Munch. Menéndez's human figures give the impression of hovering between this life and the next, as in *Destiny in Green*, where a large, naked woman sits on a swing, her stout body and long hair desperately pulling back inside the artist's canvas.

The Civil War and Beyond

The civil war traumatized all Salvadoreans, including its artists, most of whom responded to it in two principal ways: they used their art to express their personal reaction to the national tragedy, or to seek solace from the bloodshed outside their studios. Both responses, of course, are equally valid and not necessarily mutually exclusive. History is filled with artists who, by choosing to use their art as a medium to convey political or ideological messages, only succeed in compromising its aesthetic value. Political art such as muralism and graffiti did flourish in El Salvador during the civil war, but with very few exceptions its treatment is best left to the political analyst rather than to the student or critic of art. Accordingly, this section will focus on painters whose work was of aesthetic merit and expressed personal responses to the Salvadorean holocaust.

Antonio Bonilla (b. 1954) spent the 1970s in Mexico, where he established a reputation as an up-and-coming talent. His return to the country in 1980 coincided with the dramatic plunge into war. Over the next twelve years he developed a highly individualistic style, *feísmo* (uglyism), as an artistic strategy for commenting upon the carnage. In some ways his work of this period is reminiscent of the expressionist George Grosz, who utilized black humor to satirize militarism and bourgeois corruption in Germany between the two world wars. In 1984 as the war became entrenched, Bonilla staged a remarkable exhibition entitled *Chamber of Horrors and Other Boring Things*. Combining pre-Hispanic elements with expressionism and surrealism while borrowing techniques that Pablo Picasso used in his classic antiwar painting *Guernica*, Bonilla depicted dramatic scenes and characters from the war that was tearing the country apart. For instance, in a shocking painting ironically entitled *Discreet Charm*, a gross female body in knickers, high heels and jewels has the head of a bird, which squawks with pleasure as it is fondled lasciviously by the hand and tongue of a man. Inspired by the Spaniard Luis Buñuel's famous film *The Discreet Charm of the Bourgeoisie* (1972), the painting shouts out the message that the Salvadorean upper classes pursue their usual pleasures while the country burns. In *Chronicle of the 80s* Bonilla employed thick brush strokes of purple, green, blue, white and yellow to comment upon the attempt to conceal the truth about El Salvador, which is represented by skeletons inside twisted bodies. As in any war, women were often the innocent victims, a point made with telling impact in *Women in Storage*. Here the viewer cannot help but be moved by the thick, solid nakedness of a peasant who is trying to cover her private parts as she stares in fright and defiance at her captors. In another work, a grotesque caricature entitled *Thou Shalt Not Kill*, Bonilla sardonically applies God's commandment to El Salvador, showing that both sides of the conflict have turned into murderous monsters for reasons that they can probably no longer comprehend.

Very few Salvadorean painters have earned more national or international respect than Roberto Huezo (b. 1947). Although he has experimented with various styles, he has always remained faithful to his personal artistic creeds that art is a bastion of freedom and that the artist has a sacred obligation to seek the truth inside his/her own heart or mind, because social and political values are fickle if not ultimately meaningless. According to Huezo the only certain thing is a trinity that he describes as God-Universe-Self.[7] Thus, although his work may pay homage to both European and pre-Hispanic traditions, there is very little that is particularly Salvadorean in his paintings.

Throughout the 1980s Huezo painted his famous series of perfectly shaped eggs, which were of different colors in a variety of abstract styles. Sometimes the eggs appeared to be floating on air. At other times they were partly buried or tied down with wires. What strikes the viewer is their perfection in an imperfect world. He has also painted insects, fruits and crumpled paper, all of which seem to mean more than what they represent. The harmony of colors, the geometry of design and the symmetry of space combine to create a sense of internal unity and order that is absent from real life. Interestingly, during and since the civil war Huezo seems to have sought comfort in female nudes, which he has painted in various shades of ocher or has drawn in charcoal. Although extremely graphic, they manage to exude a spiritual, even mythical air.

Roberto Galicia (b. 1945) is one of the most tantalizing abstract painters in El Salvador. His theory of art holds that artists have an obligation to act as the conscience of society by producing works that demand the intellectual and moral input of their audience.[8] His paintings constitute a provocative illustration of this theory by forcing the viewer to decipher their symbolism, which is invariably couched in terms that demand close observation and deep concentration.

Most of his work consists of abstract objects—spheres, shafts, geometrical shapes and crumpled paper—that explode in a resplendent pattern of colors. While the overall impression is certainly dazzling, the message is not immediately clear. On examination, however, the viewer realizes that there is method in the apparent madness. One may trace Galicia's paintings from the early 1980s to the mid-1990s as his evolving response to the real-life inferno that was engulfing the country.

The Flag depicts a bloodstain upon the white and blue of the crumpled national emblem, which seems to be hanging on a clothesline that stretches across a skyline of black, the color of mourning. Galicia enjoys the technique of *trompe l'oeil* (visual tricks), and on closer viewing the flag seems to turn into a wounded bird that is trying to stay in flight. Without blatant politicking, Galicia draws the viewer into his private vision of a country in the throes of an historical agony. In *On the Road of Pain* his vision becomes darker still. The somber colors (black, purple, red) melt into the sky and form the outline of a mythical beast, perhaps the hound of hell presiding over an orgy of blood. By 1989 the despair appears to have been transformed into resolute anger. An example of this is *In the Depths of the Ocean*, where the folds and rocks below the blue sea seem to form the contours of a pre-Hispanic face. By 1994, two years after the peace accords, Galicia's mood changed dramatically. In *Birth* he portrayed two huge, glowing monoliths that emerged from the dark womb of the earth to symbolize the dawn of a new era in El Salvador.

Titi Escalante (b. 1953) specializes in painting different varieties of flowers, which spring from the earth, water, jungle or baskets in all their splendor, as if to prove that beauty may yet triumph over ugliness in El Salvador. Perhaps Escalante's masterpiece is *Explosion*, an almost photographic painting of lilies in a wicker basket.

Titi Escalante is also one of the few professional sculptors in El Salvador.

She is renowned for her dark green frogs with spidery legs. On the surface there could not be a greater contrast than that between the ugly amphibian and the elegant lilies. However, upon reflection it becomes apparent that there is a philosophical link between the two: the beautiful flowers need compost to bloom, while inside the animal's body beats the heart of a prince. Titi Escalante demonstrates that while an artist's quest for beauty and truth can be a solitary and often painful affair, it is not necessarily at odds with a sense of humor.

El Salvador entered the new millennium with well-established painters who can serve both as teachers and as inspiration to their younger compatriots. With peace, enthusiastic galleries and societal support, the future augurs well for the country's most important art.

ARCHITECTURE

Due to the havoc that numerous earthquakes have caused, architecture can only be considered to be a footnote in the history of the arts in El Salvador.[9] Apart from the aforementioned colonial churches (see section on art in the colonial era) the visitor to San Salvador, Santa Ana, San Vicente, San Miguel and other towns will find a small number of stately homes that date back to the first half of the twentieth century. Salvadoreans also point with pride to a few majestic buildings that have survived the ravages of earthquakes and fire, such as San Salvador Theatre, Santa Ana Theatre and the National Palace in San Salvador. Apart from the archaeological ruins that dot the country the oldest building standing is Casa Ambrogi, a handsome building made from wood and sheet metal, two materials that are particularly resistant to seismic activity. The economic boost that the liberalization of banking laws and the growth of foreign investment in the 1990s provided has had an interesting side effect. There are now many modern buildings with long, straight lines and reflective glass, such as the Torre Cuscatlán, the headquarters of a major bank. Of doubtful aesthetic taste, such buildings are nevertheless a welcome sign of the spirit of entrepreneurship that is slowly but surely helping to construct a more prosperous, confident El Salvador.

THEATER

A Spanish-born actor and director, Edmundo Barbero (1899–1985), did more than anybody else to promote theater, El Salvador's most neglected genre.[10] As the head of theater at the National Centre of Fine Arts in the 1950s and, subsequently, as the director of Teatro Universitario (University

Theatre), Barbero almost single-handedly revitalized the moribund theatrical scene. He staged both classical plays from Europe and modern, in some cases iconoclastic works. The performance of Jean-Paul Sartre's *Huis clos* (Behind closed doors) under his direction in 1956 caused a sensation among El Salvador's conservative theater-going public. Barbero was instrumental in inspiring a brief period of theatrical activity that has never been repeated in El Salvador. An exciting and talented group of dramatists worked in the 1950s and 1960s. Among them were Walter Bénecke (1930–80), Walter Chávez Velasco (b. 1932), Roberto Arturo Menéndez (b. 1930), Alvaro Menéndez Leal (1931–2000), José Rodríguez Ruiz (b. 1930), Italo López Vallecillos (1932–86), Roberto Armijo (1937–97) and José Roberto Cea (b. 1939), all of whom won awards in the Juegos Florales (Literary Awards) of Quezaltenango, Central America's most prestigious playwrighting award.

Apart from guerrilla theater in the zones that the rebels controlled, and light entertainment in San Salvador (reviews, variety shows), theater came to a near standstill during the civil war. Since then, however, there has been a minor revival. A few theatrical groups (Hamlet, Vivencias, Artteatro) have staged serious works by reputable national and international playwrights. Moreover, a campaign has been launched to foster interest in the theater among the younger generations by producing children's theater and by printing plays by important national dramatists in high-school textbooks. Two universities (UCA and Universidad Tecnológica) now have active theatrical groups. The status of theater was given an important boost in 1999 with the award of the Premio Nacional de Cultura (The National Prize for Culture) to Dorita de Ayala, a well-known actress who has devoted her life to promoting this art in El Salvador.

MUSIC

El Salvador does not have the rich musical tradition of some of the other Latin American countries (see Chapter 5). Nevertheless, for a small, developing country its musical archives reveal a surprisingly large number of reputable composers, and the quality of its orchestras and choirs has always been high. The national fondness for military music dates back to 1841, when an Italian, Juan Gido, and two Spaniards, José Martínez and Manuel Navarro, established the first band in San Miguel. Even today for the vast majority of the population a military band is as close as it is likely to get to a musical performance.

Composers: The Long Nineteenth Century

The first composer of note in the country was the Guatemalan-born Escolástico Andrino, who arrived in the country around the middle of the nineteenth century. Among his best-known works is a symphony that was unusual for the time in that it was written in a classical style reminiscent of Haydn and Mozart. Although a capable teacher, Andrino was not able to instill an interest in the classical style in his pupils, who preferred the Romantic tradition that was popular in Europe in the early part of the century. Andrino was also a conductor, directing a famous requiem mass in January 1860 for the funeral of President Gerardo Barrios's mother.

Most Salvadorean composers preferred the Romantic tradition between 1850 and the first decade of the twentieth century. Preeminent among them were Nicolás Roldán (1851–90), Felipe Soto (1885–1913), Rafael Quintero (1890–1946) and José Napoleón Soto (1901–86). The taste for light music meant that countries like Mexico, Brazil, Argentina and Cuba had national composers who were developing modern traditions while El Salvador was trapped in the nineteenth century with salon music, rhapsodies and flowery symphonies. According to Germán Cáceres, El Salvador's most outstanding musical scholar, the prolongation of European Romanticism retarded the development of serious music in the country.[11]

Ion Cubicec and the First Generation

An invigorating wind of change entered El Salvador with the arrival in 1950 of the Romanian Ion Cubicec (1917–98), an outstanding composer and director. At long last local musicians and music lovers were exposed to modern European styles, particularly in piano and strings. Cubicec founded the Salvadorean Choral Society, which performed an outstanding version of Carl Orff's *Carmina Burana*. Cubicec's *String Quartet* is an excellent work that combines expressionistic features with a powerful feeling for his adopted country in a manner reminiscent of Bela Bartók.

Cubicec paved the way for what is known as the First Generation of professional composers in El Salvador. Hugo Calderón (b. 1917), who completed his musical education in the United States, has written admired pieces for the piano (*Central American Suite, Piano Sonata*), for the flute and piano (*Nocturn*) and a major symphonic work (*Prelude, Sound and End*). Esteban Sevellón (b. 1921), who studied in Rome, caused a sensation at the age of twenty-nine when he wrote the first major Salvadorean ballet, *Rina*, and a symphonic poem, *Phaethon*. Since then he has continued to evolve as a musician, consolidating his reputation with such works as *Sihuehuet*, a symphonic poem for narrator and orchestra, and *Soliniquital*, a serenata for strings that was performed with distinction in Mexico in 1980.

Víctor Manuel López Guzmán (1922–93) was admired for his research into pre-Columbian music, whose tonalities and rhythms he incorporated into his own compositions, most notably in *Quartet for Strings*. In symphonic works he utilized mood effectively to evoke visions of the national landscape. The most innovative member of the First Generation is Gilberto Orellana Sr. (b. 1920), who for many years experimented with harmony and orchestration. He has concentrated on symphonic poems, among them *Fantasy in the Woods, Emmanuel, Route to Paradise* and *Psychosis*. The latter work consisted of explosive sounds that recalled Stravinsky's *Rites of Spring*. Late in life Orellana changed course, opting for a nationalistic style that praised the natural beauty and pre-Columbian heritage of El Salvador.

Contemporary Composers

A group of composers who were born between 1939 and 1950 can be credited for consolidating the tradition of serious music in El Salvador, which was not an easy task given the country's painful circumstances in the last twenty-five years. The oldest member of this group is Gilberto Orellana, Jr. (b. 1939), whose *Concert for Violin and Orchestra* is an inventive composition that conveys the contrast between good and evil. Orellana is also one of the first Salvadoreans to experiment, however timidly, with electronic techniques. He has also employed a complex, mixed technique in *Pipil Symphony*, a combination of diverse styles and instruments that includes the use of a seashell. Josep Karl Doestch (b. 1944), who resides in the United States, is admired for one outstanding piece, *Sonnet 87*, a neo-Romantic interpretation of a Shakespearean sonnet for soprano or tenor, choir and orchestra. Probably the most talented member of this second generation of composers is Alex Panamá (b. 1940), who studied and worked in France and Germany. In the 1960s he was considered the bad boy of Salvadorean music because of his extremely imaginative, neoclassical compositions that were influenced by such European masters as Paul Hindemith. When he was eighteen, Panamá composed *Septet for Wind Instruments* (for two flutes, oboe, two clarinets and two bassoons). In the 1960s he wrote a splendid series of innovative pieces, including *Two Suites* (for piano) and *In Praise of Patrice Lumumba Noiminis* (for flute and percussion). A misunderstood figure in his country, he has lived in seclusion for many years.

A slightly younger generation of composers, born during the 1950s, are currently at the height of their creative powers. Angel Duarte (b. 1952), who studied in Mexico, is considered a radical experimentalist who is capable of combining the most diverse styles in the same work. Manuel Carcach (b. 1955), a guitarist who subsequently took up composition, has written interesting pieces for guitar, percussion, oboe, piano, flute and orchestra. However, by far the most public and charismatic figure of this group is Germán Cáceres (b. 1953), who studied at the Julliard School of Music in New York and completed a doctorate in Musical Composition at the University of Cincinnati. Given his academic background it is not surprising that he is a meticulous, self-conscious musician who composes, theorizes and writes about his craft. He has based two compositions on Latin American literature. *Sonatinas for Guitar and Piano* is inspired by a short story by the Argentinian Julio Cortázar, and *Songs of Light Words* is inspired by poems by the Salvadorean Hugo Lindo. Currently Cáceres is experimenting with ensemble theory, which he defines as the "infinitude of possibilities offered by the application of algebra to music."[12] Among his outstanding compositions that utilize ensemble theory are *Concert for Violin and Orchestra* and *Trio for Violin, Cello and Piano.*

According to Cáceres the future of composition in El Salvador has two very promising figures in Carlos Mendizábal (b. 1968) and Carlos A. Colón Quintana (b. 1968). His advice to them and to all young composers in the country is that they should impose no restrictions upon their creativity but one: "To thine own self be true."[13] Cáceres's principal worry is that while El Salvador has a conservatory of music, it is not possible to study beyond the high-school level. Ambitious musicians must travel to the United States or Europe to pursue higher degrees in composition or performance. Cáceres warns that there is always the danger that they may not return to El Salvador.

Orchestras and Choirs

In 1875 a Belgian conductor, Alejandro Coussin, founded the Philharmonic Society of El Salvador, which in 1910 was replaced by the National Orchestral Society under the direction of the Italian Antonio Gianoli. This in turn was replaced by the current National Symphonic Orchestra, which was founded in 1922 by the German Paul Muller. Since 1941 Salvadorean conductors have assumed the direction of the National Symphonic Orchestra. The first of them was the revered Alejandro Muñoz Ciudad Real (1902–91), who broke new ground by organizing public performances of works by Igor Stravinsky, Richard Strauss and Manuel de Falla. The other most influential conductor of the National Symphonic Orchestra has been Germán Cáceres, who during fourteen years at the helm (1985–99) sought to widen the popular appeal of serious music by organizing concerts for school children. He also utilized his international reputation to bring important soloists and conductors from the United States and Europe.

Apart from the National Symphonic Orchestra there are only a few other active musical groups in El Salvador. The principal ones are the Traditional Music Group, the New Salvadorean Quartet for Chords and Flutes and the National Choir, which is currently under the direction of Irving Ramírez, who studied in St. Petersburg. The National Youth Symphonic Orchestra now performs regularly, and the government, private enterprise and cultural institutions promote musical activity in the capital and in other cities. In the words of Germán Cáceres, "Hopefully our new-found spirit of peace and reconciliation will stimulate further creativity by Salvadoreans, not only in my field—music—but in all the other arts as well. The future lies with us."[14]

NOTES

1. See, for example, Luis Salazar Retana, *Colección de pintura contemporánea* (San Salvador: Tabacalera de El Salvador, 1995); and Astrid Bahamón, *Pintores salvadoreños* (Santa Tecla: Editorial Clásicos Roxil, 1999). Both these books are indispensable for the study of Salvadorean painting and feature commentary by the authors.

2. This thesis is propounded by José Roberto Cea in *De la pintura de El Salvador* (San Salvador: Editorial Universitaria, 1986). This book contains critical insights about the preeminent themes and styles of Salvadorean painting throughout the centuries.

3. For a pictorial history of pre-Hispanic art in El Salvador see William R. Fowler, Jr., Federico Trujillo and Isabel R. de Bettaglio, *El Salvador: Antiguas civilizaciones* (San Salvador: Banco Agrícola Comercial de El Salvador, 1995).

4. For a valuable illustrated history of colonial art see José Antonio Fernández and Federico Trujillo, *El Salvador: la huella colonial* (San Salvador: Banco Agrícola Comercial de El Salvador, 1996).

5. Cea, *De la pintura*, 76.

6. Ibid., 149.

7. For a representative selection of Huezo's paintings, with a critical introduction by him, see Roberto Huezo and Ana Vilma de Choussy, *Roberto Huezo: su mundo* (San Salvador: Banco Cuscatlán, 1996).

8. See Roberto Galicia, *Momento de reflexión* (San Salvador, Banco Cuscatlán, 1995). This book contains a selection of Galicia's paintings, an introduction by the painter and short essays by a number of critics.

9. For a pictorial survey of architecture in San Salvador see Walter Chávez Ve-

lasco, *Cuatrocientos cincuenta años de San Salvador* (San Salvador: Banco Cuscatlán, 1995). This illustrated history of the capital has informative commentary.

10. There are very few books on Salvadorean theater. The best are Edmundo Barbero, *Panorama del teatro en El Salvador* (San Salvador: Editorial Universitaria, 1970); and José Roberto Cea, *Teatro de y en una comarca centroamericana* (Santa Tecla: Canoa, 1993).

11. Germán Cáceres, "La música en El Salvador," *ARS* 4 (1994), 73–87. This article provides a concise history of music in El Salvador.

12. Ibid., 84.

13. Ibid., 87.

14. Germán Cáceres in an interview with the author in San Salvador on February 10, 1998.

Glossary

ARENA.   Nationalist Republican Alliance

Cacique.   Indian chieftain

Campesino.   Peasant or rural dweller

Caudillo.   Military strongman

Chicha.   Traditional, fermented corn-based drink

Cofradía.   Brotherhood of members of a parish or town

Comunidad cristiana de base.   Christian base community

Conquistadores.   Spanish conquerors

Costumbrismo.   Literature or art that depicts typical customs and manners

Criollos.   Creoles, Spaniards born in the New World

Departamentos.   Departments, the fourteen administrative units of El Salvador

Escuadrón de la muerte.   Death squad

Evangélicos.   People who worship in Evangelical churches

Fiesta patronal.   Feast day in honor of a patron saint of a town or village

FMLN.   Farabundo Martí National Liberation Front

Frijoles.   Beans

Guanaco.   Nickname for a Salvadorean

Hacienda.   Large farm or agricultural estate

Informales.   People who work in the informal economy

Machismo.   Aggressive masculinity

Maquila.   Reassembly factory

La Matanza.   The Great Slaughter of 1932

Mestizo.   Person of mixed Spanish and Indian blood

Nahuat.   The principal pre-Hispanic language of El Salvador

Pipiles.   The principal pre-Hispanic tribe of El Salvador

Pulgarcito de las Américas.   "Tom Thumb of the Americas," nickname for El Salvador

Pupusa.   Tortilla stuffed with cheese, beans, pork or other ingredients

Remesas.   International remittances

Salvadoreño.   Salvadorean or Salvadoran

Tamal.   Corn pastry wrapped in banana leaves

Bibliography

In addition to the sources listed below, the relevant issues of the following newspapers and periodicals have been consulted: *Time*, *Newsweek*, *The Guardian Weekly*, *The Washington Post*, *Le Monde*, *ECA*, *Estudios Centroamericanos*, *E.I.U. Country Reports and Profiles*, *La Prensa Gráfica*, *El Diario de Hoy*, *El País*.

Anderson, Thomas P. *The War of the Dispossessed: Honduras and El Salvador, 1969*. Lincoln: University of Nebraska Press, 1981.

Aracely de Gutiérrez, Gloria. *Tradición oral de El Salvador*. San Salvador: CONCULTURA, 1993.

Argueta, Manlio. *Cuzcatlán donde bate la mar del sur*. Tegucigalpa: Editorial Guaymuras, 1986.

———. *Milagro de la paz*. San Salvador: Adelina Editores, 1994.

———. *El valle de las hamacas*. San Salvador: UCA Editores, 1992.

Bahamón, Astrid. *Pintores Salvadoreños*. Santa Tecla: Editorial Clásicos Roxil, 1999.

Barba Jacob, Porfirio. *El terremoto de El Salvador*, 4th ed. San Salvador: CONCULTURA, 1997.

Barbero, Edmundo. *Panorama del teatro en El Salvador*. San Salvador: Editorial Universitaria, 1970.

Beverley, John, and Marc Zimmerman. *Literature and Politics in the Central American Revolutions*. Austin: University of Texas Press, 1990.

Boland, Roy C., and Marta Caminero-Santangelo, eds. *Antípodas*. Madrid/Melbourne: Vox/AHS, 1998.

Boschetto-Sandoval, Sandra, and Marcia Phillip McGowan. *Claribel Alegría and Central American Literature*. Athens: Ohio University Center for European Studies, 1994.

Brauer, Jeff, Veronica Wiles, Julian Smith and Steve Wiles. *Conozca El Salvador*. Charlottesville: On Your Own Publications, 1997.

Browning, David. *El Salvador: Landscape and Society*. Oxford, England: Clarendon Press, 1971.

Cáceres, Germán. "La música en El Salvador." *ARS*, no. 4 (1994): 73–88.

Cea, José Roberto. *De la pintura en El Salvador*. San Salvador: Editorial Universitaria, 1986.

———. *Teatro de y en una comarca centroamericana*. Santa Tecla: Canoa, 1993.

Chávez Velasco, Walter. *Cuatrocientos cincuenta años de San Salvador*. San Salvador: Banco Cuscatlán, 1994.

Cobos, Rafael, and Payson Sheets. *San Andrés y Joya de Cerén*. San Salvador: Bancasa, 1997.

Country Profile. Guatemala, El Salvador, 1997–1998. London: The Economist Intelligence Unit, 1997.

Country Profile. Guatemala, El Salvador, 1999–2000. London: The Economist Intelligence Unit, 1999.

Cuéllar, Helga. "El potencial de la Educación Superior a partir de su proceso de creación y adopción." *ECA*, 589–590 (November–December 1997): 1169–87.

Dalton, Roque. *Miguel Mármol*. Kathleen Ross and Richard Schaaf, trans. Willimantic, CT: Curbstone Press, 1992.

Erdozaín, Plácido. *Archbishop Romero, Martyr of Salvador*. Maryknoll, NY: Orbis Books, 1981.

Escobar Galindo, David, ed. *Después de medianoche (After Midnight)*, bilingual ed. Roy C. Boland, trans. Santa Tecla: Ricaldone, 1988.

———. *Indice antológico de la poesía salvadoreña*. San Salvador: UCA Editores, 1987.

Escobar, Vilma de G. *Comida típica*, 4th ed. San Salvador: Industrias Unisola, 1998.

Fernández, José Antonio, and Federico Trujillo. *El Salvador: la huella colonial*. San Salvador: Banco Agrícola Comercial de El Salvador, 1996.

Fowler, William R., Jr. *El Salvador: antiguas civilizaciones*. San Salvador: Banco Agrícola Comercial de El Salvador, 1995.

Fuentes, Carlos. *The Buried Mirror*. London: André Deutsch, 1992.

Galicia, Roberto. *Momento de reflexión*. San Salvador: Banco Cuscatlán, 1995.

Gallegos Valdés, Luis. *Panorama de la literatura salvadoreña*, 3rd ed. San Salvador: UCA Editores, 1987.

Gettleman, Marvin E., ed. *El Salvador: Central America in the New Cold War*. New York: Grove Press, 1981.

Gómez, Jorge Arias. *Farabundo Martí*. San José, Costa Rica: EDUCA, 1972.

Grenier, Yvon. *Universities, Intellectuals and Political Transition in El Salvador*. CDAS Discussion Paper No. 71. Montreal: McGill University, 1992.

Guía informativa y metodológica. Mapa arqueológico de El Salvador. San Salvador: Fundación María Escalón de Núñez/Ministerio de Educación, 1998.

Guía informativa y metodológica. Mapa de flora y fauna de El Salvador. San Salvador: Fundación María Escalón de Núñez/Ministerio de Educación, 1998.

Guía informativa y metodológica. Mapa histórico de El Salvador. San Salvador: Fundación María Escalón de Núñez/Ministerio de Educación, 1998.

Guía informativa y metodológica. Mapa de tradiciones y costumbres de El Salvador. San Salvador: Fundación María Escalón de Núñez/Ministerio de Educación, 1998.

Haggerty, Richard A., ed. *El Salvador: A Country Study.* Washington, DC: Library of Congress, 1990.

Hamovitch, Eric. *El Salvador.* Montreal: Ulysses Travel Publications, 1994.

Henríquez, Ch., Vilma Maribel, Federico Trujillo and Isabel R. de Bettaglio. *El Salvador: su riqueza artesanal.* San Salvador: Banco Agrícola Comercial de El Salvador, 1997.

Herrera Vega, Adolfo. *Expresión literaria de nuestra vieja raza.* San Salvador: Ministerio de Educación, 1961.

Historia de El Salvador, I & II. San Salvador: Ministerio de Educación, 1994.

La historia de la reforma y la reforma de la historia. La reforma en marcha de El Salvador. San Salvador: Ministerio de Educación, 1999.

Huezo, Roberto, and Ana Vilma de Choussy. *Roberto Huezo: su mundo.* San Salvador: Banco Cuscatlán, 1996.

Huezo Mixco, Miguel. *La casa en llamas.* San Salvador: Ediciones Arcoiris, 1996.

Kramer, Michael. *El Salvador. Unicornio de la memoria.* San Salvador: Ediciones Museo de la Palabra, 1998.

Lernoux, Penny. *Cry of the People.* New York: Doubleday, 1980.

Lindo, Hugo. *Obras escogidas de Salarrué, I & II.* San Salvador: Editorial Universitaria de El Salvador, 1969.

Lindo, Ricardo. *El esplendor de la aldea de arcilla.* San Salvador: CONCULTURA, 1991.

Melhado, Oscar. *El Salvador, Retos económicos de fin de siglo.* San Salvador: UCA Editores, 1997.

Membreño de Melhado, Anamaría, ed. *Secretos de nuestra cocina.* San Salvador: Compañía Hotelera Salvadoreña, 1996.

Menjívar, Rafael. *El Salvador: El eslabón más pequeño.* San José: EDUCA, 1980.

Montes, Segundo. *El Salvador 1989. Las remesas que envían los salvadoreños de Estados Unidos. Consecuencias sociales y económicas.* San Salvador: UCA Editores, 1990.

Montoya, Aquiles. *Informalidad urbana y nueva economía popular.* San Salvador: UCA Editores, 1995.

———. *La nueva economía popular: Una aproximación empírica.* San Salvador: UCA Editores, 1994.

Murray, Kevin, and Tom Barry. *Inside El Salvador.* Albuquerque: Resource Center Press, 1995.

Ochoa, María Eugenia, coordinator. *Identificación de las necesidades prácticas y estratégicas de las mujeres de las regiones de trabajo del M.A.M.* San Salvador: M.A.M., 1996.

Osborne, Lilly de Jongh. *Four Keys to El Salvador.* New York: Funk & Wagnalls, 1956.

Riding, Alan. "The Cross and the Sword in Latin America." In Marvin E. Gettleman, Patrick Lacefield and David Mermelstein, eds. *El Salvador: Central America in the New Cold War.* New York: Grove Press, 1981, 189–98.

Rivas, Pedro Geoffroy. *La lengua salvadoreña.* San Salvador: Dirección de Publicaciones del Ministerio de Educación, 1978.

Rodríguez Díaz, Rafael Arturo. *Temas salvadoreños (y unos pocos foráneos).* San Salvador: UCA Editores, 1992.

Russell, Philip L. *El Salvador in Crisis.* Austin: Colorado River Press, 1984.

Salazar Retana, Luis. *Colección de pintura contemporánea.* San Salvador: Tabacalera de El Salvador, 1995.

Sanders, Renfield. *Major World Nations: El Salvador.* Philadelphia: Chelsea House Publishers, 1999.

Schmidt, Francisco, Julio Ernesto Contreras and Luis Alberto Gómez Chánez. *Cien años de presencia evangélica en El Salvador. 1896–1996.* San Salvador: CONESAL, 1996.

Smith, Verity, ed. *Encyclopaedia of Latin American Literature.* London: Fitzroy Dearborn Publishers, 1997.

Stephen, Lynn. *Women and Social Movements in Latin America: Power from Below.* Austin: University of Texas Press, 1997.

Stourton, Edward. *Absolute Truth: The Catholic Church in the World Today.* London: Viking, 1998.

Vega, Juan Ramón. *Las comunidades de base en América Central.* San Salvador: Ediciones del Arzobispado, 1998.

Velásques, José Humberto. *Las cultura del diablo.* San Salvador: Editorial Universitaria, 1997.

Webre, Stephen. "The Politics of Salvadorean Christian Democracy." In Marvin E. Gettleman, Patrick Lacefield and David Mermelstein. *El Salvador: Central America in the New Cold War.* New York: Grove Press, 1982, 89–101.

White, Alastair. *El Salvador.* London: Ernest Benn Limited, 1973.

Zárate Martín, Antonio, and José Sánchez Sánchez. *El Salvador.* Madrid: Ediciones Anaya, 1988.

Index